ENCYCLOPAEDIA OF PSYCHOANALYSIS
5

Who Am I.

The Ego and the Self in Psychoanalysis

edited by

Bruna Seu

REBUS PRESS

Rebus Press
134 Dukes Avenue
LONDON
N10 2QB

ISBN 1 900877 28 7

CONTENTS

FOREWORD

The time is shortly before Christmas 1994 and three dreamers are ensconced in the comfortable leather armchairs of the staff bar at University College, London. The dreamers are Kirsty Hall, Oliver Rathbone and Sharon Morris. We like the idea of starting a publishing company. Single authored books, we calculate, will take three months to produce. Edited collections are a little more complicated, we note, and so might take up to six months... Our abject ignorance is a kind midwife to our project... Yet now our original idea has finally flowered. *The Encyclopaedia of Psychoanalysis* has been born. And, despite all the delays and setbacks, our vision is still intact.

Rebus Press is a non-partisan publishing company. We aim to bring a range of psychoanalytic ideas to a wide readership, namely: the experienced psychoanalyst or psychotherapist; the student, in the guise of either clinician or academic; and, last but certainly not least, the interested person in the street. We pose the question: are the original ideas which psychoanalysis brought to the world now dead, or are they alive and kicking in the work of subsequent writers, waiting to be brought forward afresh and anew for each generation of readers? In turn, we hope that through *The Encyclopaedia of Psychoanalysis*, Rebus Press will stimulate the next generation to take up the baton and produce further creative thinking.

The *Encyclopaedia* series does not set out to tell people what to think. It encourages readers to be fascinated, lured into reading 'just one more chapter', to puzzle over conflicting points of view and, on occasion, to grapple with difficult and complex ideas. Why? Well, if psychotherapists and psychoanalysts encounter the Byzantine complexity of human suffering in their daily work, then our view is that the practitioner will find assistance in this supremely difficult task by being gently helped to think for him or herself. Being told what to think and what to do does not produce good psychoanalysis or good psychotherapy, and it seems there is far too much 'instruction' of this kind already in circulation.

I wish to thank all our contributors to the *Encyclopaedia* series—past, present and future. As they have discovered—or, indeed, will discover in due course—Rebus Press is unique. We do not settle for statements such as: 'following Melanie Klein it is clear that...' or 'as Jacques Lacan has demonstrated...' We insist on *explanation*, wherever possible. As a result many of the people who have written for this series have had long, passionate, interesting, and—very occasionally—acrimonious discussions about their papers with the individual editors of our books, with the chief editor of Rebus Press, Duncan Barford, and with me. Consequently, where ideas do seem unclear, this is often because it is the intention of the author to leave the reader in doubt. Doubt *can* be a productive position from which to carry out an analysis of one's own thought, or an assessment of one's opinion about a book and—indeed—is regarded by some as the only viable position from which to conduct good psychoanalysis or psychotherapy...

The *Encyclopaedia* series has a consistent format. In most of the books you will find papers which are informed by Freudian, Jungian, Kleinian, Lacanian and Object Relations perspectives. You may also find papers where the perspective of the author is hard to pin down... Good! Keep the 'doubt' working! In each volume we attempt to offer a wide range of opinion, and the majority of papers have been specially commissioned and written for the series. In a few cases, we have published work which has already appeared elsewhere but perhaps in a format which has not been easily accessible. In some instances a paper has appeared in another language, and has been specially translated for this series.

The aim of the *Encyclopaedia* is to present a coherent body of ideas, yet within a structure sufficiently loose to allow the reader to interpret the papers for him or herself. We are hoping and aiming for a wide-ranging reaction to the contents of these volumes. Feedback, constructive criticism, ideas for future projects in the series, possible papers for future inclusion—all of these and more are most welcome.

Kirsty Hall MA
Commissioning Editor
e-mail k.hall@rebuspress.co.uk

A NOTE ON TEXTS

Quotations and references to Freud are given according to the *Standard Edition of the Complete Psychological Works of Sigmund Freud*. 24 volumes, translated and edited by James Strachey in collaboration with Anna Freud, assisted by Alix Strachey and Alan Tyson. London: The Hogarth Press and the Institute of Psycho-Analysis; New York: Norton, 1953-1974.

NOTES ON CONTRIBUTORS

MARY LYNNE ELLIS Dip. Psychoanalytic Psychotherapy (UKCP), MA Modern European Philosophy, is a training therapist and supervisor. She is a founder member of the Site for Contemporary Psychoanalysis, where she also teaches. Her most recent publications include: 'Who Speaks? Who Listens? Different Voices and Different Sexualities' (British Journal of Psychotherapy, Spring 1997), and 'Challenging Socarides, New Psychoanalytic Responses' (Feminism and Psychology, 1997).

H. SHMUEL ERLICH PhD is Sigmund Freud Professor of Psychoanalysis, and Director of the Sigmund Freud Centre for Study and Research in Psychoanalysis at the Hebrew University of Jerusalem. He is Training and Supervising Analyst for the Israel Psychoanalytic Society and Institute, and a Founding Member of OFEK: Organisation, Person, Group—The Israel Association for the Study of Group and Organisational Processes.

STEPHEN FROSH is Professor of Psychology at Birkbeck College, University of London, and previously Consultant Clinical Psychologist and Vice Dean in the Child and Family Department at the Tavistock Clinic, London. He is the author of numerous academic papers and several books, including: *For and Against Psychoanalysis* (Routledge, 1997); *Sexual Difference: Masculinity and Psychoanalysis* (Routledge, 1994); *Identity Crisis: Modernity, Psychoanalysis and the Self* (Macmillan, 1991); and *The Politics of Psychoanalysis* (Macmillan, 1987). He is joint author of *Child Sexual Abuse* (Macmillan, 1993), and co-editor of *Psychoanalysis in Contexts* (Routledge, 1995). He is currently completing a book on Young Masculinities, to be published by Palgrave in 2001.

COLLEEN HEENAN (RMN, BA Hons, MSc in Psychotherapy, PhD) is the clinical director of the Leeds' Women's Counselling and Therapy Service (England) as well as a psychotherapist in private practice and university lecturer. She is a co-author of *Challenging Women: Psychology's Exclusions, Feminist Possibilities* (Open University Press) and *Psychology, Discourse, Practice: From Regulation to Resistance* (Taylor and Francis), and the co-editor of *Feminism and Psychotherapy: Reflections on Contemporary Theories and Practices* (Sage). She is also a member of the editorial board of the journal *Feminism and Psychology* (Sage).

WILMA MANGABEIRA trained as a sociologist and received her PhD from LSE in 1991. At present she is a Research Fellow and an Associate Member of the Centre for Psychoanalysis, Middlesex University. Since 1996 she has become interested in applying the theoretical framework of radical studies of science to psychoanalysis. She has undertaken training at the Institute of Psychoanalysis, and has worked as an Honorary Research Fellow at the Anna

Freud Centre. Recent publications include: 'On Textuality of Objects in Disciplinary Practice: the Couch in Psychoanalysis' (Psychoanalytic Studies, 1999) and 'Social Studies in Psychoanalysis: a Research Agenda' (P/S: Journal of the Universities Association for Psychoanalytic Studies, 2000).

DAVID MAYERS studied and taught philosophy before training as a psycho-analytic psychotherapist. He is now a psychotherapist in private practice, Chair of Scientific Activities at the Lincoln Centre for Psychotherapy, and Honorary Research Fellow in Psychoanalytic Studies at the University of Kent. He regularly teaches Klein and Bion to students in both clinical and academic settings.

DR MARK MORRIS BA MBChB MRCPsych BPAS trained in medicine and psychiatry in Glasgow, then moved to London to train as a psychotherapy senior registrar in the Cassel Hospital in Richmond, and as a psychoanalyst in the British Psycho-Analytical Society. After three years as a Consultant Psychiatrist in Psychotherapy in St Bernard's Hospital, with part-time work in the Charing Cross Gender Clinic, he moved to his current post as Director of Therapy in Grendon Underwood Prison.

DANY NOBUS is a Lecturer in psychology ad Psychoanalytic Studies at Brunel University. He is the editor of *Key Concepts of Lacanian Psychoanalysis* (Rebus Press, 1998), and author of *Jacques Lacan and the Freudian Practice of Psychoanalysis* (Routledge, 2000), alongside numerous papers on the theory and practice of psychoanalysis.

ROBERT ROYSTON is a psychoanalytic psychotherapist and a member of the London Centre for Psychotherapy. His papers on narcissism and intellec-tual dysfunction have appeared in the British Journal of Psychotherapy.

TOM RYAN is a member of the Arbours Association and the Site for Contemporary Psychoanalysis. In addition to his clinical practice, he is a train-ing and supervising therapist for the Arbours Training Programme, and Chair of the Arbours Co-ordinators Committee. He is also co-editor with Chandra Masoliver of *Sanctuary: The Arbours Experience of Alternative Community Care*.

BRUNA SEU is Lecturer in Social Psychology at Birkbeck College, University of London. She is also a psychoanalytic psychotherapist in private practice. She has co-edited (with C. Heenan) *Feminism and Psychotherapy: Reflections on Contemporary Theories and Practices* (Sage, 1998), and has published articles on the relationship between psychotherapy, feminism, and women's shame. She is currently researching moral apathy and abuses of human rights.

INTRODUCTION

Bruna Seu

The proliferation of texts on the self in social sciences in the last twenty years is testimony to the current preoccupation with this fundamental concept. The concept itself is a very recent creation. The systematic investigation of the self as a specific subject in social sciences is very much a product of the twentieth century, even though some trace its proper birth to René Descartes' famous seventeenth-century dictum 'I think, therefore I am' (Holstein and Gubrium 2000:18). Since the advent of postmodernism, the very nature of the self has been questioned. This is a far cry from the excitement at the discovery that others and society in general can affect and shape the individual; social scientists are now struggling to find a self stable enough to be observed. The self has become an elusive entity: fragmented, contradictory, and socially constructed in the continuous fluidity of becoming. A natural offshoot of this postmodern turn is the epistemological investigation of 'how' the self becomes. If there isn't a fixed, stable core to it, what are the processes through which the self acquires a stable form and becomes understood and talked about in specific ways? The message is clear that we need to shift our attention onto dynamics external to the self *per se,* looking at historical and social contexts and, above all, the specific theoretical frameworks within which the self is constructed.

Despite the ubiquitous nature of this debate within the wider field of social science, psychoanalytic writing and theorising seems to be largely immune to its influence. Although psychoanalytic thinking and its critique has been incorporated in the discussion within the social sciences (see, for example, Flax 1990 or Frosh 1991), in clinical and theoretical writing the self is still referred to as an unambiguous, unitary entity. To make matters more complicated, differences and similarities between self and ego are often not addressed either. One gets the sense that even authors from different psychoanalytic schools assume a fundamental agreement on the meaning and the function of these concepts.

This book takes a closer look at the way psychoanalytic writers use the concepts of the self and the ego. It questions the tacit agreement on their meaning and illustrates how, in fact, the terms are totally dependent on the author's prevailing school of thought and the theoretical and epistemological assumptions underpinning that framework. The book takes a critical approach in order to challenge the reification of these concepts and enquires into their current usefulness. It suggests that psychoanalytic theories are, as Mangabeira points out, 'languages in which to discuss psychoanalytic treatment', rather than processes of discovering underlying true selves waiting to be uncovered, understood and described univocally. From this point of view the task in hand is one of 'delineating the current use and clinical applications of the concepts within different schools' (Evans in Mangabeira in this volume: 24) Thus the book aims to illustrate that self and ego are 'work in progress'.

The second aim of the book is to explore the link between the ways in which different schools of psychoanalysis formulate self and ego, and the beliefs of what constitutes human nature and psychic functioning which underpin their theoretical models. In the following chapters it will become clear how these carry crucial implications for psychoanalytic technique. This is particularly evident in the first section of the book, where the three main schools of classical psychoanalysis are examined. One of the fundamental issues at stake here is what is clearly delineated by Morris in Chapter Two as the age-old dialectic between 'nature' and 'nurture'. Morris argues for the continuing relevance of a debate around 'the nature of and relative importance of environmental contributors which might include the quality and patterns of parenting and the experience of trauma on the developing personality of the child'. He argues that Contemporary Freudians and Kleinians position themselves quite differently *vis-à-vis* this debate, with Kleinians emphasising internal constitutional factors and Contemporary Freudians arguing the importance of experiential and environmental factors. These are not as much small differences of opinion, as different paradigms. As Mayers puts it, Kleinians talk of a self 'which initiates and experiences beliefs, desires and emotions' in opposition to the Freudian ego 'which mediates between and defends against demands from other psychic agencies and the external world'. These different positions have serious implications not just for the understanding of the ego and the self, but also for technique. Hence, as Morris points out, the same child could have a very different experience of analysis if treated by a Freudian or a Kleinian analyst. Whilst the Freudian, on the basis of their belief in the influence of the real world, would relate to and engage with the child, a Kleinian analyst, in order to reach the child's unconscious phantasies, might be rather aloof and silent. Crucially, this illustrates how concepts are not intrinsically valid or self-explanatory, but are created within epistemological and political traditions.

The eternal argument of 'nature vs. nurture' does not apply to these two chapters only, but runs through the whole book as the authors take up different positions along the continuum between environmental and instinctual causal factors in psychopathology and formation of the self and the ego.

The structure of the book

The book adopts a non-partisan position, collating theoretical work from as broad a range of contemporary psychoanalytic approaches as possible. It offers trainees in psychotherapy, students of social sciences and the readership at large a comprehensive review of the development and application of two fundamental concepts in psychoanalytic discourse. It is hoped that the essays, in concentrating on key theories of the self and the ego, will form an introduction to the range of psychoanalytic concepts in this field, thus providing a useful starting point for trainees and a critical review collection for practicing clinicians. At the same time, whilst serving as an introduction to basic psychoanalytic concepts about the self and ego to academics in the wide field of cultural theory, the essays also recognise the philosophical problems of generating theory in this area.

The book is divided into three sections.

Section one sets the scene: it contains a historical chapter looking at the original formulation of 'ego' and 'self' in Freudian writing and the most important phases of their development in the history of psychoanalysis. This is followed by three chapters delineating the current use and clinical applications of the concepts made by psychoanalysts, specifically Contemporary Freudians, Kleinians, and Object Relations theorists.

Section two takes us 'beyond the couch' into a more social and intersubjective field. It explores the application of the concepts to contexts other than the 'one to one' psychoanalytic interaction. The aim of this section is to investigate what changes the concepts had to undergo to be applicable in different settings and how they have been adapted and made into invaluable tools in therapeutic communities, in groups and in the understanding of art. This further illustrates the plasticity of 'ego and self' and how their definitions and uses are flexible and adaptable.

Section three takes a much more critical and epistemological angle. The contributors to this section illustrate how the self is always culturally and historically specific. From the questioning of Freud's cultural biases in his formulation of self and ego to a radical questioning of the very idea of the self from a Lacanian perspective, this section invites the reader to approach the concepts of the ego and the self as gendered, culturally and historically constructed rather than as scientific discoveries or entities. The section ends with a comparison between the fragmented self in psychoanalysis and post-structuralist thought and how the two can be bridged in clinical practice.

Based on the assumption that concepts of self and ego are dependent on the theoretical framework in which they are based, all the contributors have endeavoured to clarify the theoretical position they were writing from, at times making comparisons between their own and those of others in the book. Overall, since the book approaches the subject from an epistemological rather than a simply clinical angle, the contributors have privileged an academic approach in their essays, where the brief clinical vignettes have the function of providing a practical illustration of what has been argued intellectually, rather than the other way round. In this sense the book is theory driven. Finally, because the book seeks to create debate and cross-fertilisation between different psychoanalytic schools, the contributors were asked to explain why it is important for clinical practitioners and/or social scientists to integrate their view into their thinking and practice, and thus to link theory back to practice.

The chapters

Chapter One, by Wilma Mangabeira, provides the first stepping stone of the book. It offers an historical and epistemological account of the concepts of ego and self in psychoanalysis from its birth to today. She reminds us first of all that these concepts are important not just *per se*, but because they reveal the different underlying assumptions about the psyches of different psychoanalytic schools. The chapter challenges the reification and representation of the concepts as clear and unambiguous entities and illustrates how instead they are constructed and reconstructed in the process of theory development. It also highlights, in its analysis of this development, the difficulties involved in theorising the relationship between mental structures (e.g. the ego), psychic agency and existential being (e.g. the self). One of the threads running through the chapter is the exploration of the view of the psyche as originally unified or fragmented. This is one of the fundamental issues in the way theories constructed the ego and the self. Are humans born with a psyche which is inherently unified and which under correct environmental support will flourish into a coherent and completely integrated self, or is the psyche inherently split and imbued with internal contradictions? In order to answer these crucial questions the chapter starts with a constructivist assessment of Freud's *Das Ich*. This is followed by an overview of Freud's frames of reference and closely follows the development of ego and self within these. The chapter continues this task by looking at post-Freudian conceptual development, in particular that of Anna Freud and Heinz Hartmann. The exploration of Jacobson's work serves as a link with the Object Relations school, in particular Fairbairn, Winnicott and Melanie Klein. The chapter concludes with an epistemological examination of the themes underlying different schools and relative formulations of ego and self.

Chapter Two, by Mark Morris, explores the Contemporary Freudian perspective on ego and self. By treating the Contemporary Freudian approach as if it were a single self, Morris starts by delineating a history of the group, explores its thoughts and ideas, and then looks at some clinical material. Hence Morris is able to illustrate clearly how theoretical trends are often heavily influenced by historical circumstances. In this case the debate between Anna Freud and Melanie Klein and the resulting controversial discussions determined the fate of the Contemporary Freudians and their specific formulation of the ego and the self. The chapter then explores the two basic approaches to the self and the ego within the group, namely functional and developmental. From the 'functional' angle Morris defines the self as a 'collective noun' for the different mental functions and structures of Freud's metapsychological frames of reference, later developed by his daughter Anna (the mechanistic metaphor of the mind in the topographical model and ego, superego and id in the structural model). In developmental terms, Morris argues that 'the self is born into a primary narcissistic fusion with mother, with object-relatedness a gradually evolving phenomenon'. The ego thus starts as a bodily ego, with a sense of identity and separateness slowly emerging in the interaction with the external world by identifying oneself as 'other' to it. Morris highlights how this differs from the Kleinian developmental theory, according to which the infant is aware of a distinction between self and other from the very beginning. These fundamentally differing views on the first stages of life have repercussions on many levels, including understanding of psychopathology and technique.

The comparison between Kleinian and Contemporary Freudian theories is continued in Chapter Three where David Mayers contrasts Klein's self and Freud's ego. He argues that the object of inquiry here is the 'self which initiates and experiences beliefs, desires and emotions, rather than the Freudian ego which mediates between and defends against demands from other psychic agencies and the external world. As discussed earlier on, there is also a marked difference between how the newborn infant is viewed, with the consequent differences in terms of technique. While for Freud the new baby is in a solipsistic state of autoerotism and primary narcissism, according to Mayers the self is seeking for objects from the very first moments. However, this is also different from the object-relating described by the Object Relations school, which views the baby's mind as a *tabula rasa*. Rather than considering the original state to be healthy primary narcissism, Kleinians view narcissistic phenomena always as a retreat from or an attack on life. The baby is born with something unbearable inside, immediately caught in the internal struggle between life and death. Hence the emergent self is the product of this struggle, albeit mitigated or aggravated by the presence or absence of internal good objects. Mayers also briefly looks at Bion's later view of the self not as a unified entity, but as a container for a host of voices, or points of view, each speaking from a significant area in the subject's life.

In Chapter Four Stephen Frosh summarises the concepts of ego and self in the work of Fairbairn, Guntrip and Winnicott. Frosh also explores the major epistemological shift in the understanding of identity, self and ego, fostered by the British Object Relations school of psychoanalysis. With Object Relations theory, the biological foundations of psychic life emphasised by Freud cease to be relevant for a genuine psychoanalytic approach to human psychology. Frosh points out that because of the shift from the individual as self-contained to being embedded in a social context, Object Relations theory holds the potential for an account of human nature and development that makes social relations central in the construction of the self. The psyche is initially a unit, a total ego that has the potential to develop into a coherent and integrated personal self. Frosh highlights the different meaning of familiar terminology. For Guntrip, for example, the ego becomes the whole person, the whole basically unitary psyche with its innate potential for developing into a true self. In this way, Frosh clearly illustrates how the fundamental existential beliefs of the author, his *Weltanschauung*, drive his theory and determine the meaning attributed to concepts. The chapter provides a clear analysis of the meaning and function of self and ego in the work of Fairbairn, Guntrip and Winnicott. The chapter ends with a critique of Object Relations theory and an examination of the school's contribution to social theory. Frosh argues that although Object Relations theory makes some important contributions to attempts to develop a psychoanalysis that deals seriously with the impact of social factors on the development of the individual, we have to be aware of the in-built limitations of its 'two-person' framework. Thus Frosh warns us of the conformist dangers present in Object Relations theory's romanticisation of motherhood, with its accompanying view that all psychological splits are produced by frustrating experiences with the maternal object.

Robert Royston's Chapter Five opens the second series of essays, looking at applications and elaborations of ego and self. Royston compares and differentiates Kohut's Self Psychology from classical, Kleinian and Object Relations theories. He argues that Kohut's formulation of self is not relevant only to psychoanalysis, but also to the social sciences since its concepts can be applied to a range of different subjects. In his essay Royston applies Kohut's formulation to art and intellectual creativity and comments on the conflict between the idea of the self as a social construct and of the self as *sui generis*. The author starts the chapter with an analysis of the schizoid self and then moves on to the detailed exploration of the self in Object Relations theory and in classical analysis. These ideas are then contrasted with Kohut's formulation of self and narcissism, with the latter viewed in Self Psychology as a less malign and more treatable phenomenon, stemming from the infant's attempt to compensate for the loss of the state of bliss and perfection of infancy. According to Royston, Self Psychology poses a challenge to value-laden western ethics and the scientific mode brought into clinical work by classical psychoanalysis. Instead Self Psychology recommends empathy as an analytic mode and intellectual instrument. The chapter ends with an investigation of the link between psychoanalysis and art. It is argued that creativity is bound up with a type of psychological struggle and that art arises from, but also transcends, psychological damage. These ideas are explored in relation to the works of Rousseau and Tolstoy.

In Chapter Six, Shmuel Erlich looks at the ego and the self in the group. He argues that although ego and self are at an opposite pole to the group, they are also what make up the group, and are in need of the group for attaining their fullest state. The chapter explores ego and self as representing different experiences of the subject's relatedness to his object, in terms of the experiential modalities of Being and Doing in group dynamics. These experiences are mainly connected to the dimensions of merging vs. separateness of self and object. Erlich argues for the need for both perspectives—i.e. the group perspective and the individual psychodynamic standpoint—to be taken into account when studying ego and self. It is not sufficient to study them from the viewpoint of the vicissitudes of the individual intrapsychic structures in the group. Erlich claims that self and ego cannot reach their fullest potential without the group. The author proceeds with his task by exploring the four levels of relationship between group and individual, then looks at self and ego as Being and Doing. Some clinical vignettes illustrate this interesting perspective.

The function of the group *vis-à-vis* self and ego is also the focus of Chapter Seven, in the specific setting of therapeutic communities. Tom Ryan argues that instead of falling into the reification of the concept of self by talking in the singular, we should rather focus on the process of 'selving', through which the self is negotiated and comes into being. Ryan is interested in the way people develop and preserve their sense of self through others, in particular those techniques through which people manoeuvre others into feeling and behaving as they require to preserve their sense of self. These dynamics are explored in the specific context of interpersonal and group dynamics in therapeutic communities. Ryan claims that the family, like structure of a therapeutic community offers a unique opportunity to observe and participate in the means by which residents attempt to induce others, through various relational strategies, to collude with their definitions, conscious or unconscious, of their selves. The author provides an in-depth epistemological critique of the problem of defining the self as singular or multiple, arguing for a view of self as relational and inter-subjective.

The theme of the self in context is continued in the chapter by Mary Lynne Ellis, who firmly positions psychoanalytic formulations of ego and self within a particular and historical context, namely a specific tradition of western philosophical thought. She argues that instead of getting over-preoccupied with debates around when developmentally the ego is formed, we should concentrate on the more fundamental questioning of the values informing our conceptualisation of subjectivity and how far the notion of ego is crucial to the practice of psychoanalytic psychotherapy. She asks 'if we adhere uncritically to this tradition how can we be sufficiently sensitive to the uniqueness and diversity of our patients' experiences, particularly those of people who are not from white western backgrounds'? Ellis sets herself the task of critiquing Freud's notions of the ego in order to unravel and reveal the social and historical biases underlying them. She demonstrates how Freud's claims of objectivity arise from the influence of Enlightenment philosophers and their view that science can offer us certain knowledge of the world. This view, she claims, does not sufficiently allow for the impact of the social context on the constitution of subjectivity. She contrasts Freud's view of the ego with Foucault's and Merleau-Ponty's theories of subjectivity. Hence, because in her view self is always embedded in a social context, Ellis argues that these alternative theories of subjectivity can contribute to the development of a psychotherapeutic approach which is 'truly sensitive and alive to difference and diversity'.

Chapter Nine, by Dany Nobus, links back to some of the questions put forward by Mangabeira around the relationship between theory and concepts. As Nobus succinctly puts it, when asked to write a chapter about the self in Lacanian theory, he found himself having to face the 'assignment of having to include something that is simply not there'. Through a scholarly review of Lacan's work, Nobus proceeds to elucidate his claim that 'there is no such thing as a notion of the self which can lay claim to conceptual status' by critically examining the views endorsing the 'Lacanian self'. What is most interesting in this chapter is the reflection on the reasons behind the eagerness of Anglo-American authors to read the concept of the self into Lacanian texts. Nobus identifies several. The first is a political and strategic desire to gain acceptance for Lacanian contributions amongst scholars and practising therapists alike by aligning them to prevalent paradigms within the Anglo-American social sciences. This is explained with reference to the ubiquity of the notion of self in the Anglo-Saxon world, not only as a technical term or as a smidgen of academic jargon, but also as a word in everyday language. Then having entertained the idea that the problem is simply caused by ignorance and intellectual blindness, Nobus rejects it. He argues instead that behind the investment into the concept of the self there are much more fundamental existential and historical pressures. The desperate need to find the self in every theory and to invent it when it is not there, Nobus claims, is due to the 'fundamental longing for the maintenance of psychic mastery—a craving that is as private as it is political, as personal as it is ideological'. In this way Nobus makes a fundamental point, illustrating how the motivation of the reader and the demands of the social climate can influence the construction of a theory and a concept to such an extent that it might override what was originally intended by the author. In this case, the self is made a central notion for Lacan, who in fact never considered it a valuable notion for psychoanalysis, to the point of arguing that 'the degree to which human beings are convinced that they possess a strong identity is more indicative of psychosis than anything else'.

Continuing with the theme of construction of selves, in the final chapter Colleen Heenan looks at how notions of self are constructed in the consulting room by the practitioner and the patient. Heenan investigates overlapping concerns of post-structuralism and psychoanalysis with understanding the self and the construction of meaning. She claims that a deconstruction of the discursive process of psychotherapy allows for an awareness of the clinician's historical, cultural and gendered specificities of their practice. At the same time, she argues, psychoanalysis could offer anchoring to post-structuralist ideas in the form of a distinction between a 'core' self and a 'true' self. Heenan starts with a brief outline of key ideas within postmodernist and post-structuralist thinking. She then illustrates the practical use of these ideas by a strategic deconstruction of text taken from some psychodynamic psychotherapeutic group work with women suffering from eating disorders. She suggests that reading therapeutic text from a discursive perspective makes public the private world of psychotherapy. This enables not just the practitioner, but also the patient, to reflect on the various discourses, which position and thus constrain both psychoanalytic and feminist notions of 'selves'. Her fundamental message is that 'truths' about the self are not lying inside, waiting to be 'discovered'; instead, they are constructed and reproduced between patient and therapist.

Thus, coming full circle, the book ends. From a narrative point of view, the book could be viewed as a very rich and interesting collection of stories about the ego and the self. Some of them have assumed the self to be observable and discovered through analytic work, some have taken a more strategic view and explored the positive plasticity of the concepts, and others have focused on and explored their constructed nature. I hope this fascinating range of perspectives will stimulate further thinking and discussion around a crucial concept which is clearly still in the making.

Section One

CONSTRUCTING THEORY—FREUD'S CONCEPTS OF THE 'EGO' AND THE 'SELF' AND POST-FREUDIAN DEVELOPMENTS

Wilma Mangabeira

This chapter presents an historical review of the concepts of the ego and the self and is structured as follows. Section one introduces the reader to the different ways in which an epistemological history of psychoanalytic concepts can be discussed. It adopts a constructivist perspective and addresses the contemporary controversy regarding different assessments of Freud's concept of *Das Ich*.

Section two undertakes an overview of Freud's three frames of reference with regards to mental functioning. It also spells out the intricate theoretical definitions of the concepts of the ego and the self. It closes by suggesting that Freud's ideas cannot be encompassed within a single unified framework and that his models of the mind overlap rather than supersede each other.

The sections that follow take up post-Freudian conceptual developments, which came to shape different schools of thought, as we know them today. Section three presents the work of 'ego psychologists' such as Anna Freud and Heinz Hartmann.

Jacobson's work on 'self and the object world' provides the basis for a link with Object Relations theory in section four. This section also examines the contributions of other psychoanalysts, such as Melanie Klein, Fairbairn and Winnicott.

Sections three and four argue and demonstrate that there is no clear-cut unified contemporary theory regarding the concepts of the ego and the self and that each of the reviewed authors have selected and elaborated upon different aspects of Freud's work. The sections also suggest that a comparison between different post-Freudian approaches allow us to pinpoint different underlying assumptions about the psyche. From one perspective, the psyche is viewed as inherently and essentially unified, and under supportive environmental conditions will flourish into a coherent and completely integrated self. From an alternative perspective, a more polyvalent and fluid view is adopted. The ego and the self are seen as constantly being re-drawn in contradictory and multi-layered ways.

Section five revisits the themes discussed in the previous sections. It concludes with the idea that although contemporary psychoanalysis has developed into different schools of thought, which provide for alternative readings of the concepts of ego and self and the role of the environment in shaping selfhood, adherence to particular schools of thought is not directly translated into day to day clinical work.

Considering that, as pointed out by Evans (1996: ix), 'psychoanalytic theories are languages in which to discuss psychoanalytic treatment, the challenge becomes one of delineating the current use and clinical applications of the concepts within different schools'. Such an endeavour will be carried out by the other contributors to this book.

1. 'Internalist' versus constructivist accounts: an introduction to the treatment of psychoanalytic concepts

There are two ways in which a historical review of concepts can be undertaken. One mode is to present the developments of a knowledge system such as psychoanalysis as if it had emerged in a smooth, linear and progressive way and predominantly by a single author. This is the method employed in traditional epistemological histories and is adopted by some psychoanalytic writers.

The underlying assumption of this mode is that of ideas being neatly 'discovered', in an ever-unfolding process from 'ignorance' to full-fledged knowledge. The account is mainly 'internalistic' and theory development is seen as the result of an evolving process, free from biographical constraints as well as from social, political and institutional influences. The result is usually the reification of concepts and their representation as clear and unambiguous entities.

In psychoanalysis, for example, its theoretical bedrock is sometimes presented as the exclusive outcome of Freud's intellectual quest, evolving from the 'affect-trauma' model, to the 'topographical model' and finally to structural theory. The development of psychoanalytic knowledge is portrayed as the outcome of Freud's clinical experiences, *vis-à-vis* his attempt to understand pathologies and create a metapsychology.

In the second mode, by contrast, ideas and theory development are seen as 'constructed'. The underlying assumption is that they are the outcome of a variety of influences and debates between members of a particular knowledge community, such as the psychoanalytic community, and are also shaped by social and institutional dynamics and constraints. Theory development is seen as the outcome of a struggle. At one level, it consists in defining the empirical basis of theory—or, in other words, what is considered to be legitimate data. Who is in a position to provide such data and who sanctions its legitimacy? At another, interrelated level, as expert communities expand and new members are brought into the discipline, we see the role of controversies, theoretical differences and institutional practices playing a part in clarifying and rendering concepts more sophisticated, but also in closing and reifying them as dominant principles.

Even though in the history of psychoanalysis Freud's genius and influence unquestionably marked the birth of this discipline, and his writings on the concepts of the ego and the self provided the basis for the theory development that took place later, this chapter will adopt the second mode in its review of the concepts. It hopes to provide the reader with a much more complex and multifaceted account. It will demonstrate how these concepts emerged within the particular specificities of theoretical and empirical debates, and developed as a result of questionings and controversies in psychoanalysis.

When comparing the first and second modes of theory presentation, it is possible to see that the main point of contention is whether we adopt what Kerr has critically termed an 'official' stance[1], or if we treat theory development in a critical and non-idealised way, tolerating and accepting its sometimes untidy, incomplete and contradictory features.

The chapter will deconstruct the concepts of the ego and the self as reified entities by exploring two themes. The first theme is the problem of whether environmental variables influence intra-psychic development and the extent to which they should be integrated in a general theory of the mind. In psychoanalytic theory there is a constant tension between accounting for the role of instinctual drives on the one hand, and the extent to which the relations between the infant/child and its primary caretakers should be incorporated as explanatory terms in the constitution of the psychic structure. This raises the question of whether emphasis should be placed on pre-Oedipal or Oedipal relationships as the seat of development as opposed to the original role of pathology.

This theme covers the way theories account for how the symbiotic and undifferentiated baby develops functional ego activities, as well as constituting itself as a subject, and what is considered 'normal' and 'pathological' development. The ways in which these questions are answered will result in different clinical diagnoses as well as different therapeutic procedures.

In the history of the concepts of the ego and the self it is possible to detect a constant swinging of the pendulum between the significance of the environment on the one hand and intrapsychic factors on the other, in explaining the development of the personality.

The second theme explored in the chapter refers to a controversy which I have identified in the literature regarding Freud's use of the term *Das Ich*. As discussed in detail in the section below, the different readings provided by authors of this German term have significant implications for our understanding of the concepts of the ego and the self.

There are varying assessments about the extent to which Freud differentiated the concepts of the ego and the self. For some, Freud did not clearly distinguish the two terms; this original theoretical problem was accentuated by Strachey's somewhat problematic translation. According to others, Freud deliberately used *Das Ich* indiscriminately in order to maintain a creative ambiguity and an internal theoretical tension. According to yet a third view, Freud's theory clearly defined the concepts of ego, self and character.

I hope that by bringing out this controversy at the same time as providing a historical review of the concepts of the ego and the self, I can demonstrate how even such core psychoanalytic concepts have not been taken up by the community in a consensual or linear way. This constructivist stance may prove quite a demanding task for the reader, since it stresses how theories are constructs and that they never achieve complete closure. On the other hand, such an approach can be rewarding to the extent that it deconstructs reified concepts and invites the adoption of a critical and creative stance towards theory.

2. Freud's models of the mind and the concepts of the ego and the self

When reading contemporary psychoanalytic literature addressing Freud's concepts of the ego and the self, it is possible to identify a central controversy regarding the term *Das Ich*.

In one view, authors refer to the multi-faceted and undifferentiated *Das Ich*—which refers both to the ego and the self—as a 'terminological ambiguity' that should and can be resolved by various means. This problem is alleged to have been accentuated by translating the original German text into English.[2]

Moore and Fine, for example, have tried to eliminate what is seen as a problem by suggesting that the term 'ego' in Freud has an early and a later meaning:

> In his early writings, Freud sometimes used the term to refer to the total (mental) self; sometimes it meant an organised group of ideas. In modern usage, the term most often refers to Freud's 1923 redefinition of the ego as one of the three major functional divisions of the mental apparatus... One aspect of the ego in its earlier meaning has now been replaced by the concept of the self. (Moore and Fine 1990: 58)

Hartmann (1956) commented on the ambiguity in Freud's use of the term *Das Ich* and proposed that in the writing preceding structural theory, this term should be translated as 'the self', of one's own person.

Additionally, there are two radically different views to the ones presented above. The first is suggested by Kernberg (1982), Laplanche and Pontalis (1988) and Padel (1986). They have rejected as untrue and simplified the interpretation according to which Freud used the term ego sometimes in a nonspecific way to designate the personality as a whole and at other times in a precise and specific way, referring to an organ which is gradually differentiated from the id. These authors suggest that *Das Ich*, contains a creative ambiguity, as it is at times used to indicate the self, which pertains to the experiential domain, while at other times it refers to the ego as a mental structure.

It is suggested that this is a creative ambiguity which portrays the very difficulties in theorising the relations between mental structure and psychic agency on the one hand, and being—as an existential dimension—on the other.

As pointed out by Kernberg (1982: 894),

> ...Freud never separated what we think of as the metapsychological ego from the experiencing self. His ambiguous use of *Das Ich* resulted in a sacrifice of clarity and precision, but it kept the meaning of *Ich* open-ended.

Laplanche and Pontalis have stated that although it is impossible to ignore Freud's own testimony in *The Ego and the Id* (1923) regarding the essential modifications to the concept of the ego, the notion of a so-called turning point of the 1920s should not be unreservedly accepted.[3]

A further point of view has been proposed by McIntosh (1986). This author has suggested that there is a clearly delineated concept of 'the self' in Freud, which 'he developed precisely and used consistently'. I shall return to McIntosh's views later on in this section.

Bearing in mind these different assessments of the extent to which Freud clearly differentiated between the concepts of 'the ego' and 'the self', let us look at his three theoretical models of the mind.

Freud's first theoretical framework—the 'affect trauma' model (mid 1890s to 1897)—coincides with his initial attempts at creating a new knowledge system as well as developing a therapeutic technique. His early collaborative work with Breuer and experiments with hypnosis with hysterical, obsessional and phobic patients was followed by attempts to theorise the aetiology of such disorders and differentiate between 'actual neuroses' and 'psycho-neuroses'. While the latter were explained as the outcome of sexual frustration and abnormal sexual life—by which Freud meant coitus interruptus, sexual abstinence and masturbation—the former was seen as related to the experience of sexual seduction in childhood.[4]

During this period of Freud's thinking, the mental apparatus is described as creating a clear-cut division between conscious and unconscious material. Defence and resistance are observable features of an underlying dynamic set about by a mechanism of dissociation (what will later be called repression). The ego is synonymous with consciousness and 'conscious self', and has the capacity to repress mental content which it finds unacceptable. A central theme is that of conflict, which has its source in the external world—sexual frustration and trauma—*vis-à-vis* the ego's tendency to reinstate equilibrium.

In the 'affect-trauma' model of the mind the mental apparatus is conceived of as being relatively rudimentary in early childhood and increasing in complexity during the course of development. This psychological organisation functions as a vehicle for adaptations to demands from both internal and external sources, but the adaptation to experiences deriving from external reality, such as trauma, is emphasised. Among the functions of the mental apparatus are the control and discharge of excitation, as wall as the function of defence against distressing affects and unacceptable ideas.

As pointed out by Sandler et. al. (1997: 44), in this model development brings about differentiation within the apparatus. One of the differentiated agencies is referred to as the ego. It is used in this frame of reference to designate both consciousness and a capacity to perform a function of defence.

The ego is thought of as coming into existence on the basis of the interaction between innate traits and thoughts, and the external world.

By 1897, the year when Freud carried out his self-analysis, a fundamental shift in theory can be observed. By that time, Freud was clearly dissatisfied with the outcome of his clinical work and questioned the effectiveness of his theoretical model. The shift resulted from Freud's scepticism about the widespread occurrence of sexual abuse, as recounted by his patients. It was also the result of his self-analysis and his uncomfortable discovery of unconscious, forbidden sexual wishes and fantasies of his own, as revealed by his dreams.

In this theoretical shift, patients' material is no longer taken at face value, as factual instances of sexual abuse. Rather, they are seen to communicate wishful sexual fantasies that, owing to their unacceptable or potentially disturbing nature, have been pushed out of consciousness and seem to operate as if they were indeed memories of real events. Patients' utterances were now interpreted as representing wishes, gratified by fulfilment in fantasy. Patients were recounting fantasies rather then recalling actual events.[5]

The change from the affect-trauma frame of reference to the 'topographical model' (1897-1923) moved the focus from external reality and its impact on psychological processes to the inner world itself. This shift inaugurated Freud's view of the internal world as dominated by man's struggle with his innate drives. The basis for the theories of the second phase can be found in *The Interpretation of Dreams* (Freud 1900), particularly in the seventh chapter.

In this transition it is possible to observe the abandonment of the theory of trauma to explain the origins of the psychoneuroses and a shift of emphasis instead to the history and vicissitudes of the patient's inner drives and of the struggle to deal with them. The change in Freud's ideas allowed him to make a major distinction between 'historical' (objective) and 'psychical' truth as well as to formulate key concepts of psychoanalytic theory, such as repression, conflict, repetition compulsion and projection.[6]

In the affect-trauma model there was the distinction between conscious and unconscious aspects of the mind this distinction is further elaborated in the topographical model, by the introduction of three systems—conscious, preconscious and unconscious.

In the latter model, everything above the barrier to the preconscious conforms to reality, to laws of time and space and distinctions between past, present and future. Below this barrier, this law no longer operates and does not conform to reality as we normally recognise it. In this other portion of the mind—the dynamic unconscious—we believe and think what we want to believe, we are free of constraints. It operates according to wishful law, to desire. This is so because there are two principles of mental functioning: primary and secondary processes. Primary-process thinking can be defined as the way in which drives express themselves, discharge tension. Secondary-process thinking constitutes the basis of rational and goal-oriented thought. It also has delay functions.

On the basis of these principles, Freud systematised a theory of drives (or instinctual drives) to try and explain what governs the inner portion of the mind, arising from our bodily being.[7]

Freud contended that during the phallic phase a universal and recurrent process took place, the development of the Oedipus complex and its resolution in positive or negative forms.[8]

For Freud instinctual wishes were predominantly sexual in nature and he gave the energy of these drives the name 'libido'. Later in his theoretical development, Freud added aggressive wishes to the contents of the unconscious.[9]

In *Totem and Taboo* (1912), Freud examined infantile omnipotent fantasies and explored the psychosexual stages at which the self is cathected as the first libidinal object. Here was the beginning of the concept of narcissism, which was to be presented two years later.

In the paper 'On Narcissism' (1914a), Freud attempted to clarify the complicated problem of the person's relation to his love-objects and himself in both normal—'primary narcissism'—and pathological states—'secondary narcissism'.

In this paper, two central concepts were spelled out, those of identification and introjection. As I will discuss in detail at the end of this section, the distinction between an identification with the father and the choice of the father as an object can be treated as a core clarification for understanding the differences between the ego and the self.

According to Tuttman (1984a), the theory development carried out by Freud during this period was significantly influenced by the collaborative work taking place between himself and some of his close followers. Moreover, the ideas of identification, internalisation and introjection, developed during this period, mark the beginnings of developmental psychology and of Object Relations theory. Ferenczi and Abraham stressed the importance of early life dyadic interaction between mother and baby. Even though they neither theoretically differentiated between objects and their mental representations, nor elaborated on the stages in development of a sense of self in relation to objects, the beginnings of a theory of object relations was in the making.

In the 1914 study, Freud was also concerned with the child's formation of ideals on the basis of his parents as models. He introduced the concept of the ego ideal, which was later subsumed in the concept of the superego. As pointed out by Bateman and Holmes (1995: 56), primary narcissism persists into later life in the form of an 'ego ideal', which informs our aims, values and ambitions.[10]

The ego ideal represents internalised parental standards and expectations, including culturally determined ideas conveyed through parents. The conscience is seen as a separate but related self-critical organisation which functions to motivate the child to conform to the standards and precepts of the ego ideal.

In the metapsychological paper on 'The Unconscious' (1915b), a further conceptual development occurred: what had been described as the ego now became the 'system' conscious. Further developments in the concept of the ego followed. By 1917, in 'Mourning and Melancholia', Freud looked at pathological states of mourning. He wrote about the object relationship and clarified the concept of identification even further. The mechanism of identification was described as the archaic way by which the ego chooses an object and incorporates that object into itself. In discussing mourning and melancholia as reactions to object loss, he concluded that the lost object is incorporated and regressively replaced by means of identification.

Finally, the work published in 1920, *Beyond the Pleasure Principle,* may be regarded as introducing the last phase of Freud's theory development. In it, he postulated what later came to be seen as one of his least popular concepts and the locus of heated debate in contemporary psychoanalysis. Freud suggested that the aggressive drive was a derivative of a biologically based death instinct (Thanatos).

The use of the topographical model by Freud lasted for roughly twenty-six years. During this time psychoanalysis became well established as a movement, with national and international organisations. It also consolidated public arenas for the exchange and debate of ideas through the creation of specialised publications and the organisation of

conferences and scientific meetings. By 1923 the psychoanalytic movement had a fully developed system of training as well as an established
clientele around the world. It is also worth mentioning that this period
was marked by many schisms between Freud and his early collabora-
tors and, as these controversies took place, Freud was able to consolidate many aspects of his theory as well as his technical prescriptions as
the legitimate psychoanalytic principles to be adopted by others.[11]

The shift from the topographical model to the third frame of reference—Structural Theory—can be explained by Freud's continuing clinical experience as well as an awareness of an increasing number of
inconsistencies in the topographical model. Among the conceptual
problems was the acknowledgement that there was no clear place
within his topographical map of the mind for ideals, values and conscience. Also, he recognised that the influence of both the external
world on mental structures and the unconscious nature of defence
needed more exploration.

Another conceptual problem was that the word 'unconscious' was
being used in two senses: the 'descriptive' sense (which merely attributed a particular quality to a mental state) and the 'dynamic' sense
(which attributed a particular function to the psyche).

At this point in theory development, Freud was also struggling to
achieve a clearer understanding of the interaction between the internal
world and external events, especially in his discussion of internalisation and identification, which began in the papers 'On Narcissism'
(1914a) and 'Mourning and Melancholia' (1917).

In the structural theory of the mind, Freud put forward a model that
represented a tripartite division of the mental apparatus into three
major structures or agencies, which he called id, ego and superego. In
the topographical model, what had been most clearly differentiated
from the 'unconscious' had been the 'ego'. It now began to appear that
the ego itself ought partly to be described as 'unconscious'.

It thus became apparent that in regards to both the concepts of the
'unconscious' and 'the ego', the criterion of consciousness was no
longer helpful. Freud therefore abandoned the use of consciousness in
this capacity: 'being conscious' was henceforward to be regarded simply as a quality that might or might not be attached to a mental state.
The old 'descriptive' sense of the term was in fact all that remained.
The new terminology describes the id, the ego and the superego in the
following way.

The id is the agency containing the primitive instinctual drives, with all their hereditary and constitutional elements. It is dominated by the pleasure principle and functions according to the primary process. During development a portion of the id undergoes modification, under the influence of the child's interaction with the external world, to become the ego.

This latter agency is seen to deal with the task of self-preservation and the acquisition of means whereby a simultaneous adaptation to the pressures of the id, the superego, and the demands of reality can be brought about. The ego gains the function of delaying instinctual discharge and of controlling it by means of a variety of mechanisms, including mechanisms of defence.

The third agency, the superego, develops out of the residue of the child's early conflicts in relation to his parents, caretakers or other figures of authority. It is the vehicle of the conscience, of parental and cultural values, and of the child's own ideals.[12] Developmentally speaking, the genesis of the superego is derived from a transformation of the child's earliest object-cathexes into identifications: it takes the place of the Oedipus complex.

The ego is portrayed as an organisation trying to serve three masters at once—the id, the superego, and the demands of the external world. Anxiety could be aroused by threats from any of these three sources. Instead of anxiety being regarded simply as the way in which a threatening instinctual wish shows itself in consciousness (via a 'transformation' of libido), it is now seen quite differently, i.e. as a specific response of the ego. As will be shown in section three, after the structural theory was developed, the ego's mechanisms of defence came to be more intensely studied and interpreted in the treatment situation.

The concern with the way in which the ego adapted to the various and often conflicting demands made upon it was reflected in changes in psychoanalytic technique. The real world, whose significance had been de-emphasised in the second phase, was now endowed with great significance.

With the evolution of the structural theory, developmental notions became more intrinsic to Freud's vision of the mental apparatus. The ego and the superego, in particular, were conceived of as structures appearing and evolving in the course of development. The id too, is subject to developmental and maturational changes that give rise to the unfolding sequence of instinctual development from orality to adult genitality. On the other hand, the variety of experiences in the course of life, together with repressed ideational content, introduces ever-changing objects and modes of satisfaction of the drive impulses (i.e. instinctual wishes) into the id.

As development proceeds, the balance between the ego and the id shifts as the ego becomes more and more capable of controlling and delaying instinctual drive demands. In this third phase, the concept of the ego is extended. Freud now spoke of the ego as an active agency of the mental apparatus, an active participant in conflict with other agencies and the external world. The ego now is seen as a coherent organisation of mental processes, which is distinguished by being able to organise and to integrate different aspects of the person's experience and capacities. The ego's task, as seen by Freud, is to control the more primitive id impulses and to adapt these to outer reality in accordance with the reality principle, as well as to mollify the requirements of the superego.

The structural ego is also defined through its functions. These are primarily control over perception and activity, on the one hand, and control over drive impulses and wishes, on the other. Another important ego function is that of reality testing. The term ego now also describes the more rational, reality oriented and executive aspects of the personality and is partly conscious and partly unconscious.

After having outlined Freud's three models of the mind and the concept of the ego as delineated in the structural theory, we can go back to trace a better clarification of its distinction from the concept of 'self'. As already suggested at the beginning of this chapter, there are different assessments about the extent to which Freud differentiated the concepts of the ego and the self.

Kernberg (1982) has asserted that Freud used *Das Ich* indiscriminately—that is, as ego and as self—in order to maintain ambiguity and internal tension. This was Freud's way of indicating its system properties as well as the fact that, as part of these system properties, the ego is the seat of consciousness and, consequently, the consciousness of one's self or of the self as a person.

By contrast, McIntosh (1986) has argued that Freud's theory clearly differentiated between ego, self and character. This author suggests that Freud departed from common-sense words such as 'I', 'me', 'self' and 'myself' and took them as raw materials from which to build up his theories. Let us look at how McIntosh describes the differences he has identified in Freud's concepts.

First there is the person as a *subject,* who acts, thinks, feels, desires, suffers, enjoys... In [Freud's] work this common-sense usage grades off into the more technical and specialised concept of the system-structure ego... It is the system-structure ego which plays the central functioning role in organising the individual into a coherent subject capable of acting consciously in the world.

Second, there is the 'I' of one's own person as *object,* the 'I' that we think about, perceive, enjoy, love, hate, that we believe or wish ourselves to be... (McIntosh 1986: 430, my italics)

McIntosh provides a detailed and complex analysis of several of Freud's texts which cannot be fully discussed here. The following quotes will be used, however, since they provide core insights into Freud's thinking. McIntosh analyses concepts present in 'Project for a Scientific Psychology' (1950), 'On Narcissism' (1914a), 'Instincts and their Vicissitudes' (1915a) and the *Ego and the Id* (1923), and discusses the centrality of notions of: (a) the progression from primitive auto-erotism to 'primary narcissism' and genuine object choice, and (b) the centrality of the notion of 'identification' for an understanding of the concept of self. Let us look briefly at these.

The first is the notion that primitive auto-erotism of infancy and early childhood precedes the development of the self. Both developments are seen as completely dependent upon the acquisition of ego functions. As McIntosh points out:

In the primitive auto-erotic stages there can be pleasurable experiences to one's body, and this experience can have a mental content, be remembered and sought after, etc. but a 'self' in the form of a coherent and relatively stable intentional object has not yet emerged. The development of such an object requires the binding of psychic energy via linguistic (hyperinvested) processes, and the organisation of the psychic content of the investment into at least a semicoherent whole. In short, investment of the ego-as-object (the self) presupposes at least a minimal development of the ego-as-subject (the system ego)... The successor to primitive auto-erotism is *primary narcissism.* The special feature of primary narcissism, Freud points out, is that while an invested self-object has been formed, its content has not yet been articulated and differentiated into something clearly distinct from the world at large... (McIntosh 1986: 438-439, my italics)

The second issue is how Freud progressively clarified the role played by identification, a concept that is inter-related with those of differentiation, internalisation, introjection and identity.

McIntosh (1986: 441) suggests that, for Freud, it is identification which shapes both the self and the ego:

In order for the child to form a self which can become the object of an investment, it must be able to look at itself through the eyes of another person, i.e. it must see itself as someone else does, most basically as a distinct person, and more specifically as, e.g. 'little girl', 'naughty boy', etc. So from the start there is a twofold identification. First, the child adopts the parent's attitudes and modes of thought as its own, i.e. the ego-subject identifies with the parent. Second, via these attitudes and modes of thought, the child defines its self as the parents do, i.e. the self is formed via identification with the parent(s).

The second process requires the first, and in that sense the first is the more basic. Indeed, Freud states that identification 'is the earliest expression of an emotional tie with another person.

McIntosh (1986: 441) then quotes the following passage in Freud:

It is easy to state in a formula the distinction between an identification with the father and the choice of the father as an object. In the first case one's father is what one would like to *be,* and in the second he is what one would like to *have* [Freud's italics]. The distinction, that is, depends upon whether the tie attaches to *subject* or *object* of the ego [McIntosh's italics]—the former kind of tie is therefore already possible before any sexual object-choice has been made. It is much more difficult to give a clear metapsychological representation of the distinction. We can only see that identification endeavours to mould a person's own ego after the fashion of the one that has been taken as a model. (Freud 1921: 106 and 1923: 31)

McIntosh goes on to say:

Freud's point is that there cannot be an object without an ego to have the object, and since it is identification which shapes the ego, this process is in a sense prior to any object relation. In that sense the ego is prior to the self, but in practice the two develop, via identification, side by side. The primitive ego builds a primitive object, and as the ego evolves, so does the self. (However, the two develop by layers not by replacement).

Finally, McIntosh touches on the issue of self representation which, although it goes hand in hand with that of the self, is separate from the latter:

It must be noted, however, that identification is not the only process that creates the self. In addition... there is self perception, which builds the self according to what the subject perceives itself to be, and psychic need, which tends to make the self into what the subject wishes, hopes, or fears itself to be. (McIntosh 1986: 441-442)

Although the above quotations seem successful in arguing that Freud differentiated between the concepts of the ego and the self, McIntosh's contribution is unique. It contrasts sharply with the views of other authors, who either believe that ambiguity was maintained for a purpose (Kernberg, Laplanche and Pontalis and Padel), or that we can only fully understand Freud's concept of the ego if it is taken from the last stage of his theory development, i.e. the structural theory.

In the following sections, I will address the themes opened up by this outline. I will show how contemporary psychoanalytic thinking took up and developed different aspects of Freud's theory.

3. Ego Psychology

In *An Outline of Psychoanalysis* Freud stated that the child's attachment to the mother is the first and strongest object relationship, and that this unique bond becomes the prototype for all later love relations (1940: 188). While Freud himself did not empirically investigate the details of this basic relationship, we see in this formulation a change in psychoanalytic theory to include the pre-Oedipal phase of development in a systematic way. Indeed, after the 1940s, clear-cut theories of child development were put forward with important implications for the concepts of the ego and the self.

From the 1940s onwards the empirical basis of psychoanalytic knowledge expanded from what in its early days was based on Freud's self-analysis and the systematisation of clinical experience into case histories, to include child analysis and observations of children by analysts.[13]

Two contributions written towards the end of Freud's life seem to illustrate clearly this new trend and had a significant impact on later developments: Anna Freud's *The Ego and the Mechanisms of Defence* (1937) and Hartmann's *Ego Psychology and the Problem of Adaptation* (1939). They were relatively immediate outcomes of the theoretical developments in the structural model and initiated an important line of psychoanalytic thinking known in the postwar period as 'Ego Psychology'.

Anna Freud's work focused on the angle of ego's defence activity against the drives, which came to be known as the ego's defence mechanisms. She systematised Freud's 1926 formulations about conflict, anxiety and adaptation and considered defences as a means of maintaining functioning rather than succumbing to conflict (see especially her fourth chapter, 'The Mechanisms of Defence'). In some cases, defences allow the ego to bind anxiety and avoid displeasure. This can help the ego avoid anxiety and channel instincts so as to provide some gratification, 'thereby establishing the most harmonious relations possible between the id, the superego, and the forces of the outside world' (Anna Freud 1937: 176).

She re-emphasised the importance of the relationship of the ego to the external world and the normal and adaptive aspects of the personality. She considered defence mechanisms as not only responding to the dangers of the internal world but also to those of the external world.

In a paper where Anna Freud (1966) compares her own work with that of Hartmann, the reader is informed of the fact that their views appeared and were openly discussed at the same time, in the 1930s, in the Vienna Society. Moreover, we learn that Hartmann's idea of ego autonomy was initially met with a great deal of opposition from the analytic world.[14]

This is an important point to emphasise for it reveals the tensions within the psychoanalytic movement at that time. On the one hand, there was a perceived need by some psychoanalysts to expand

Freudian ideas, while others viewed any post-Freudian theoretical expansion as a threat to orthodox psychoanalysis. When Hartmann began his work, psychoanalytic treatment was based primarily on Freud's psycho-sexual theory. However, through the challenges posed by their clinical work, some analysts realised that the psychology of the self and important interactions with others were not adequately explained by drive theory alone. As we shall see, shortly after Hartmann emigrated to the United States, not only did his ideas become accepted, but for many years came to dominate mainstream American psychoanalysis.

Hartmann claimed an angle of autonomy for the ego and suggested that although the ego grows on conflict, these are not the only roots of ego development. Instead of the ego simply being a mediator between the demands of the id and the external world, Hartmann conceived of the ego as, in part, outside this area of conflict and thus able to interact with the external world, free from internal influences. He stressed the non-defensive aspects of the ego. This 'conflict-free sphere of the ego' develops independently, and flourishes unimpeded by conflict if environmental influences are reasonably favourable. It contains such functions as thinking, perception, language, learning, memory and rational planning. Development of these aspects of the personality may influence the experience of pleasure and satisfaction.

The ego's repertoire of adaptational resources usually develops in a 'conflict-free sphere', except under serious traumatic circumstances. In an 'average' expectable environment the individual gradually acquires the capacity to act upon himself and to elicit helpful environmental responses. Hartmann described the earliest stages of ego development from several angles, 'as a process of differentiation that leads to a more complete demarcation of ego and id and of self and outer reality; as the development of the reality principle; and as the way leading from primary narcissism to object relationships'.[15]

Whilst Freud had moved the focus from the external world to an emphasis on the internal workings of the mind, within the topographical theory, and back again in the structural model, Hartmann moved the focus further towards reality by suggesting that the experience of pleasure did not arise simply from satisfaction of instinctual wishes but *also depended on what good experiences the external world was able to offer*. Hartmann emphasised the crucial role of the caretaker in providing the infant with psychological as well as psychical nurturance, thereby facilitating maximal adaptational potential.

According to Hartmann (1950), psychoanalytic theory of the time did not offer a clear distinction between the terms ego, self and personality. The author suggested the following differentiation:

> In using the term narcissism, two sets of opposites often seem to be fused in one. The one refers to the self (one's own person) in contradiction to the object, the second to the ego (as a psychic system) in contradiction to other substructures of the personality. However, the opposite of object cathexis is not ego cathexis, but cathexis of one's own person, that is self-cathexis; in speaking of self-cathexis we do not imply whether this cathexis is situated in the id, in the ego, or in the superego. This formulation takes into account that we actually do find 'narcissism' in all three psychic systems; but in all of these cases there is opposition to (and reciprocity with) object cathexis. It therefore will be clarifying if we define narcissism as the libidinal cathexis not of the ego but of the self. (Hartmann 1950: 84-85)

Hartmann, therefore, introduced the term 'self' to refer to the whole person (both body and psychic organisation). For him, the psychic self contains, among other components, the ego and the psychic representations (of oneself and of objects). He also introduced the term 'self representation' as contrasted with 'object representation'.

Hartmann emigrated to the United States in 1941 and together with Kris, Loewenstein and Rapaport consolidated the ego psychology approach. On arriving in America Hartmann stated that 'adaptation to social structure and cooperation is essential to humanity'.[16] His theoretical task would be to explore the relevant mechanisms of such 'adaptation' by focusing on intrapsychic conflict and the resulting integration and coordination of contradictory drives, in line with the ideas Freud proposed in *The Ego and the Id*.

According to Kurzweil (1995: 202), such an approach was acceptable to native Freudians. It appealed to the American scientific ethos and resonated with issues that social scientists of the time were trying to solve.[17] Hartmann's views dominated American psychoanalysis from the 1940s well into the 1960s.

For many critics, the fact that the ego psychology approach came to be so widely accepted resulted in the shaping of American psychoanalysis into a conservative position, since the emphasis was placed on adjusting the demands of the instincts to fit in with what was socially possible or acceptable, i.e. on social adaptation.[18]

On the other hand, however, as Frosh (1987: 90-91) has suggested, there is much that is attractive in Hartmann's approach in that it takes account of the impact of external reality on personal development. By making the energy of the ego into a basic building block of development, Hartmann moved reality to centre stage. By claiming that there is a direct link between the psyche and reality through the ego, Hartmann implies that the internal economy of the mind can be affected by the external world in a way not described by Freud.

4. Object Relations

Although Jacobson is sometimes located within the ego psychology approach, her work may also be classified as a major contribution to American Object Relations theory. Jacobson's work inaugurated a view that was based in the structural theory and, at the same time, provided a developmental frame of self and objects.

It has been suggested by several authors (e.g. Tuttman 1984b), that Edith Jacobson's valuable contribution can be summarised as having put knowledge of external realities, and internal representations of the self and its key object relations, into the centre of psychoanalytic thought. She was also the first to attempt to trace the developmental lines of the self and its mental representations.

Perhaps, more than any of the above reviewed authors, Jacobson's writing allowed for bridging the gap between the ego as a structural unit, which is moulded under the impact both of reality and instinctual drives, and the growth of the ego with the development of object relationships. Edith Jacobson took up Hartmann's distinctions but developed them further. She stated that:

> The term 'self' which was introduced by Hartmann will, in agreement with him, be employed as referring to the whole of the person of an individual, including his body and body parts as well as his psychic organisation and its parts. The 'self' is an auxiliary descriptive term, which points to the person as a subject in distinction from the surrounding world of objects. (Jacobson 1965: 19)

Jacobson provided an important focus for Object Relations theory. She proposed that:

> The meanings of the concept of self and self representation, as distinct from that of ego, become clear when we remember that the establishment of the system ego sets in with the discovery of the object world and the growing distinction between it and one's own physical and mental self. From the ever-increasing memory traces of pleasurable and unpleasurable instinctual, emotional, ideational, and functional experiences and of perceptions with which they become associated, images of the love objects as well as those of the bodily and psychic self emerge. Vague and variable at first, they gradually expand and develop into consistent and more or less realistic endopsychic representations of the object world and of the self. (Jacobson1965:19)

Jacobson clarified a constellation of early defence mechanisms intimately connected with the vicissitudes of self and object differentiation, which predate the definitive emergence of the tripartite intrapsychic structures of ego, superego and id. Her developmental frame is thus:

> Intrapsychic life starts out as a primary psychophysiological self in which the ego and id are not yet differentiated, and in which aggression and libido drives are undifferentiated as well. The first intrapsychic structure is a fused self-object representation which gradually evolves under the impact of the relationship between mother and infant...
> This symbiotic phase of development comes to an end with the gradual differentiation between the self representation and the object representation.
> At this stage pleasure principle and 'primary process' prevail. Unconscious early (pre-Oedipal) fantasy life, pregenital sexual affect motor activity begin to develop, although affective organ language is still predominant. Multiple, rapidly changing and not yet clearly distinguished part images of love objects and body part images are formed and linked up with the memory traces of past pleasure-unpleasure experiences and become vested with libidinal and aggressive forces. (Jacobson 1965: 52-54)

When the child learns to walk and talk and acquires urinary and bowel control, a more organised stage sets in. Object and self awareness grow, perception and organisation of memory traces expand. The object imagery gradually extends to the surrounding animate and inanimate world. Language symbols, functional motor activity and reality testing develop. However, magical animistic fantasy life, preverbal at first, predominates and remains concentrated on the mother until pre-Oedipal and later Oedipal triangular confirmations form. Object constancy develops.

As the child progresses:

Infantile sexuality reaches its climax; fusion and neutralisation of sexual drives set in. Though processes are organised, functional motor activity and object relations develop rapidly. Emotional and instinctual control is being established; tension tolerance increases. Predominance of libido and enduring libidinal object investment develop. As tender attachments grow and affects become attached to ego functions, awareness of self begins to extend to awareness of emotional and thought processes, of ego attitudes and ego functions. *A concept of self as an entity that has continuity and direction is formed.* Reality principle and 'secondary' process become more dominant. Signal anxiety (castration fear) exerts a drastic influence on repression and counter-cathectic formations. (Jacobson 1965: 53, my italics)

As outlined by Kernberg (1984), in Jacobson's scheme, the Oedipal and latency periods are marked by the integration of self representations into an organised self concept. Furthermore, ego identity, which originally stemmed from the integration of good and bad self representations at the time when object constancy was established, is further consolidated. Pathological conditions such as the breakdown of ego boundary and loss of reality testing can be seen as the result of the refusion of self and object representations.

The focus on the pre-Oedipal relationship between infant and mother is also the starting point of Ronald Fairbairn's theory. For Fairbairn, the quality of the mother's loving care is seen as crucial to early development. According to this author, the deprivation of love in early childhood can lead to a withdrawal from spontaneous relations with the mother and an overinvestment in one's inner world.

Fairbairn attempted to develop an overall model for psychoanalytic Object Relations theory, but, as we shall see, established his own unique theoretical stance. He was greatly influenced by Melanie Klein's work, particularly by the concepts of the paranoid-schizoid and depressive positions (see below). Like Klein, he also attributed great importance to the first year of life and suggested that core structural developments took place during that time. Fairbairn departed from Klein, however, on his views about fantasy and the ego, and rejected her conceptualisation of the death instinct.

For Fairbairn, moreover, Freud's libido theory needed to be reassessed. For the former, psychoanalysis should be concerned with events within relationships of dependence on others, rather than on the vicissitudes of instincts. Fairbairn conceptualised libido as a function of the ego and aggression as a reaction to frustration or deprivation. He dispensed with an independent id. Fairbairn conceived of the ego as a unified structure present from birth, rather than developed from the id, as a result of its relation with reality.[19]

Thus the ego is central and active from early life. Its relationship with objects is primary. Fairbairn's theory is based on an original state of infantile dependence and the struggles of a vulnerable ego, which is oriented towards external reality and motivated to seek out and develop secure relationships.

Fairbairn's second departure from Freud relates to his views on psychic energy itself. Although Fairbairn retained the term libido, for him, the psychic economy is object seeking rather than pleasure seeking. The infant is oriented towards reality from the start and the quality of interpersonal relations structures and transforms the libidinal drives themselves.

Fairbairn proposed an alternative to Freud's model of the mind and developed a framework for normal development and pathological conditions in terms of dynamic structures within the self. He replaced the structural model of id/ego/superego with the basic endopsychic structure, a unitary, all embracing model, for which he retained the term ego. The ego is seen as a source of energy and is from the start oriented towards reality, seeking a relationship with the primal object. The central ego is an undivided ego. The structure of the mind develops from this pristine ego through processes of internalisation, splitting and subsequently repression of the maternal object.

Fairbairn also replaced Freud's body-dependent developmental phases of the oral, anal, phallic and genital, with a scheme based on the quality of relationships with objects. The three stages of development are: infantile dependence, quasi-independence and mature dependence.

Infantile dependence involves primary identification, something akin to fusion with an object not yet fully differentiated from the self. Infantile dependence, primary identification and narcissism are thus connected in the model. In this stage, whole objects are treated by the infant as part objects.

Since Fairbairn conceived of the ego as attached libidinally to objects, the splitting of the object involves the splitting of parts of the ego associated with it. The ego can split into two parts, one dealing with external figures and another linked to internal objects.

The infant's early life is characterised as unconsciously splitting and internalising subjectively experienced components of important external figures. The first objects to be treated in this way are the frustrating aspects of needed persons (i.e. the 'bad mother') with the aim of gaining control over them.

Quasi-independence is a long transitional stage when the infant establishes firmer relationships with external objects, which are progressively better differentiated, and organises his or her internal world with the internal representations of objects. Discrimination, acceptance and rejection characterise this stage.

For Fairbairn, the individual develops from the early stages of dependency through a transitional stage, and finally to a mature dependency stage. The latter reflects the achievement of full self-object differentiation and a give and take relationship with whole objects.

As pointed out by Grotstein and Rinsley, an important consequence of Fairbairn's theory is that internal object relations are a compensation for environmental deprivation:

Fairbairn differentiated between 'interpersonal relationships' and 'object relationships'. A nonpathological relationship with a real person, he maintained, does not require internalisation because the interpersonal interaction is inherently satisfying. In contrast, an intolerably ambivalent relationship results in a splitting of one's attitude about the person, such that a rejected part of that person is transformed into the status of an 'internal object'. Thus, the shadow of object relations falls upon interpersonal relations and inexorably constrains them.

In Fairbairn's object-relational view, then, it is the external person who is the disappointing object. Pathological relationships are characterised by 'object relatedness' in terms of their need to adapt to or comply with a disappointing real-life situation by internalising the very badness of the needed (but rejecting) person. Indeed, the more unsatisfying an object (e.g. mother, father) has been in actual reality, the more a child is compelled to internalise it. Specifically, the child takes in those images of the mother or the father that cause fear or shame. (Grotstein and Rinsley 1994: 5-6)

Thus, a significant aspect of Fairbairn's theory is that continuous splitting of internal objects and the fantasies associated with them arise as a consequence of a failure in the maturational environment. To Fairbairn fantasy is a substitute response to external frustration, while, as we will see below, for Kleinians it is a basic element of psychological functioning. For Fairbairn, the inadequacy of real external relations ,therefore, leads the infant to create internal fantasy objects, yet these compensatory fantasies limit the child's capacity for healthy development and real interpersonal interaction. The underlying assumption about normal development is of ever higher degrees of unity of the ego and of self—'real' object differentiation.

There is a strong sense of essentialism in Fairbairn's postulation of an innate, unified and integrated ego. For transition from one stage of development to another is seen as a fundamentally natural process, as a gradual unfolding of needs and potentials that take place within the context of a carefully graded pattern of separations.

Similarly to Jacobson, Donald Winnicott's work has provided a bridge between Freud's drive theory and an interpersonal perspective.

Although Winnicott did not conceptualise along metapsychological lines, his concepts invigorated psychoanalytic thinking of the time. His developmental steps include: the stage of dual union, the stage of hallucinatory wish fulfilment; the stage of playing, and the stage of creativity in adult life.

For Winnicott early infant development begins with a particular mind frame of the mother of a newborn baby. Primary maternal preoccupation is a state of great attunement between the infant's needs and the mother's responses. This allows for the child's illusion of omnipotence. The drive-driven child conjures up in his mind an object suited to his needs. By responding as a 'good enough mother' and presenting the baby with such a dutiable object, complementary to his wish, a moment of illusion is created in the baby, who feels he has made the object himself. This omnipotence works as a basis through which frustrating experiences can be dealt with and progressive differentiation between me-not me, self and objects can take place. Only once this process is under way can a healthy development of a creative and playful self be born.

Object relating is something that the maturational process drives the baby to achieve, but cannot happen securely unless the world is presented to him or her well enough. The adaptive and flexible mother presents the world in such a way that the baby starts with a ration of the experience of omnipotence, this being the proper foundation for his or her later coming to terms with the reality principle. The mother's mental health and proper attunement are the basis upon which an inner world in the infant can develop:

> [W]hen the baby is living in a subjective world, health cannot be described in terms of the individual alone. Later it becomes possible for us to think of a healthy child in an unhealthy environment, but these words make no sense at the beginning, until the baby has become able to be clear about the not-me as distinct from the me, and between the shared *actual* and the phenomena of personal psychical reality, and has something of an internal environment. (Winnicott 1986: 23)

Furthermore, the mother's attunement with the baby allows her to provide just the 'right dose' of frustration. As the infant works through developmentally adequate challenges, the emergence of a sense of self is enabled:

> In health the mother is able to delay her function of failing to adapt, till the baby has become able to react with anger rather than be traumatised by her failures. Trauma means the breaking of the continuity of the line of the individual's existence. It is only on a continuity of existing that the sense of self, of feeling real, and of being, can eventually be established as a feature of the individual personality. (Winnicott 1986: 22)

If environmental support is 'good enough' this sense of self will evolve into what Winnicott called the 'true self'. Only once this has been established can omnipotence be given up and the reality of pain and loss be faced. The infant then gradually consolidates differentiations between internal and external, reality and illusion, realising and accepting that there is an outside reality that is not the result of ones own projections.

According to Winnicott (1986: 31), the achievement of a 'true self' includes a sense of feeling real, of being, and of the experiences feeding back into the personal psychical reality, enriching it, and giving it scope. As a result, the healthy person's inner world is related to the outer or actual world and yet is personal and capable of an aliveness of its own. Introjective and projective identifications are constantly taking place.

In contrast to a 'true self', Winnicott refers to a 'false self' as a pathological condition where a complete schism of the mind takes place. Its most extreme example can be found in schizophrenia. The emergence of a 'false self' is related to environmental failure at an early stage of emotional development. It is a highly organised defence mechanism, and is experienced by the individual as a sense of futility, irrelevance and unreality. The false self is totally compliant to the environment and conceals frustrated and sequestered drives:

> I refer to those people who have unconsciously needed to organ-
> ise a false-self front to cope with the world, this false front being
> a defence designed to protect the true self. (The true self has been
> traumatised and it must never be found and wounded again.)
> The false self, from our point of view here, though a successful
> defence, is not an aspect of health. It merges into the Kleinian
> concept of manic defence... (Winnicott 1986: 33)

The sense of futility and unreality experienced by those with a 'false self' is strongly associated with its complaint nature. As suggested by Elliott (1994), due to the loss of maternal sensitivity, the small infant tries to make an emotional connection with the mother by abandoning its own wishes and incorporating her demands, desires and feelings. It is as if the child, unable to find an adequate representation of its own needs and psychic states, turns defensively against itself by internalising the attitudes and reactions of others.

As critically emphasised by Frosh (1987),[20] although Winnicott accepts that the newly born infant has a fragmented ego (even accepting the existence of the id), he stresses the naturalness of the process whereby the child's sense of integrated selfhood is formed—what is required is simply a supportive, non-intrusive environment and it is environmental failure that gives rise to internal splitting.

As we have already discussed, the view of a basic unity of the psyche, and that psychological splits are introduced by frustrating experiences with the maternal object, is shared by Fairbairn. Others play an essentially facilitating role in the construction of the self. It is only if there is environmental failure that a debilitating, unconscious fragmentation of the self arises. This suggests the existence of a human 'essence' that stands outside the social world, even if it needs certain environmental conditions to apply before it can be brought to fruition.

According to Frosh (1987), a 'primary unity' view of the psyche has been challenged by other post-Freudian approaches, including that proposed by Melanie Klein. Klein asserts the inherently split nature of the mind, as an entity imbued with internal contradictions in its fundamental nature.

Melanie Klein's theory is simultaneously an instinct theory and an Object Relations theory. Like Freud, she thought of the individual as driven by life and death instincts, but she never spoke of instincts in and of themselves or divorced from objects; they are inherently attached to objects. Thus object relationship is fundamental to this approach, even if she wrote relatively little about it as an end in itself.

According to Klein, unconscious phantasy is the primary content of unconscious mental processes. Phantasy refers to the psychic representation of instincts, but because of the indissoluble link between instincts and objects, it is also the arena in which the child's object relational drama is experienced. This does not, however, mean that the experiences are not in any important sense real: phantasy is not merely an escape from reality, but a constant and unavoidable accompaniment of real experiences, constantly interacting with them. In contrast to Fairbairn's view of phantasy as a substitute response to external frustration, in the Kleinian view it is a basic element of psychological functioning, without which there would be no mental process at all.

As pointed out by Bott Spillius (1988), since in Klein's view instincts are inherently attached to objects, relationships with external objects are assumed to become the focus of unconscious phantasy as soon as any form of mental activity is possible. Klein assumes that the individual has a rudimentary ego at birth involving the capacity for some organisation. It can experience anxiety and can attempt to do something psychically to fend it off. Similarly, Klein assumes that the new-

born baby has a rudimentary capacity to relate to objects in external
reality and in phantasy, though she makes it clear that the capacity to
distinguish internal from external is at first very limited. Through the
constant operation in phantasy of projection, introjection, and identification, an inner world of objects and self is built up which is used
throughout to give meaning to events in the external world.

Klein's conception of the paranoid-schizoid position is a constellation of anxieties, defences, and object relationships characteristic of
early infancy. This position is the first and most primitive organisation
of the mental apparatus, distributing the emotional experiences in relation to internal and external objects into a dynamic framework that
continues to exert influence throughout life, despite modification by
the attainment of its counterpart, the depressive position. The defensive mechanisms predominating in the paranoid-schizoid position are
splitting, projective identification, fragmentation, introjection, idealisation and magical omnipotent denial.

The infant projects love and hate onto the mother's breast, splitting
it into a 'good' (gratifying) and a 'bad' (frustrating) object. The good
object is idealised, perceived as capable of providing unlimited gratification. The bad object, by contrast, becomes a terrifying persecutor.
The paranoid-schizoid position is therefore characterised by persecutory anxiety as the infant fears being destroyed by the bad object.
Omnipotent denial is a mechanism used to divest the persecuting
object of reality or power.

As suggested by Moore and Fine (1990), the language adopted by
Klein to describe this position reveals its core characteristic. The designation *paranoid* refers to over-threatening anxiety and phantasied anni-
hilation by persecutory internal objects. It is also called *schizoid,* to indicate the splitting the infant's self undergoes in phantasy in order to
achieve a suitable relationship to the goodness of the object.

The depressive position is a constellation of characteristic anxieties,
defences, and object relationships that normally develops in the second
trimester of infancy but continues throughout life, never totally
worked through. The distinctive features of the depressive position are
the integration of part objects to form the whole object and the painful
recognition by the individual that his/her feeling of love and hate are
directed to the same, whole object. The concern for the object is central
to this position. Object separateness and independence are also its hallmark. Klein also suggests that there is an intricate relationship between
the depressive position, symbolic thought and creativity.

In order to transcend the schizoid poles of paranoid displacing and projective idealisation, and arrive at the depressive position, the infant needs to integrate conflicting feelings and come to terms with the fact that the mother is an independent and whole person. Such a transition involves reparations, which proceed from the infant's first experiences of gratitude, resulting from the acceptance of the reality of dependence upon the maternal object.

These 'restorative' attempts are also closely associated with creative capacities, which reparation and gratitude seem to enhance. The attainment of the 'depressive' position entails experiencing guilt and ambivalence as well as negotiating depressive feelings.

According to Klein,

> In normal development, in the second quarter of the first year, persecutory anxiety diminishes and depressive anxiety comes to the fore, as a result of the ego's greater capacity to integrate itself and to synthesize its objects. This entails sorrow, and guilt about the harm done (in omnipotent phantasies) to an object which is now felt to be both loved and hated; these anxieties and the defences against them represent the depressive position... Internalisation is of great importance for projective processes, in particular that the good feelings can be projected on to external objects. It strengthens the ego, counteracts the process of splitting and dispersal and enhances the capacity for integration and synthesis. The good internalised object is thus one of the preconditions for an integrated and stable ego and for good object relations. (Klein 1997: 143-4)

In closing this review of Kleinian ideas, I would like to raise some important points. First, the Kleinian approach has been criticised by many Freudians, sometimes resulting in quite fierce debates.[21]

Second, although to the best of my knowledge Melanie Klein and Kleinian authors have not explicitly addressed the ways in which the structural ego relates with the experiential self, there are some indications in the theory that provide for a dynamic view of how these two levels of mental functioning might work.

The central idea is that on one level the paranoid-schizoid and the depressive positions are a developmental account. They can be seen in a continuum, in which the latter supersedes the former, as the maturational process takes place. This allows for a greater understanding of certain pathologies, such as of patients who have never completely outgrown the early phase of development—the paranoid-schizoid position—or have regressed to it at some stage in their lives.

At another level, however, these two positions can be seen *as states*. Individuals operate within different states, with one predominating over the other, throughout their lives. There is a constant shift between states of greater splitting and dissociation, and of states of a greater degree of integration and completeness. Steiner has suggested that the analytic situation is a privileged place to see this constant shifting of states:

> [Through analysis] we can learn to evaluate whether (the patient's) anxieties, mental mechanisms and object relations are primarily depressive or primarily paranoid-schizoid, and this will determine the way we interpret. A continuous movement between the two positions takes place so that neither dominates with any degree of completeness or permanence. Indeed it is these fluctuations which we try to follow clinically as we observe periods of integration leading to depressive position functioning or disintegration and fragmentation resulting in a paranoid-schizoid state. Such fluctuations can take place over months and years as an analysis develops, but can also be seen in the fine grain of a session, as moment to moment changes. (Steiner 1988: 324-325)

Kleinian framing of mental structures and functioning, therefore, provides us with a far more multi-layered view of the psyche and of the individual's experience in the world. If, as suggested, we take the paranoid-schizoid and the depressive positions as states, the issue then becomes one about *differing degrees* of integration/disintegration, at a particular point in time.

As we have seen, in Fairbairn there is a 'natural' unity of the psyche, which only fragments and splits as a result of trauma. Similarly, in Winnicott, it is only if the child is deprived of a good-enough environment that a debilitating unconscious fragmentation of the self arises, in the form of a 'false self'.

For Klein, on the other hand, a sense of self emerges in its relations with and distinction from unconscious internal objects. As pointed out by Elliott (1994), the central role played by phantasy processes can be seen as a kind of continual shuttling of inner and outer worlds, from which a sense of self emerges as an outcrop of unconscious 'internal objects'.

We can thus suggest that the view of normal development as a linear and progressive process, leading to the emergence of a self which is stable and wholly integrated, as proposed by Fairbairn and Winnicott, should be questioned. Perhaps this view should be replaced by another concept of the self that accepts that there are different degrees of self-object separateness, and of integration/disintegration between part-selves. Furthermore, a notion of personal identity as unique and clear-cut should be replaced by one that is more multi-layered and polyvalent.

The different approaches reviewed in this section throw light on the lack of a clear-cut unified theory of the ego and the self. The main questions one should raise are: what are the presuppositions in each of the approaches reviewed, in regards to normal and pathological development; what is the role played by environmental factors; and which approach to the psyche should be adopted, a model with a notion of an inherent unity of the ego/self, or models which incorporate more multi-layered and polyvalent notions of selfhood? As I hope to have shown, Kleinian ideas provide some theoretical concepts which may lead us in the latter direction.[22]

5. Concluding Remarks

As we have seen from the above review, there is no clear-cut unifying theory regarding the concepts of the ego and the self.

Freud's ideas cannot be encompassed within a single unified framework. His models of the mind overlap rather than supersede each other. The theory of dreams, for example, is still most explicitly formulated in terms of the topographical model, rather than related to the second phase in his development of theory.

Although McIntosh offers us an outline of how the concepts of the ego and the self could be clearly identified in Freud, the very problem of theorising the relations between mental structure and psychic agency, and the self as an existential dimension, is not resolved.

Post-Freudian approaches—including ego psychology, American and British Object Relations theorists and the Kleinian approach—have attempted to tackle this problem. However, although they offer us a more sophisticated reading of our knowledge about the ego and the self, with the exception of Fairbairn, they do not constitute alternative metapsychologies.

In post-Freudian developments we see that each author has selected and elaborated upon different aspects of Freud's work. New ideas overlap rather than replace original formulations and, to a certain extent, each approach provides a partially incomplete formulation.

The underlying differences between the authors reviewed in this chapter concern their different attempts to strike a balance between environmental and intrapsychic factors in the development of the personality. As a result, the various approaches may be classified as intrapsychic, interpersonal or mixed.

Another important contrast that can be identified refers to underlying assumptions about the psyche. In other words, whether it is viewed as inherently unified and able under correct environmental support to flourish into a coherent and completely integrated self, or whether it is considered to be inherently split and imbued with internal contradictions. In the latter view, the ego and the self are entities that are constantly being re-drawn in contradictory and fragmented ways.

In the chapters that follow, contributors will indicate the current use and clinical applications of the concepts reviewed above. It should be stressed, however, that adherence to particular theoretical frames does not translate directly in the day to day clinical work. While the adoption of a theoretical framework by a clinician can be seen as the result of the way a psychoanalyst positions himself/herself in relation to broader philosophical and political standpoints, the way clinical work is carried out is effected by one's socialisation into the psychoanalytic and psychotherapeutic professions.

As emphasised by Bateman and Holmes (1995), an analyst's adherence to one particular strand of psychoanalytic theory and therapy results from positioning oneself in relation to quite abstract themes, including the following: the extent to which experience is determined by the environment, and the extent to which it is innate; whether a mechanistic or humanistic view of the mind is taken; the balance between determinism and freedom; the emphasis on mental forces as opposed to meanings and language; and whether a position of mentalism, realism or constructivism is adopted.

In addition to the analyst's positioning within these abstract debates, psychoanalytic research and reflections on clinical practice have demonstrated that the clinical work of psychoanalysts is not a direct translation of general theoretical concepts. Rather, it is influenced by a variety of personal, biographical variables as well as sociological and cultural processes.

Firstly, as argued by Sandler (1983), there is a wide gap between the 'official' or 'public' formulations sanctioned by psychoanalytic institutes and different psychoanalytic schools of thought, at a particular point in time, and analysts' 'implicit, private theories' which emerge from their attempt to understand a particular patient.

Secondly, as Hamilton (1996) has demonstrated, analysts' interpretative practices are not directly informed by abstract theoretical formulations, but undergo 'local translations' of different kinds. The analyst's preconscious, for example, mediates how theory is applied at the clinical level.

Thirdly, as I have argued elsewhere (Mangabeira 1999), since the transmission of psychoanalytic knowledge is highly dependent upon the 'personal equation', i.e. the style of one's training analyst and supervisor, and the general outlook of one's training process, socialisation into a particular psychoanalytic culture is far more relevant in shaping the professional identity of an analyst than the clear-cut adherence to one particular school of thought.

Notes

[1] It seems worthwhile to point out that Kerr (1992: 358-359) used the terms 'official', 'orthodox' and 'loyalist' with hesitation since there has never been an appointed committee of the International Psychoanalytic Association whose function was to sanction 'approved' work. Kerr used these terms, however, to indicate a universe of discourse that was largely, though not exclusively, produced and consumed by practising psychoanalysts. This discourse had its heyday in the two decades after The Second World War.

[2] It is argued that the ambiguity resulting from Freud's use of *Das Ich* was compounded by Strachey's translation into English in the Standard Edition. For a detailed discussion, refer to Kernberg (1982) and Richards (1985).

[3] According to Laplanche and Pontalis (1988: 138) '[I]t is impossible to assign two senses of the word 'ego' to two different periods: the word is used in its full sense from the start, even though this sense is gradually refined through a series of (theoretical) developments... It seems inadvisable to draw an outright distinction between the ego as a person and the ego as a psychic agency, for the simple reason that the *interplay between these two meanings is at the core of the problematic of the ego*... The attempt to identify and eliminate a supposed 'terminological ambiguity' is in this case merely a way of avoiding a fundamental problem'. (My italics)

[4] For a very interesting discussion on how Freud's ideas were at the same time revolutionary and conservative, particularly his adherence to nineteenth century sexual prejudices, see Breger (1981).

[5] Freud's abandonment of the seduction theory has been the subject of a heated controversy in contemporary psychoanalysis. This controversy was inaugurated by Masson (1984) with strong accusatory overtones. For details on this debate, see also Kerr (1992) and Malcolm (1997). For a discussion on the relevance of Freud's theoretical shift and its implications for psychoanalytic theory, see Blass and Bennett (1994).

[6] Interestingly enough, the controversy around Freud's abandonment of the seduction theory has been re-ignited in the US in recent years as a result of an increase in the number of patients being diagnosed with 'multiple personality disorder'. Since the origin of this condition is seen to reside in childhood sexual abuse, Freud's conceptual differentiation between 'historical' (objective) and 'psychical' truth is being questioned. The 'false memory syndrome' has emerged as a reactive category, used by therapists and lawyers who are defending parents who, allegedly, have been wrongly accused of abusing their children. For references on this discussion, see note above. For references on the history of these two conditions, see Acocella (1998), Borch-Jacobsen (1997) and Hacking (1992, 1995).

[7] The 'drive' theory of psychoanalysis had its first elaboration in 1905 in *Three Essays on the Theory of Sexuality*. In this formulation Freud emphasised the role of sexual drives in normal development and in the origins of pathologies. The psychosexual phases of childhood were outlined as the oral, anal, phallic and genital.

[8] Freud's proposition of the Oedipus complex has been the subject of important controversies which question, for example, whether the complex is in fact universal or only deemed to be so due to Freud's ethnocentrism. Feminist writers in particular have taken issue with Freud's view of female sexuality, as proposed by the complex, and its notions of 'penis envy' and 'castration anxiety'. For feminist critiques, refer to Chodorow (1978a), Dinnerstein (1976) and Seu (1998).

[9] The emergence of the concept of 'libido' and the second drive theory, developed in 1920 to include the 'death instinct', are very good illustrations of how theory development is the result of negotiations, outcomes and dynamics which extend beyond the boundaries of 'clinical work'. Their stabilisation as theoretical principles and questions about their centrality to psychoanalytic theory provided for the emergence of many controversies during the early 1900s, such as those with Adler and Jung as well as in the 1940s, in the disputes between Anna Freud and Melanie Klein. For details on the former, see Freud (1914b), McGuire (1991) and Ellenberger (1994). For details on the controversial discussions in the British Psycho-Analytical Society, see Baudry (1994), King and Steiner (1991) and Kohon (1986).

[10] At this time Freud distinguished clearly between 'ego ideal' and the 'institution of conscience' which he saw as 'an embodiment, first of parental criticism, and subsequently of that of society' (Freud 1914a: 96) For a detailed discussion about the concepts of 'ego ideal' and 'ideal self', refer to Sandler et. al. (1963).

[11] For details on the history of psychoanalysis during this period and Freud's central role in closing and stabilising psychoanalytic principles, see Mangabeira (1999).

[12] As pointed out by Richards (1985), after the publication of *The Ego and the Id* and the two or three shorter works immediately following it, 'ego ideal' disappears almost completely as a technical term.

[13] The introduction of child observation and child analysis exerted a major impact on psychoanalytic theory development. It is alleged that they brought a more 'respectable' and 'scientific' outlook to psychoanalysis by allowing for the testing of major psychoanalytic hypotheses. Among those engaged in such a project were Hartmann, Anna Freud and Melanie Klein. It is worthwhile pointing out that this view can and should be questioned. There is a debate, for example, about whether child observation can in fact be used as evidence for theory building. Bell (1995: 223) has suggested that 'observation of infants can never be evidential for psychoanalysis, as it excludes that which is central to psychoanalysis, namely the internality of experience and its roots in the unconscious'.

[14] According to Anna Freud (1966: 17) 'There were many who feared that the explicit introduction of an ego psychology into psychoanalysis endangered its position as a depth psychology, a discipline concerned exclusively with the activity of the instinctual drives and the functioning of the unconscious mind'.

[15] Quote from Hartmann 1939: 165-166, in Tuttman 1984a.

[16] Quoted from Kurzweil (1995: 200).

[17] According to Kurzweil, Talcott Parsons, a prominent figure of American sociology during this period and well known as a conservative, not only took up ego psychology as a framework but also celebrated it in his papers and lectures.

[18] For details on this controversy, see Frosh (1987), Kernberg (1997) and Kurzweil (1995).

[19] In 'Experimental Aspects of Psychoanalysis', Fairbairn clearly spelled out his disagreements with Freud regarding the structural theory. Refer to Sharff and Fairbairn Birtles (1994).

[20] Frosh has also provided an interesting critique of how Winnicott's emphasis on the mother-child relationship can pose conformist dangers. This is so because it presupposes a biologically determined role that must take priority over all other aspects of a woman's life. It reveals an ethnocentric stance, since patterns of infant-mother relationships are relative culturally and historically. For more details see Frosh (1987).

[21] Refer, for example, to the controversial discussions that took place in the British Psycho-Analytical Society between 1941 and 1945, in which Melanie Klein and Anna Freud were the central protagonists. The debates were around disagreements with the following Kleinian ideas, among others: 1. The centrality accorded to Freud's most speculative idea—the death instinct—and Klein's stress on the aggressive drive, 2. Her timetable, 'compressing' into the earliest period of life ego functioning as well as unconscious phantasies and object relations purported to exist from birth. This controversy illustrates in a very clear way the theme of the socially constructed nature of knowledge development in psychoanalysis. It was, at the same time, a confrontation between different theories and a political and institutional crisis. Moreover, as Klein and Freudians claimed that their theories had support from child analysis and child observation, this controversy also raised debates about what should be considered legitimate in terms of empirical basis of knowledge development in psychoanalysis.

[22] Indeed, the concepts of 'the ego', 'the self' and 'selfhood' are core themes in debates about psychoanalysis and the postmodern turn. See, for example, Elliott and Spezzano (2000).

Section Two

Section Two

THE EGO AND THE SELF: A CONTEMPORARY FREUDIAN PERSPECTIVE

Mark Morris

Fundamentally, it could be said that psychoanalysis is the study of the self from the perspective of the self. Other academic disciplines that study the self do so from different starting points, sociology from a society of selves, social psychology from the social interactions of selves, behavioural psychology from the observable actions of the self, and so on. Neuroanatomy and neurophysiology explore the structures and processes of the parts of the brain whose functions contribute to aspects of the experience of being. The psychoanalytic study of the self is perhaps closer to neurology in that the focus of study is directed at the minute detail of the self, with psychoanalysis starting from the mind side of the Cartesian dualistic divide between the mind and the brain.

Within psychoanalysis, the analytic practice and theory of analysts from the different schools have vastly more in common than not. There is a broad acceptance of the existence and overwhelming importance of the unconscious; there is broad agreement about the centrality of the Oedipus complex and the importance of the developmental task of negotiating a solution. Clinically, there is no controversy about the nature of the setting, namely regular sessions held three to five times a week with the patient on a couch facing away from the analyst and with the only injunction being to say whatever comes in to their mind. Nevertheless, there are differences in emphasis and in practice. In this chapter I try to elucidate some of the perspectives that analysts who might consider themselves Contemporary Freudians bring to a debate about the ego and the self.

Given the centrality of the self both in the discipline, and also in this volume, it would seem appropriate to try to identify and define the different terms as I use them in this chapter, with the caveat that these terms and definitions are personal, and are included for clarity rather than claiming to be definitive statements. Firstly, the 'self' refers to the psychological and physical entirety of the person, inclusive of conscious and unconscious parts of the mind, the body and the somatosensory interface between the two. Within this broad and inclusive notion of the self lie two sets of terms that describe the self from different perspectives; firstly the self in its environment, and secondly the self as an internal or mental environment. Considering the notions from the outside, from an environmental perspective, a person's 'identity' refers to the psychological component—a continuous sense of self which need not necessarily be linked to the biological self, but which distinguishes them from other 'selves' with different 'identities'. As an 'individual', the person is being considered as a part of a social system; the self defined by their role in a social structure that surrounds them. Within this structure the individual can operate as an 'agent' demonstrating volition and choice within the structure of the social setting that surrounds them.

In contrast to these inclusive notions of the self, the 'ego' has a narrow technical definition. The term 'ego' refers to a specific psychic function that maintains balance and sanity between the gratificatory pleasure principle demands of the id, and the prohibitory moralism of the superego. The ego maintains balance by the referential use of the reality principle in the mitigation of the demands of the id, and the ego maintains sanity via the use of 'ego defences' to protect the self from unpleasant aspects of reality. When the term 'ego' is used in common language to refer to consciousness, or the sense of 'I' or self, this is not so much a mistake as a side effect of the terms passing into popular parlance—rather like the popular 'fact' that leukaemia is a cancer of the blood, when it is actually a disease of bone marrow and lymph tissue.

The subjective sense of 'I' is consciousness. This has most helpfully been described by a combination of the philosophy of mind, and the anatomy and physiology of the brain. Philosophically, Descartes' dualist riddle about how the mind and body interact has been solved by Ryle's notion of the mind as function rather than entity. From the other side, the task for the neurophysiologist studying mind is to use the science of brain to track down this function. Some of this can be mapped out, by establishing which bits of the brain contribute which aspects of mind. For example, the sum of the content of consciousness—the perception of the five senses—can be attributed with considerable accuracy to parts of the cerebral cortex. The quality of form of consciousness is more difficult, although the level of consciousness (the spectrum between sleep to acute wakefulness) is a particular pattern of neural impulses in the 'reticular activating system' which facilitates the experiencing of perceptual and stored memory stimuli. Thus my Contemporary Freudian perspective of the 'self and the ego' does not confuse these terms with issues of consciousness which are the preserve of the neurophysiologists and does not ponder over the existence of mind which is assumed. It dispenses with the notion of 'ego' as a technical description of an important mental function to leave the issue as a debate about Contemporary Freudian perspective on the self.

I hope to illuminate some Contemporary Freudian ideas about this by using a kind of parallel process to introduce and describe the Contemporary Freudian group and its perspectives as if it were itself a single self. In the process, the Contemporary Freudian way of approaching what is rather a diffuse issue under my definition above will become clear. In the same way as a Contemporary Freudian might approach a patient by eliciting a history, then moving on to explore psychic contents, to examine the Contemporary Freudian 'self', I shall first elicit a history, secondly explore the thoughts and ideas of this 'self' and thirdly examine how it actually functions by looking at some clinical material.

The self as defined by its history

A brief historical overview of the Contemporary Freudian group is particularly important because the influence of actual reality and experience on the nature of the 'self' are emphasised by the Contemporary Freudian group. This reflects the central influence of Anna Freud's interpretation and development of her father's work. Prior to the forced emigration of the Freud family to London in 1938, there had already been some debate about the different clinical approaches proposed by Anna Freud and Melanie Klein. These differences became more difficult to avoid with the two women in the same psychoanalytic institute, and culminated in a series of special meetings—the 'controversial discussions' (King and Steiner, 1991). At stake were a variety of theoretical and clinical differences between psychoanalytic practice as it had evolved in London, and a more traditional model identified with Vienna and brought over by analysts fleeing from the persecution of the Nazis.

These differences were crystallised by the clinical approach of the two women to the analysis of children. On one side of the argument is the technique employed by Anna Freud. Using her background as a teacher, she emphasised the importance of the person's experience of parenting, life and trauma in the forging of the self. This more pedagogic approach was translated in the consulting room to a need for the analyst to provide a structure and context for the patient. The reality of the personality of the analyst was employed as an anchor to stabilise the vessel of the analytic process in the choppy seas of the clinical material. Linked to this approach was a theoretical position based on a more literal reading of Freudian developmental theory; for example positing the development of the superego in the second or third year of life. The notion that the superego begins with the internalisation of the parent was extended to the analyst. Thus the importance of the analyst clearly being a person with whom the child might engage and perhaps internalise as a fair and reasonable superego became a focus of the work. The Contemporary Freudian group, who are essentially her followers, derive from this position an emphasis on the influence of the real external world on the self.

The other side of the controversy was crystallised by Melanie Klein's analytic approach, demonstrated in her celebrated accounts of her analyses of children (Klein 1975). This involved the re-creation of the adult analytic situation with the largely silent analyst responding to and interpreting the material of the patient. The short-term reassurance of the child and reduction of their anxiety in the setting was less important than achieving access to the child's unconscious phantasy wherein might be found extreme emotional reactions and fantasies. This discussion remains contemporary and relevant. For example, Klein's young patient Richard, in an analysis carried out in Scotland during the war years, describes fear of the falling destructive bombs. Was Richard's fear more to do with a fear of the effect his father's destructive 'bomb' penis might have on his mother, as suggested; was it an accurate comment on the current situation in the war at the time; or was it a comment on his fear of this woman he was sent to see who 'bombed' him with disturbing ideas in a central European accent? Almost certainly all three views are true, but the first in particular represented a theoretical and clinical breakthrough that caused debate and dissent.

The controversial discussions ended without resolution, but with differences clarified. In the British spirit of compromise, members of the society informally resolved to recognise three broad groups with differing theoretical and clinical standpoints. The first were followers of Melanie Klein with an Object Relations theoretical position. The second were followers of a more classical approach, which had been espoused by Anna Freud, who as they have evolved, have become Contemporary Freudians. The third were a group recognising value in both sides, and wishing to be independent—who became known as the Independent Group (see Kohon 1986). This latter group were later identified with the work of Donald Winnicott, whose writing illustrated the combination of influences from both sides. With the presence of the divergent theoretical and clinical positions in the same institution, the British society has been a place of lively and creative debate. A particularly fruitful area of development has been the effort to synthesise the undeniable clinical realities of minute to minute interaction with patients in the consulting room captured by Object Relations theorists with the more structured model of the psyche of Freud's earlier work. As part of an open-minded eclecticism, the Contemporary Freudian group has mapped modern Object Relations theory and technique onto the more traditional models of the mind and analytical clinical practice (Sandler 1987). This pluralist approach to theory is also illustrated by efforts made to synthesise Freudian theory with developments in other allied fields such as attachment and experimental psychology.

The self and ego functioning

Contemporary Freudian theoretical positions on the self can be broadly grouped into two areas, functional and developmental. From a functional perspective, Anna Freud's work, 'The Ego and the Mechanisms of Defence' (1937), extended the mechanistic metaphor of the mind that had begun with Freud's topographical model. The hydraulic notion of unacceptable mental contents being pushed down (repressed) from consciousness into a layer beneath (the unconscious) provided a model for symptom formation. A symptom emerges when the pressure of all the repressed material becomes too great for the system, and the repressed returns again in symbolic form. Thus, the Viennese housewife with an overwhelming urge to slap her husband for his infidelity develops a paralysis of the hand she would have used to administer the blow.

Freud's second model was structural, refined to propose superego, ego and id. Anna Freud extended the conception of the ego as a broker between the dark instinctual forces of the id and the moralistic constraints of the superego by describing the variety of defensive psychological mechanisms that the ego can employ to help it in its task. Processes such as denial, projection, reaction formation, repression and sublimation were described and their meanings extended beyond Freud's original formulations. The United States, where more Viennese psychoanalysts had settled during the war, had a stronger classical Freudian tradition from which grew the 'ego psychology' approach (Hartmann 1939). Central to this was the notion of the 'conflict free sphere of the ego', with which the analyst could ally in the task of understanding the patient, creating the 'ego alliance'.

Critics of these mechanistic models of the mind argue that the theoretical rigour of description of the type of defence and the nature of the symptom of this approach somehow interfere with the reality and immediacy of the clinical encounter between the self of the analyst and the self of the patient. Freud originally trained as a neurologist during an era of all-consuming faith in materialistic science. Underlying his earlier work was a belief that eventually the mysteries of the mind would be completely scientifically explicable. Thus, psychoanalytic understandings of the self that stem from this mechanistic and functional approach have an inclusive and decisive quality, which resembles an empirical scientific 'certainty'. The question 'what do we mean by the self'? is answered simply by reference to the different mental structures and functions for which 'the self' is a collective noun. For many, this theoretical complexity and certainty remove the sense of surprise and unexpectedness that make psychoanalysis so interesting. For example, one might argue that analyst and patient can happily engage via their 'ego alliance' in constructing theoretical formulations about the nature of the patient's defensive strategies, and yet the patient does not change. Perhaps the 'ego alliance' assumes the very thing that the analysis sets out to explore. If a patient is healthy enough to be able to form an alliance with the analyst, then perhaps they do not need treatment in the first place. The question is whether the task in a psychoanalytic treatment is analysis of the ego, or analysis by the ego. The functioning of the self becomes pathological at the point at which the ego can no longer be the honest broker between the superego and id, and it starts to deal dishonestly instead. It may be a first principle that the ego will deal dishonestly with the analyst as well. Exploring how the ego does this may be the central analytic task.

British Kleinian theorists, in their expositions of the paranoid-schizoid and depressive positions, further extended the notion of the ego defence, emphasising the sequence of splitting followed by projection and projective identification. The standard metaphor to illustrate these defences invokes the mother-infant dyad. The infant is enraged at the mother for being imperfect, and splits the mother into two aspects, one good, and one bad. The hatred of the bad part is projected onto the mother so that she is perceived as aggressive and wishing to destroy him. Then the infant's projected aggression becomes identified with her (projective identification) and the infant loses touch with and control of these aggressive feelings (Segal 1973). It has been suggested that one might distinguish between those defences of the ego that are more mature and defences that are more primitive. Anna Freud's defences of the ego represent mature ego functioning; the mature ego can decide to sublimate or deny reality. These defences are distinct from more primitive ego functioning which makes more use of splitting, projection and projective identification, and where the only defence that works is dishonesty, and the fragmentation of the ego itself.

The self as a product of its development: narcissism

Developmental perspectives of the self, in particular the issue of primary narcissism, underlie much theoretical difference in position between Kleinian and Contemporary Freudian analysts. For both, the central preoccupation and task of the self is to be able to engage in relationships in a productive manner. For both, a central difficulty is that the frustrations and vulnerability that this process engenders lead to a variety of pathological manoeuvres to mitigate the risks entailed. Perhaps the most severe and persistent of these is narcissism. Contemporary Freudians regard adults who function at a narcissistic level as exhibiting a regressive phenomenon. In developmental terms, the primary narcissistic phase would be before the baby (or the foetus) has a notion of the distinction between the self and the outside world. It proposes that there is a time for the self, before Object Relations, a time when the self cannot distinguish itself from everything else around it. The early phases of development, therefore, are characterised as a gradual emergence into a realisation of separateness from mother and separateness from others and the world. The trauma of birth is a concrete cleavage of a physical union with the mother and is cushioned psychically by a belief of oneness and fusion with the mother. More accurately, this is not a belief, but rather the lack of a conception of the possibility of separateness from the mother.

In this model the self is born into a primary narcissistic fused oneness with mother. Object-relatedness is a gradually evolving phenomenon that is dependent on two factors. Firstly, it is dependent on the infant's cognitive and intellectual capacity to grasp the concept of separateness from the object, the cognitive ability to conceive of the notion of 'otherness'. The second factor is the development of increasing physical ability and co-ordination which enables the infant to see the outside world as something that it can interact with. Margaret Mahler's account of maternal fusion and the gradual capacity of the infant to tolerate moving away from mother could be seen as the recapitulation in the concrete world of a psychic process, which the infant has been negotiating in its mental world (Mahler et al. 1975). The Winnicottian account of this emergence of a distinct self differentiated from the other views certain traumatic events in the infant's early life as piercing this fog of primary narcissism (Winnicott 1971). These events form memories that can be identified as occasions when there was clearly an outside world that impinged. These events or memories constitute 'ego nuclei', parts of the psyche which demonstrate the existence of a self as distinct from other and which will eventually coalesce to form a broader conception of self. In this model, a sense of self develops as a raft of separate memories that have been sufficiently significant to represent the impingement of the external world.

The Lacanian model proposes a point in time when the mother holds the infant up in front of the mirror with pride. The infant sees itself as a physical whole which provides a model for a psychological whole self. A paradox resides in this account, namely, that psychological wholeness is never as complete as that first perception of the physical self. In the same way, the Winnicottian model contains within it the seeds of fragmentation and breakdown with the re-dispersal of the coalesced ego nuclei. A more Freudian hypothesis is that the 'skin is the first organ of the ego', and that the physical integument with the outside world forms the basis of a notion of psychological separateness. There seem to be as many different theories as theorists. For example my own children seem to have displayed a 'nappy phase', when they realise that there is an alternative to me putting on their nappy; that is, they resist it. Out of the recognition of this alternative to what daddy wishes to do emerges a sense of self and identity as distinct and differentiated. It seems to me that this process can only occur when there is a confluence of psychological and physical development to such a degree that independent thought is possible at the same time as independent purposeful movement is becoming possible.

In contrast to these varied accounts, the Kleinian developmental theory is simpler and more consistent. From the beginning of experience, the infant is object related and aware of a distinction between self and other. In these very early stages of life, prior to the acquisition of cognitive or motor skills, the baby is entirely and totally dependent for survival on the object, the mother. Aware of its utter state of vulnerability, helplessness and dependency, any experience that is sub-optimal, for example, hunger, cold, or fear, is experienced as a life threatening and terrifying attack by the object. This model is supported not only by regressive phenomena observed in adult psychoanalytic patients, but also by a tradition of infant observational study and interpretation which is hard to refute. The sound of a crying distressed baby is not indicative of a Winnicottian 'harmonious mix up' or primary narcissistic indifference. The sound of a baby crying invokes a conception of a traumatised individual in a frightening world, a state that elicits an almost biological response of comforting, soothing or an attempt to meet the need. Perhaps babies are very good at communicating their needs to their objects.

This distinction between Contemporary Freudian and Kleinian notions of the earliest days of the self is a function of these entirely different perspectives on narcissism. A Contemporary Freudian perspective might see it as a regression to a kind of default state of the personality—hence 'primary' narcissism. This regression might perhaps be to recharge the batteries, and as such be relatively benign. Indeed, the concept of the 'narcissistic wound' incorporates an idea that people have a fund of narcissism which enables them to get through life, but which can become depleted. The omnipotence and self-centredness of narcissism is best understood as a return to this pre-object related state. The task of the mother with an infant is to gradually disabuse them of their omnipotent narcissistic fantasy; the task of the analyst with a narcissistic patient is similarly to gradually enable the patient to relinquish their need for narcissistic regression. This perspective contrasts with a Kleinian view where narcissism is not a regression but rather a destruction of reality; the destruction of the real world of unsatisfying object relations and the creation and substitution of this unsatisfying real world with a fantasy world of omnipotence and self-aggrandisement. A self that is narcissistic is always secondary and almost always pathological, since it represents not being object related, and thus is not conceived to be a natural developmental state.

The self as instinctually driven: Eros and Thanatos

These two distinct models of narcissism point up a second broad theoretical difference between Contemporary Freudian and Kleinian perspectives on the self, namely differences in relation to theories of the instincts. More specifically, there is a difference in the perceived relative importance of the life and death instincts, Eros and Thanatos, as primary drivers of the self. The Contemporary Freudian perspective emphasises the struggle of the self to pursue Eros, or the life instinct, by striving for adaptation. A Kleinian perspective emphasises the contribution of the death instinct, of destructiveness. For example, a more Freudian perspective would see the regression to narcissism as an adaptive response in the circumstances to anxiety; a more Kleinian perspective sees it as a destruction of the object related world of reality.

This difference is also illustrated with reference to developmental accounts. In the Kleinian theory of infant development, the 'prime mover' is the baby, who, frustrated at being hungry, feels murderous and then projects this murderousness into the mother who is then experienced as a terrifying persecutor. A Freudian account might emphasise the role of the anxiety and helplessness of the baby and its fear. The link between frustration and murderousness seems to run through a Kleinian account of the self. Thus a principle task for an individual is to find a way to tolerate the frustration engendered in dependent relationships and deal with the murderousness and destructiveness engendered that does not involve destroying either the dependent relationship or the object.

A Contemporary Freudian perspective does not directly contradict this account. It would agree that this conflict is a central one for the self to tackle. The difference is in terms of emphasis—that tolerating the frustration engendered in dependent relationships is a significant task. However, it is a significant task alongside other life tasks such as growing up, leaving home, negotiating sexual relationships, establishing a job or occupation, establishing a family, approaching old age and so on. From a sociological perspective of looking at agency and structure, the Contemporary Freudian view is that the self is an agent who, in good faith, is struggling to negotiate a way through the various complexities and complications that are the structures of life. The task of the analyst is to help the individual with the difficulties that they encounter. A Kleinian perspective would see the agent, the individual, as compromised by their thoughts and actions. The latter would be determined by the pervasive operation of a mind conceptualised as a structure where dependency oscillates with destructiveness, and a paranoid-schizoid resolution oscillates with a depressive position. These conflicts will affect and distort the analysis as they do everything else and the task of the analyst becomes that of examining the way in which these distortions manifest themselves in the analytic process, and thereby to understand them better. Thus a Freudian analyst might see the fact that a patient comes to analysis as optimistic evidence that they wish to improve their lives and their lot. A Kleinian analyst would not disagree with this, but would focus more strongly on the patient's wish to destroy the analytic process and the understanding and progress that might derive from it. This may sound extreme, but it merely reflects the truism that none of us really wants to face the realities about oneself that psychoanalysis reveals. We all find it difficult to bear how we really are.

The self in clinical practice

There is an argument that suggests that session 520 of a four- or five-times-a-week analysis would be very similar, whoever your psychoanalyst is and whatever school or theoretical model they are using. By this time, in the third or fourth year, the analytic process will have settled down to a steady rhythm of psychic exploration. However, even if this argument is true, and many would dispute this, there are technical differences between the practice of psychoanalysts, and these can be traced to the differences in theoretical positions on the self touched on above. This is well-illustrated using Freud's celebrated metaphor of the personality as an onion. Like an onion, the self consists of layers that progress from the superficial, easily observable outside to deeper layers that are more private, hidden and difficult to access. A psychodynamic process proceeds by investigating and exploring those truths about the self that are relatively superficial in order to gain access to those truths that are deeper, more hidden, and more fundamental. One might oversimplify the difference between a Kleinian and a Contemporary Freudian analysis by suggesting that the Contemporary Freudian analysis goes from the surface and the Kleinian one from the depths. A Freudian might start by exploring the self at a relatively superficial level, and then, as trust in the setting and the analyst develops and as the patient feels comfortable about disclosing more difficult and hidden things, the analytic work moves to greater depths. This might be contrasted with a model of a Kleinian analysis. This might start in depth with interpretations and formulations at an early stage about very fundamental aspects of the patient's mental functioning. Then by working through the issues and associations that radiate out from these interpretations, through mutative changes and understandings at the core of the self, the analysis might work its way through to the more superficial and surface layers. So a more Freudian approach goes from surface to depth whereas a more Kleinian approach goes from depth to surface.

The difference in technique that underlies this distinction is to be found in the use of the counter-transference. Again, clarification requires oversimplification and generalisation to the point of parody, but going to see a Contemporary Freudian analyst as a patient, you are more likely to be greeted with a 'Good Morning' or a 'Good Afternoon', with some comments about the weather or about your journey. The analyst is more likely to structure the session, putting you at your ease, asking questions or taking a history. The Contemporary Freudian uses (superficial) aspects of their personality to engage with (superficial) aspects of the patient's personality, and then uses the (superficial) rapport so established to enquire about the (superficial) problems that you think have brought you along to the consultation. All the while, there is a recognition by the analyst that the engagement is superficial and that the business of the work will be the deeper material. However, it is thought that this material is better accessed by analyst and patient working together to look sequentially more deeply. A more Kleinian orientated analyst might not engage in superficial banter, they might say nothing or clarify the time available for the session before lapsing into a silence that is uncomfortable for both parties. In the silence and the way that the patient responds to it, the analyst will be thinking about the encounter and examining their counter-transference, examining the effect that the patient is having on them. As the consultation progresses and they gather information about the patient's current situation and past history, they will form hypotheses and propose them as interpretations. Since these interpretations are heavily influenced by the effect that the patient has had on the analyst, and because they, as psychoanalysts are able to examine in considerable depth their own reactions, these hypotheses and interpretations may present fundamental propositions about the patient. One may spend the next few sessions or, indeed, the rest of an analysis, working through these initial insights.

The Contemporary Freudian analyst may arrive at the same hypotheses or conclusions via a different route, but he or she would be less likely to formulate it in the early stages. Instead they might file it away to be brought out again at some point in the future when both patient and analyst are ready and the dynamic under consideration had been illustrated in some other setting. It might be argued that for the Contemporary Freudian, the counter-transference is one of a range of resources to be drawn upon in understanding a patient, together with the reported history, the current circumstances and other theoretical and developmental factors. A Kleinian clinical approach focuses more strongly on the counter-transference, using the latter as the prime clinical tool. Perhaps the Kleinian argument is that one can be more sure of how the patient makes you feel than you can be about what the patient says or how they present themselves. A further issue is that the Freudian notion of transference is that it is a long-term and gradually developing phenomenon—the classical term was the 'transference neurosis'. Over time, aspects of this become clear and available for interpretation. A more Kleinian perspective sees transference as a much finer grain moment-to-moment flux taking place between the two people in the consultation room. A Kleinian analyst might therefore at times say more in a session, commenting on these transferential eddies as they take place, whereas a more Freudian analyst might sit back and evolve a formulation about the session as a whole process.

Thus, the Contemporary Freudian perspective of the self as a product of its evolution, history and environment is extended into the clinical technique, where the analysis is an evolutionary process. Just as the infant is born in a confused state and the parent structures the environment, enabling the perception of separateness and independence, in the analytic process, the patient begins in a state of confusion, and needs to have the environment structured until they become more able to operate independently within it.

Clinical example

Ms M is a 27-year-old woman from Birmingham who engaged in eighteen months of twice-weekly work. She had presented to her general practitioner with an increasing number of hypochondriacal concerns which prompted referral to psychiatry and then on to psychotherapy. With two older sisters and a younger brother, she had grown up in a family where father was largely absent; as children they were told he was working away from home on building contracts, which was true for some of the time but he had also spent time in prison. Mother had intermittently worked as an auxiliary nurse, and Ms M gave an impression of a bustling and capable woman. Ms M lived in a shared flat paid for through housing benefit. Her life seemed to revolve around her social life, pubs and clubs, and it seemed as though she had an uncomfortable sense of having grown out of this existence but having nowhere else to go. At school she was bright, but in the same way she drifted, losing interest in her studies and instead beginning a long series of part-time jobs waitressing or in bars. As part of the night club culture she drifted in and out of drug use just as she had drifted in and out of relationships. An attractive woman, there was a cycle of being pursued, realising this was 'Mr Right', followed by a waning of the relationship. These relationships did not so much end; rather they faded, belying the flimsiness of the initial engagement.

This sense of flimsiness was fairly characteristic in the sessions. She would miss them frequently, and it would seem she had attended just because she happened to be in the area and had remembered on the off chance. She never actually accepted that she had psychological difficulties that needed to be attended to, rather she half-maintained that her GP had been wrong in his diagnosis of her physical difficulties as hypochondriacal. Nevertheless she bore him no malice and went along with the (psychodynamic) treatment. It seemed as though this rather ephemeral attachment might reflect something of a relationship with her father; she had drifted in and out of life and relationships and now analytic therapy as her father had drifted in and out of her life. In other ways also, her identity seemed insubstantial; when presented with problems in her heterosexual relationships she would muse about homosexual attractions and hint that there had been some leaning towards this. As the third girl—her mother had wanted a boy—it seemed as though the arrival of her younger brother prompted her to be forgotten or scotomised in the family and to drift in and out of the family consciousness, establishing what became a prevailing pattern.

Following the summer break in the second year her attendance was poor for a few weeks. In one session she arrived five or ten minutes late (as was common) and in her usual way she did not so much sit down as drape herself across the chair as one might drape a coat. A slim woman in blue jeans and a cropped T-shirt, she looked around the room nonchalantly for a few minutes before starting. She began by commenting on my dark blue suit, saying that she didn't like it, it was black and it reminded her of evil things. She said that she didn't like me wearing suits and preferred me in jackets. She complained

that the last time I had worn it she had mentioned this and now I was wear-
ing it again (an accurate claim). After a pause she went on to talk in some
detail about what had happened the previous day. By chance she had met a
man whom she had met before the summer break. She rather fancied him but
had not seen him again. He had been free for the afternoon and after a boozy
lunch they had gone for a walk in a local park, then gone back to the pub to
spend the evening together. Characteristically, her account of events became
increasingly hazy, and it was not clear how the evening had ended up.

In the session I had felt rather overwhelmed by her comments about my
suit, but I was not sure of their significance. Instead, at this point I com-
mented on the fact that she had not attended the previous session, and won-
dered whether I might be someone she had met before the summer break who
was interesting but who she did not feel she had a connection with. She
appeared to ignore this comment and sat looking out of the window. After
some time she said that she didn't think she would be able to get along to the
session next week either because she had arranged to go out of the city to visit
some friends that week. There was another lengthy pause during which time I
became aware of a familiar dynamic with her; the fact that I would be sitting
waiting for her at the time of her next session, but she might not be there. I
wondered about a connection between this and the 'black' suit, that Ms M
seemed to feel that she should be able to control me into waiting for her, for a
session that she may or may not attend, and to decide what suit I was and was-
n't allowed to wear. I formulated this for her, linking it with her experience in
childhood of her father over whom she had had no control, who had left her
waiting without an explanation. After a further pause she said that he was
just a bastard, that he was an evil and horrible man whom she didn't like me
mentioning. As the session ended I reflected to myself that this was not the
way she always spoke about her father, but there seemed to be a link between
father as evil for her that day, and my 'evil black' suit.

This brief account of a session illustrates several aspects of a
Contemporary Freudian perspective on the self, which are translated
into elements of clinical practice. Firstly, rather than pre-empt the
development of the session with an early interpretation about me
being 'clothed in evil' in my suit, I sat back to see what would emerge;
to see if the significance of the material came forward gradually, rather
than making an early interpretation. I might instead have said that she
had an evil and destructive feeling about the summer break or something else she might be projecting onto the suit, and more importantly
she might be enacting this destructiveness by missing sessions. Not

intervening early echoes the Contemporary Freudian approach to the session as an experience which will evolve and need time to develop without interference. More broadly, this reflects a perspective on the analytic process and the development of the self as being evolutionary rather than constitutional. An early interpretation might have derailed the process of the session before I really had a grasp on what was going on.

A second theme that emerges is about the notion of the 'ego alliance' or the therapeutic alliance. It may be that the reason for not immediately interpreting the patient's attribution of evil to the analyst is that to do so might undermine or seriously question the somewhat precarious treatment alliance. A more Freudian perspective argues that the treatment alliance is a real phenomenon which one needs to be aware of; the treatment alliance brings the patient to the sessions, prompts the patient to pay analytic bills, prompts the patient to work and to free associate in the sessions. From a more Kleinian perspective, the nature of the treatment alliance or lack of it becomes a central problematic to be analysed. It is assumed that the connection between analyst and patient will contain within it the seeds of the pathology that need to be explored. It was clear that Ms M's alliance with me was decidedly precarious, and being further undermined by her. Her missing sessions and dismissing of my ideas represent a destroying of links, a destruction that maintains her lack of substance and connections with the world. It is unfortunate that Ms M grew up in a world where relationships that many of us take for granted were absent, for example, links between fathers and daughters, or links between mothers and their daughters. Ms M's mother wished she had had a son. It is not in question that these sorts of links were absent for her in her childhood. What is significant is that now in her adult life she was actively engaged in destroying such links as were available (such as with me) to recreate this environment, by attenuating the link to her psychotherapy so that it appeared as if I was as unreliable as her father was. Ms M continues in an insubstantial world after the original need for this has passed.

The third issue is that I link what takes place in the room with her experience of her father. I 'reconstruct' her historical reality for her by reference to events in the transference. A Kleinian perspective might be that this takes the issue out of the room, and dilutes it. By understanding these phenomena in relation to previous developmental experiences one removes the emotionality and sense of 'realness' of the dynamic, substituting instead a much less robust intellectual process. A more Freudian perspective might be that the roots of trauma are to be found in these historical formulations, and that this is where the real work is situated. Furthermore, an analytic process restricted to what happens in the consulting room runs the risk of solipsism and unconnectedness to the patient's real world. Clearly, both of these positions have merit, and there are genuine and significant issues at stake.

Although I have presented Contemporary Freudian views in contrast with Object Relations and Kleinian perspectives, in some ways the clinical material of this young woman illustrates their complementarity. The pervasive sense of flimsiness indicates that she has a disorder of the self, or a disorder of identity. It may be that more 'healthy' patients who have a relatively intact ego structure or a more robust sense of self do have the capacity to ally with an analyst to engage in the process of exploration. However, more borderline or narcissistic people whose ego or sense of self is much more fragmented or confused may not have the capacity to form such an alliance. In these circumstances a more Object Relations or Kleinian clinical approach may be more appropriate, or may be the only way that the patient can be contained in a situation where a compulsive undermining of the therapeutic process is taking place.

Conclusions

In this chapter, I have proposed a Contemporary Freudian perspective on the self and the ego first by dispensing with the 'ego' as a term describing a function of the mind of the self, and then by using the device of examining the Contemporary Freudian group as if it were a 'self' to illustrate the way that I conceive Contemporary Freudians approach the concept. Thus the Contemporary Freudian emphasis on history as structuring the self is illustrated with reference to the origins of the group in the British Psycho-Analytical Society; the rootedness of the Contemporary Freudian perspective in traditional Freudian metapsychology has been mentioned, and an account of some of the theoretical underpinnings have been followed by some comments on analytic practice and how this is predicated on theories of the self.

In considering the nature of the self, a Classical Freudian perspective might emphasise developmental and historical factors in the definition of the self; a Kleinian perspective might emphasise the characteristic ways in which the individual deals with the inherent frustrations and fragmentation of psychic life, and the Contemporary Freudian perspective combines the two by incorporating Object Relations developments in psycho-analytic practice and theory into the more classical framework. In defining and describing the self, therefore, historical and developmental aspects are important, as well as the characteristic defensive, splitting and projective identificatory mechanisms that the individual may have become accustomed to using. Whereas a Classical Freudian analyst might assume that the primary motivation and aim of the self is adaptive and based on the life instinct, a Kleinian analyst might be more interested in the destructive and narcissistic aspects of the self. A Contemporary Freudian position recognises the role of the patient's destructiveness in the creation of their symptoms while trying to balance this with recognition of more constructive, life instinct and adaptive aspects.

If a more classical perspective is that the analyst forms an alliance with the self and the patient, and that the analyst and patient then explore together the nature of the patient's difficulties, then a more Kleinian perspective is that the very nature and tenor of the 'alliance' or otherwise that is formed is the central analytic problematic. A Contemporary Freudian perspective tries to steer a path between these two views, acknowledging the importance and reality of the 'real' aspects of the relationship between analyst and patient, but also acknowledging that the patient will bring their past into the consulting room by transferential and projective-identificatory mechanisms. Perhaps subsequent development of psychoanalytic theory after both Freud and his daughter, Anna, has demonstrated that notions of 'the ego' or 'the self' massively oversimplify very complex and fragmented psychic systems. Perhaps all one can say is that for some people these systems of fragments work in harmony or in tandem to enable the self or the ego to function as if it were whole. For others, the complexities and fragments that make up the self or the ego are so contradictory and conflictual that they need help.

MELANIE KLEIN'S CONCEPTION OF THE SELF: THE SUBJECT OF EMOTIONAL RELATIONSHIPS

David Mayers

Introduction

The Kleinian group of psychoanalysts in the British Psycho-Analytical Society has functioned as a coherent and productive work group for some sixty-five years. It would be senseless to attempt to give an overview of the whole tradition in one chapter. I have therefore limited myself to an account taken from Melanie Klein's own writings: both those on general psychology (Klein 1926, 1959) and those on specific psychic configurations (Klein 1935, 1940, 1946). Despite its inevitable lack of completeness, I think my account will be recognised by contemporary Kleinian practitioners, analysts and therapists working with adult, adolescent or child patients.

A centrally important component of Kleinian psychoanalysis is that the analyst seeks to understand, describe and interpret the patient's life in terms of the patient's own subjective experience, rather than from the position of an external objective observer. Thus, Kleinians speak of unconscious phantasies which have the form of object relations rather than of instincts; of an internal world inhabited by internal objects as opposed to using a term such as psychic structure; of a self which initiates and experiences beliefs, desires and emotions, rather than of the Freudian Ego which mediates between and defends against demands from other psychic agencies and the external world. Klein continued to use the terminology of Freud's structural theory, but this should not obscure the very different emphasis she gave to it.

The Kleinian programme, then, aims to be psychological, and the psychology is one of Object Relations. Now many analysts have spoken of object relations. The Kleinian use of the term is distinctive and must be understood as such if the Kleinian account of the self is to make any sense.

In Freud's thinking, an instinct has an aim and an object: the identity of the object is secondary to the achievement of the aim and the subsequent relief of tension. Therefore, if I am hungry, I feed and I become relaxed: whose breast I feed from is, relatively speaking, unimportant. Indeed, Freud considers that the new baby believes it feeds itself, discovering the existence of an external breast only after successfully negotiating stages of auto-erotism and primary narcissism.

Klein believes that the baby comes into the world equipped with a primitive capacity to believe, to desire and to feel. Thus, I believe that there is a breast which will feed me and relieve my hunger; I want to find it and feed from it and I approach it with love or with hate. This is crucial; the objects that Kleinians speak of are objects of psychological acts committed by the self/subject; and it is a feature of such objects that they do not have to coincide with things in the external world. Thus, if I stroke a dog, there exists a dog which I stroke; if I am afraid of a dog, there does not have to exist a particular dog which I fear. This is quite different from the literal use of the word 'object' in the sense of speaking about objects as one might when asking how many objects there are on the table and then counting the plates, the glasses and so on.

For the self to function psychologically at all involves its relating in some way or other to an object. The emotional state of the subject will endow the object with certain qualities—being loveable, being hateful, and being interesting, for instance. The Kleinian baby self is born with a primitively furnished mind that seeks out and creates a world in its own image. This is a very different sort of object relating from that described by members of the Independent School of British psychoanalysis, for whom the baby's mind is a *tabula rasa*, to be written on by a pre-existent environment already endowed with welcoming or hostile properties. We will explore, in subsequent sections, how the Kleinian baby, mainly by means of projection and introjection, learns to differentiate itself from its objects and its world.

It is perhaps worth a mention that Kleinian Object Relations have often been seen as one case of the post-Hegelian Self/Other dialectic so much spoken of and so much misunderstood since the 1960s. This is quite erroneous, since the Kleinian object, to the degree that its identity is determined by the subject's state of mind, is precisely not Other. This will become clear in the subsequent discussion of the paranoid-schizoid position.

The legacy from Freud

Before we turn to the work of Klein herself, we should think about some elements of Freud's thought that were fundamental to her development of psychoanalysis. I want to draw attention to Freud's analysis of different phenomena of identification during the second decade of the twentieth century.

In 'Mourning and Melancholia' (Freud 1917) Freud explores the differences between the process of normal mourning for the loss of a loved one and the pathological state that we would now call depression. For mourning to be successfully accomplished the multitude of emotional investments (cathexes) have to be withdrawn so that psychic energy can be redirected to new loved objects. In everyday speech we might speak of 'letting the lost object go'. Depression is the state of mind where we will not let go. Instead, in phantasy, we take the lost object into our mind and make it part of ourselves; we then become prey to the reproaches and revenges that we visit on the object for leaving us in the first place. The level of worthlessness, uselessness, damage or deadness that we feel in a state of depression will reflect the damage that, in phantasy, we have inflicted upon the object. When the internalisation has been organised round a phantasy of cannibalistic oral sadism, the result is a sense of a chewed-up, fragmented self. This is a case of the self's identifying with its object by introjection.

In *Group Psychology and the Analysis of the Ego* (Freud 1921), Freud discusses what happens when individuals identify themselves with bodies such as the Army, the Church or the State, seeming voluntarily to delegate their powers of thought, judgement and choice to generals, clergy, politicians or whomever. The gain is a sense of solidarity with other members of the group and of safety, protection from the group's enemies. There is also an anaesthetising of one's personal sense of danger—if I risk enemy gunfire not because I choose to but because my admired leader tells me to, then danger becomes safety, foolhardiness bravery. But I may also feel depersonalised, unsure of my own identity, with no sense of knowing why I am doing certain things. When the externalisation has been organised round a phantasy of defecation, the pleasure or pain of the excretory act will determine our feelings about our leaders and our relations to them. This is a case of the self's identifying with its object by projection.

Freud introduced the terms ego-ideal and super-ego respectively in 'On Narcissism' (Freud 1914a) and *The Ego and the Id* (Freud 1923). The ego-ideal is an introject combining one's own narcissistic self-admiration with the loved and admired qualities of parents (and later of group leader); the super-ego is an introject comprising parental and social discipline and moral judgement. The first relates to shame, the second to guilt. Both the ego-ideal and the super-ego are precursors of Klein's internal objects.

In the structural theory of the mind as presented in *The Ego and the Id* (Freud 1923), the ego has to mediate between the demands for instinctual satisfaction from the id, the commands and prohibitions from the super-ego and the consciously perceived requirements of society. Thus, the notion of self has to be deconstructed into the different psychic agencies. We shall see that Klein uses the term 'ego' in a much more informal way, coming more and more to equate it with an untheorised notion of self—that part of the personality which contains and processes psychological experience, whether conscious or unconscious.

The events of the First World War caused Freud to turn his attention to an aspect of human behaviour that he thought could not be accounted for by his earlier formulations of the pleasure principle and the reality principle. During the war, millions of soldiers had offered themselves for destruction, in full knowledge of what they were doing, rather than taking evasive or defensive action. Freud could account for this only by revising his instinct theory in terms of mutually opposed life and death instincts—only a death instinct could account for such determined self-destruction. The title of his work *Beyond the Pleasure Principle* (Freud 1920a) is derived from this insight. Prior to this time Freud considered the drive towards pleasure to be the most basic of human functions; now it seemed that the struggle between life and death was even more fundamental.

Freud admitted that his postulation of a death instinct was on the level of philosophical speculation. However, Klein, who was amongst the few analysts to take the idea seriously, put clinical flesh on the theoretical skeleton by paying special attention to patients' attempts to undermine and destroy the analytic work—the negative transference.

Melanie Klein

Klein was analysed first by Ferenczi and then, for a short time before his early death, by Abraham. Ferenczi encouraged her to work with children, and her election to the Budapest Psychoanalytic Society followed a paper on a child analysis. However, she found Ferenczi's theorising lacked a sufficient appreciation of the negative transference. It was from Abraham that she learned about very early sadism. Abraham subdivided Freud's oral stage into the sucking and biting stages; and his anal stage into the anal retentive and the anal sadistic. So began Klein's distinctive contribution to the study of the infant mind and to psychoanalytic technique: she found that children could be understood before they had learned to speak, since her use of play technique (discussed below) demonstrated that infantile symbolic functioning existed and was also a key to understanding it. Klein considered that object-relating began much earlier than Freud had postulated.

Klein's first major development of psychoanalysis was the invention of the play technique, which served that same function in understanding child patients as free association does for adults. Children are given basic play materials—dolls (male and female, large and small), animals, cars, etc, drawing materials, water, containers and Plasticine. What they do with these items represents what is happening in their unconscious minds—or, as Klein came to say, their internal worlds. Play technique is geared to the concreteness of early psychic functioning. For instance, we might say that we are hungry, or that we love someone we are with—but this calls for considerable symbolic sophistication. In the hungry infant's experience, there is something horrible in his tummy which is hurting him; his mother's love for him takes the form of her putting a warm precious part of herself into him and removing the bad hurting thing. As she worked with her child patients, Klein was able to fill out Freud's early insight that the primitive ego is a body-ego, demonstrating that we experience our psychic life in bodily terms. The mind is a space into which objects are brought—introjection—or from which they are expelled—projection. Or they might enter and leave in an unwilled way, welcome or unwelcome. These activities are demonstrated in the analytic playroom, where objects are brought together and separated, damaged and repaired, treasured or thrown away, loved or hated. The toys can be seen to have symbolic equivalence with the important things in a child's life—members of the family, parts of his own body and parts of his parents' bodies.

Her observation and interpretation of children's play made Klein believe that the new-born baby mind is already furnished with basic templates round which it organises its experience of the world: the feeding breast in the mouth, the space in mother's body where babies live, father's penis which gives babies to mother, the activities of taking in and putting out. These are called unconscious phantasies—the psychic expression of instinctual impulses and of defences against such impulses. Kleinians believe that this is a superior way of thinking to instinct theory, because the operation of unconscious phantasy can be observed, not just theoretically inferred. It is of great importance that unconscious phantasy always takes the form of an object relation, and that this is never neutral: the subject always has beliefs about, desires and feelings for, its object. For example, feeling hungry may relate to a phantasy of a breast which I believe to be full of love and nourishment which I want to feed me; or a feared hostile breast, which I believe to be full of poison, which I wish to destroy or hide from.

We have by now arrived at an account of the primitive self very different from Freud's. He saw the newborn baby as living subjectively, in a solipsistic state—auto-erotism; then of developing an image of its own body and taking that for its object—primary narcissism; only then being able to reach out to other objects, a contact which, should these prove too threatening, is withdrawn, so that primary narcissism always remains the foundation of psychic life. For Klein the healthy self is always seeking for objects—that is what psychic life is. There is no such thing as primary narcissism (nor what some people speak of as 'healthy narcissism'). In her view, narcissistic phenomena always involve a retreat from or an attack on life.

* * *

So far we have a sketch of Klein's account of the furniture of the mind, how she observed and investigated it. Next must come Klein's account of how psychic life is lived.

The newborn baby's first experience is of the struggle inside itself between the forces of life and death; it is terrified by an internal presence which threatens its existence. To put it more simply, it is acutely conscious of something unbearable inside itself which must be got rid of. But where can it be put? For the orally organised baby, the only other place than inside itself is inside its (oral) object—the mother's breast—and at this stage mother is breast. But if the breast is filled with something deadly, it will become a death-dealing breast. So how will the baby feed? In phantasy, the baby solves this problem by splitting both self and object into two: the good part of the self remains while the bad part is expelled into the breast; the good part of the breast remains loving, feeding, desirable, while the bad part is poisonous, hateful and to be avoided at all costs. Klein calls these split-apart good and bad bits, part-objects, and the mechanism by which the self creates them, projective identification. (We can recall here the putting of a part

of the self into group leaders in Freud's Group Psychology paper.)
Now we have a new constellation: the purged self faces two objects
(breasts), a good one which loves it and wishes to feed it and a bad one
which hates it and wishes to take a tit-for-tat revenge by feeding it back
the poison which the baby first expelled into it. Being fed by the good
breast is experienced, in phantasy, as taking a good loving object inside
and being strengthened and nourished by it; being fed by the bad
breast means being invaded by a hating destructive object, so that the
self is internally split again. In this drama, the primary anxiety relates
to the survival of the self in the face of its own self-destructiveness. The
self's characteristic defences against the threat are the repeated patterns of splitting, projection and re-introjection. Klein calls this phenomenon the paranoid-schizoid position, 'paranoid' because of the fix-
ation on the need to survive, 'schizoid' because of the splitting mechanism and 'position' because a psychological pattern, a characteristic
anxiety and defences against it, have replaced Freud's biologically
based notion of a developmental stage.

The above account, left as it is, sounds theoretical and speculative.
Let us recast it in terms of everyday experience.

There is a distressed howling baby. Mother comes, picks him up,
cuddles him, and offers him her breast. He starts to feed, visibly
becomes calmer and happier, and feeds until he has had enough. The
baby then relaxes with a contented smile and goes peacefully to sleep.
Here the self has been threatened by a bad object, but a good one has
come to the rescue. As a result, the baby feels loved and strengthened,
the bad object is put to flight and fear is replaced by security.

Alternatively there is a distressed howling baby. Mother comes and
is obviously unsettled by, perhaps impatient with, his distress. She
picks him up and offers him her breast, but he feeds reluctantly, or
turns away altogether. His distress continues and even increases.
Mother cannot comfort him and becomes herself more anxious at her
helplessness, or irritated by his rejection of her. Here the baby is threatened by a bad object, which, when he tries to expel it, takes over the
breast and threatens him from outside. He is now prey to attacks from
inside—he is still hungry—and from outside because he has alienated
the good object and called into being the bad one. It should be noticed
that the states of mind of both mother and baby are important here.
Klein is often accused of denying the importance of the external world.
However she stresses over and over again how the mother's reception
of the baby's feelings can change things and how a confident relaxed

mother can reinforce good feelings in the baby and detoxify bad ones. Thus when the baby re-introjects what it has put into mother its internal good objects are strengthened and its bad ones weakened.

It must not be thought that everything happens in terms of sucking or biting, though the pattern of splitting, projection and introjection, and the subsequent peopling of the internal world with loved and hated objects, is neatly introduced this way. The primitive self has a far wider repertoire—just as passing water or faeces can be a good experience, so the baby can express love by making presents of the contents of its body. When anal or urethral phantasies are dominant, this is how babies are imagined to be born. Equally, passing water or faeces can be painful experiences, used to attack the object by burning or poisoning. However, as long as the self's primary concern is survival in the face of death threats (whether oral, anal or phallic), the cycle of splitting self and object, and the projective identification of part-self with part-object, continues.

* * *

If things go badly for the emergent self, if the loved good objects and the feared bad ones have to be kept too far apart so that hate and fear cannot be lessened, then the foundations of psychotic illness are laid. However, when things go well and when good internal objects are strong enough to mitigate the threat of destruction, then a new position emerges. As the forces of good—love, trust, fidelity, honesty and so on—are strengthened, so the forces of destructiveness—hatred, jealousy, envy—are lessened. The self begins to realise that, far from there being two objects, one loving/loved, one hating/hated, there is only one. The breast that I have loved and gratefully fed from is the same breast that I have hated and filled with my poison. In Klein's language, part-objects come together to form a whole object. This calls into play a new set of emotions, guilt and shame at having attacked the loved breast—or by now we can say mother—a wish to repair the damage and a wish to make amends for having been so hateful. Fear for the survival of the self is replaced by fear for the survival, or wellbeing of the object. Or to put it another way, fear of death by biting or poisoning—my own projected destructiveness—yields to fear of death by starvation, since I have bitten the breast that fed me. This new anxiety brings with it a new set of defences. In phantasy I deny that I hurt my object; or I denigrate the object, saying that it deserved to be hurt; or I control the object, waving the hurt away magically. These defences are easily recognised in everyday life: 'What are you making that silly fuss for, I hardly touched you'!; 'Well, it serves you right'!; 'There, kiss it better'!. Klein calls this position the depressive position, and its characteristic defences the manic defences. This is because just as an excess of persecutory anxiety and a massive deployment of schizoid defences leads to schizophrenic illness, so an excess of depressive anxiety and corresponding manic defence leads to manic-depressive conditions.

Once the depressive position is securely established and fear for the survival of the self lessened, we do not need to resort so frequently to projective identification to rid ourselves of our feared parts. This means that we can begin to see our objects as having qualities of their own, rather than seeing them in terms of what we have projected into them. It is only now that real inter-personal relations can be established, because it is only now that we can believe in persons with an existence separate from our own. This has widespread implications beyond the scope of this discussion. It is important to emphasise that in Kleinian theory objects are not persons, that objects belong essentially to the internal world and persons to the external, that commerce with the latter is always conditioned by the position of the former. However far we advance from infantile concrete thinking, however adept we become in the deployment of symbolic thought, unconscious phantasy remains as the bedrock of life.

In Kleinian psychology, the paranoid-schizoid and the depressive positions are the polarities between which the self lives and relates to its objects. There is constant commerce between them. We have seen how, under the influence of good objects, splits are healed and thus persecutory anxiety yields to depressive anxiety. If wounds are felt to be genuinely healed and if real rather than manic reparation is felt to be made, then a secure life can be lived under the aegis of the surviving good object. The position of Raskolnikov at the end of *Crime and Punishment* is a good example. However, if depressive anxiety becomes unbearable and the manic defences break down, then we can become so persecuted by our depression that we resort to schizoid functioning. Macbeth provides a good example, since he cannot cope with his guilt after murdering Duncan and, instead of trying to make amends, seeks to secure his position by murdering again and again.

EGO, SELF AND SUBJECTIVITY: CONTRIBUTIONS FROM THE OBJECT RELATIONS SCHOOL[1]

Stephen Frosh

The critique of Freudian instinct theory which comes from the Object Relations school[2] is of great contemporary interest, because it shares in the fundamental psychoanalytic position that gives centrality to the concept of the unconscious, whilst arguing that the appropriate level of explanation to be used in psychoanalysis is psychological or psycho-social, not biological. In this chapter, key components of this critique are outlined and elements of the Object Relations position on ego-object relations are presented, paying particular attention to implications for social theory. Some recent developments in 'intersubjectivist' thinking are also acknowledged, but it is nevertheless suggested that there are in-built limitations to the extent to which the 'two-person' framework adopted by Object Relations theory can offer a way forward for a socially aware psychoanalysis.

For Object Relations theory, it is not that the biological foundations of psychic life emphasised by Freud do not exist, but rather that they are not relevant for a genuinely psychoanalytic approach to human psychology. In the words of a prime propagandist of the object relational view, Harry Guntrip, biology is only:

> a study of the *machinery* of personal life, not of its *essential quality*, to use Freud's own term, a study of the mechanisms of behaviour and not of the meaningful personal experience that is the essence of the personal self. (Guntrip 1973: 49)

This is a revealing quotation: with his reiteration of the term 'personal', his use of the notion of the 'self', and his concentration on the 'experience' of the individual, Guntrip aligns himself firmly with humanistic psychologists who advocate a focus on each person's potential for a meaningful existence as the true subject for psychology. Given this, not surprisingly, Guntrip (1973) argues that Freud's reliance on nineteenth-century biological and physical concepts resulted in an impersonal instinct theory which is inappropriate for a psychology that is actually about people in their relationships with themselves and others. He suggests that the instinct theory side of Freud's work should be jettisoned because it ties analysis to an overly reductionist viewpoint which only acknowledges meanings as residing in physical impulses. This provides no information when one wants to discuss humans as people whose fates are dependent on the quality of the relationships they form with others. 'Here the important concepts are needs, purposive activities, meanings and significances' (Guntrip 1961: 145).

The fundamental proposition of Object Relations theory is reflected in its name. In the traditional psychoanalytic view, human psychology is driven by the impulse to give expression to the drives, and it is in order to do this successfully that relationships with others are formed. In Object Relations theory, this order of events is reversed, Freud's sexual and aggressive drives being replaced by an assumption that humans are fundamentally relationship-seeking creatures. In Fairbairn's terms, libido is object-seeking rather than pleasure-seeking. The substance of the Object Relations argument is thus that the dominating feature of human psychology is an impulse to form relationships—a social orientation. Hence Winnicott's idea that there is no such thing as a baby, only a baby-and-mother field, and Fairbairn's refusal to distinguish between energy and structure to indicate that the ego is always in motion, striving to form relationships with others. Although, according to Winnicott at least, instinctual satisfactions occur, they are merely 'orgiastic' experiences, and it is the non-orgiastic activities of personal relating that form the basis of psychological development and experience. The tendency to form, or try to form, relationships is the motivating force to which most aspects of behaviour or experience can be reduced and which gives meaning to pleasure. For Fairbairn (1941: 34), 'It is not the libidinal attitude which determines the object relationship, but the object relationship which determines the libidinal attitude', with maturity defined in interpersonal rather than individualistically genital terms.

The human individual's basic reality is expressed in her or his relationships. These are organised to meet fundamental needs very different from the instinctual 'needs' that are the stuff of Freudian theory, being concerned instead with the interpersonal conditions required for healthy psychological development. Thus, Greenberg and Mitchell (1983: 198) list the basic 'needs' implicit in Winnicott's theory as including 'an initially perfectly responsive facilitation of [the infant's] needs and gestures; a nonintrusive "holding" and mirroring environment throughout quiescent states', and so on—no mention here of feeding or the gratification of any incipient sexual impulse, the usual bases for a biological drive theory of human social development. Nevertheless, it is hard to envisage the origin of the impulse to form relationships that Object Relations theorists postulate as basic, unless it is in biology: as everything reduces to this impulse, and as it is the defining characteristic of human existence, it possesses a function not unlike that given to sexual energy by Freud or, perhaps, general libido by Jung. It may be that viewing libido as object-seeking is more accurate or more morally acceptable than viewing it as pleasure-seeking, and there is certainly an argument to be made from observations of infant behaviour that children are born with a fundamental affinity for social interaction which is not connected with any obviously Freudian drive gratification. However, none of this represents a complete escape from biology; it simply alters what it is that is regarded as innate. But the significance of this difference should not be underestimated, and nor should its political possibilities: whereas Freud viewed the individual as a self-contained world, comprehensible in terms of the way energy is inputted to, and outputted from, the system, Object Relations theory embeds each individual in a social context and suggests that there is no way of understanding the one without the other. This means that whereas classical Freudianism always views the individual as in essence separate from the social world that influences her or him (an 'essentialist' notion), Object Relations theory holds the potential for an account of human nature and development that makes social relations central in the construction of the self.

Fairbairn insisted that from the start of life instincts or 'impulses' operate in the service of a relationship-seeking ego, which initially constitutes the whole of the infant's mental structure. Thus, it is not necessary to postulate the existence of a separate realm of the psyche which contains a pool of impulses that fuel psychological functioning, and it makes no sense to describe the ego as somehow 'precipitated' from somewhere else. Importantly, it is not the *concept* of an unconscious that is disputed, but its localisation in a *structure* which is somehow split off from the other parts of the mind. This is a characteristic and central point for Object Relations theory: that the psyche is initially a unity, a total ego which has the potential to develop into a coherent and integrated personal self. Psychic splitting is a secondary phenomenon, a derivative of something else, and signifies a distortion of optimal development. Fairbairn's claim is that the child is a whole being from the start of life and would ideally remain whole however much her or his complexity might alter during development. In Guntrip's (1973: 93) gloss, 'the human infant is a unitary dynamic whole with ego-potential as its essential quality from the start'. More fully:

> Fairbairn believed that we must be aware of the fundamental dynamic wholeness of the human being as a person, which is the most important natural human characteristic. To Fairbairn, the preservation and growth of this wholeness constitutes mental health. (Guntrip 1973: 93)

The emphasis on *naturalness* is noticeable here, suggesting a normative view of mental health as the 'unfolding of a human essence' (Elliott 1994: 24) that is very similar to that of humanistic psychology and rather different from the more cautious presentations characteristic of Freud. In addition, the passage implies an identity between ego development and the creation of a true self that is representative of the use of 'ego' terminology in Object Relations writing. For instance, Guntrip's rejection of the concept of the id is in order to extend the notion of the ego, so that the ego becomes the whole person, suffused with its own energy and gradually enabling the organisation of all experiences within its unifying framework.

> The only escape from a dualism of radically opposed structures is to banish the term 'id', and reserve 'ego' to denote the whole basically unitary psyche with its innate potential for developing into a true self, a whole person. (Guntrip 1973: 41)

The psyche should not be seen as the container of incompatible desires and impulses which operate in a way that cannot be integrated; rather, everything that exists within the psyche is consistent with its wholeness, is, in that way, all ego.

Instead of the ego being formed as a precipitate of the id when desire comes into conflict with reality, Object Relations theory suggests that it is the unconscious that is an epiphenomenon, formed only when the 'innate potential for developing into a true self' is frustrated. Hence the fervour of Guntrip's attack on the notion of the id: it is anathema because it suggests the permanent existence of a psychic region which can never be integrated with the rest of the personality, belying the concept of a whole, mature self. The following is presumably meant as damning criticism:

> Thus Freud could take the term 'id' from Groddeck, who wrote, 'We should not say "I live" but "I am lived by It"'. This completely destroys the unique and responsible individuality of the person. (Guntrip 1973: 105)

Whether the phrase 'I am lived by It', though unpalatable, nevertheless might be an accurate representation of experience, does not seem to be at issue, because the idea of an It/id smacks of biology and hence is regarded by Guntrip as reductionist and mechanistic. Greenberg and Mitchell (1983: 213) note that in this respect Guntrip's critique of Freud is moral rather than empirical: 'he considers drive theory degrading to mankind and, on that basis, unacceptable'. As will be apparent, optimism over human nature is a characteristic attribute of Object Relations theory and is coupled with a positive view of the possibilities for psychotherapy; the political consequences of this optimism are worthy of debate.

The maturational environment

The concern of Object Relations theorists with personal relationships leads to an emphasis on the type of environment available for maturational purposes. Instead of impulses originating from the id driving the individual, with other people being literally 'objects' used to relieve the tension produced by the drives, Object Relations theory proposes that there is an ego embedded in human relationships from the start, the developmental history of which takes place in the context of these relationships. In line with this, Fairbairn replaces Freud's developmental scheme of oral, anal, phallic and genital stages, which refers to parts of the infant's body and which is therefore individualistic in its conception, with a scheme based on the quality of relationships with objects: immature dependency, transitional (latency and adolescence), mature dependency. What distinguishes the first and last of these stages is the ability of the maturely dependent adult to differentiate her or himself from the parent or other object, whereas the immaturely dependent infant is in a state of 'primary identification' with the mother, unable to experience her or himself as in any way separate. The differentiations of maturity also allow for a degree of reciprocity which is unavailable to the dependent infant.

The transition from one stage or pattern of relating, to the other is a long and potentially difficult one, but in Fairbairn's view it is fundamentally natural, a gradual unfolding of needs and potentials that take place within the context of a carefully graded pattern of separations. This idea, incidentally, has influenced workers outside the Object Relations school: for example, Margaret Mahler's intricate account of the phases of ego development is based around a 'separation-individuation' structure that is very similar to Fairbairn's, describing how the child's total embeddedness in the mother becomes a gradual position of separation and identity (Greenberg and Mitchell 1983). What is distinctive about Fairbairn's account, however, is the position it takes up with respect to *internal* object relationships—the inside of the mind, as it were, which is the primary focus of psychoanalysis. For Fairbairn, the entire world of internal object relations is a compensation for environmental deprivation, for the frustrating aspects of the relationships that the infant experiences with real, external objects —predominantly or exclusively the mother of early infancy. The ideal situation is the perfectly gratifying mother, leading gradually and naturally to the perfectly poised individual at peace with the world, functioning with a whole ego and able to form totally fulfilling, mature relationships with others. Under such circumstances, psychology would consist of an exploration of the way in which people relate to real, external others. What actually happens, however, is that society interferes with the bond between mother and infant, creating unnatural separations too early, and resulting in the infant experiencing objects as depriving and frustrating ('in a state of nature the infant would never normally experience that separation from his mother which appears to be imposed upon him increasingly by conditions of civilisation'—Fairbairn 1944: 109). Because it is so distressing to desire an object which is also so unsatisfying, the infant sets up substitutive ones inside—or, rather, she or he *internalises* the object in an attempt to control ('coerce') it more successfully. Thus, internal objects are compensations for the deprivations experienced in the real world: their source lies not in the biologically determined ambivalence of the instincts, but in the frustrations of maternal failure. Psychodynamics—the internal world of unconscious phantasy and mental structures, the primary material for psychoanalytic exploration—is thus the product of environmental events. Freud's notion that fantasies are substitutive satisfactions has been taken to extremes in this theory: as Greenberg and Mitchell (1983) note, all psychopathology and virtually all psychodynamic life is hypothesised to have maternal deprivation at its root.

Fairbairn's (1944) description of how the originally unified ego of the child becomes split in the face of failures in the early environment has proved seminal for Object Relations thought. According to Fairbairn, the first defensive manoeuvre that the infant undertakes to cope with the frustrations of the external maternal object is to internalise it in an attempt to control it or make it palatable. The unitary ego is thus faced with an ambivalent object which is the focus both of libidinal desire and hostile aggression. To cope with this painful, internal circumstance, the object becomes split into an acceptable, rewarding, 'good' object, and an unsatisfying 'bad' one. In fact, Fairbairn postulates that the unsatisfying object has two aspects: 'On the one hand, it frustrates; and on the other hand, it tempts and allures' (Fairbairn 1944: 111). To deal with this situation, the bad object is split again into its two elements, with the newly created exciting and rejecting objects being repressed as another defensive act. The crucial point here is that this process also creates a specific psychic structure. This follows from Fairbairn's fundamental postulate that ego and object only exist in relationship with one another: hence, as the object is internalised so part of the ego is redirected from the external to the internal world; and as the internal object is split so is the ego. Fairbairn describes a psychic structure organised around three ego-object pairs: between a libidinal ego and an exciting object; between an anti-libidinal ego (or 'internal saboteur') and a rejecting object; and between a central ego and an idealised object. The last of these is the residue of the healthy relationship between the original unified ego and the accepting outer world, and contains the self of ordinary consciousness; the other two pairs represent the attachment of the ego to bad objects which are nevertheless desired. The libidinal ego's attachment to the exciting object fills it with greed but also leaves it deprived, while the anti-libidinal ego's link with the rejecting object makes it the repository of destructiveness and hatred. These two ego-object pairs provide the focus for psychopathology of all kinds; they are maintained in a repressed state and are split off from, and rejected by, the central ego. Thus, Fairbairn (1944) proposes that it is infantile dependence rather than the Oedipus complex that is the 'ultimate cause' of psychic organisation; more fully, it is the child's response to external difficulties with the mother that create an internal world of splitting and repression.

Although Guntrip sets himself up as simply an elaborator of Fairbairn's theory, Greenberg and Mitchell (1983) point out that he alters this theory in some important ways. These centre on his concept of the 'regressed ego', which he introduces as an addition to Fairbairn's scheme. Guntrip was impressed by observations, in himself and in his patients, of the severity of the schizoid withdrawal from relationships with objects, and the intense fear combined with neediness that such relationships could provoke. He therefore proposed that the libidinal ego undergoes a final split, leaving part of it attached to the exciting object, but hiding away another part in an even more withdrawn state, characterised by a renunciation of all objects, internal as well as external. The motivation for this withdrawal derives from early deprivation; what is novel about Guntrip's formulation is that it proposes that this deprivation is structurally embedded in the mind as an infantile ego that longs for a return to the objectless but whole state of the womb, when it was entirely one with the mother, before frustration and rejection set in.

Guntrip suggests that the early traumas generated by inadequate mothering are essentially frozen in time: the helpless and terrified infantile ego, overwhelmed by unrequited longings and dread of abandonment, remains alive within the regressed ego, in the heart of the personality (Greenberg and Mitchell 1983: 212).

Regressive longing is at the core of psychopathology as a mixture of desire for good object relationships and a fear of forming any at all. This is distinct from Fairbairn's proposal that it is attachment to bad object relations that forms psychopathology and it also offers a new view in proposing that an objectless ego state is possible. Guntrip can even be read as proposing that 'withdrawal is primary, and object seeking is a secondary defensive reaction against the terror of regressive longing' (Greenberg and Mitchell 1983: 215). But the crucial point remains the same for all Object Relations theorists: that the painful structuring of the psyche is a consequence of environmental failure, and in important ways embodies that failure in the structure it produces. Splitting, fragmentation and withdrawal are observable aspects of personal life, but they are not essential; given a good enough social world, they would not occur at all.

Mothering the true self: the contribution of Winnicott

In what has been described above, the characteristic concern of Object Relations theorists with the early mother-infant bond is revealed, as well as their tendency to play down the Oedipus situation and find a source for all psychological conflict in failures of maternal gratification. In the work of Donald Winnicott, there is to be found the quintessential instance of romanticisation of the possible relationship between mother and child. However, this is achieved with a considerable degree of subtlety and with such a strong focus on the interpersonal aspects of the developmental (and psychoanalytic) encounter that it has proved to be of great value for recent theorists intent on using psychoanalytic ideas in the service of social theory. As will be seen, there are some concepts in Winnicott's work that have the paradoxical effect of simplifying the interpersonal context towards a conformist politics (particularly gender politics) whilst also producing playful and creative associations that have spawned some very radical insights, particularly in the realm of what has come to be called 'intersubjectivity'— the development of selfhood in relation to other people's minds.

Winnicott (1956) suggests that the mother has the role of providing a 'facilitating environment' in which the child's inner potential to develop her or his true self can be unfolded. At birth, the infant is in an unintegrated state, unable to piece together the portions of experience that become available—a description which, incidentally, distances Winnicott from Fairbairn's insistence on the primary unity of the neonate ego. It is the mother's role to support the infant's ego after birth by falling into a state of 'primary maternal preoccupation' in which she has complete oneness with her baby and can provide her or him with perfect 'holding', allowing the child to gain a sense of trust in the world and a security in her or himself. At first, the mother-child dyad centres on periods in which the infant is excited and the mother magically anticipates the object suitable to the child's desires, conjuring up a sense of omnipotence in the infant which serves as the basis for a solid and creative sense of a powerful self. In between these periods, when the child is quiescent, the mother's role is to be a solid but non-intrusive figure, allowing the child to feel secure in the presence of someone else—the foundation for the important capacity to be alone that is another mark of the healthy ego. Gradually, as the child's sense of hallucinatory omnipotence becomes strong enough for her or his self to begin to be established, the mother has to learn how to 'fail', to recover in stages from the 'illness' of primary maternal preoccupation, so that the child can learn the limits of her or his power and can start to experience her or himself as a separate being in a real world. In all this the mother functions as a kind of mirror to her child, mediating reality gradually, at a pace appropriate to the infant's development, geared to presenting the child with a picture of the strength of her or his presence in the world. This is the foundation of 'good enough mothering', and if managed leads to the formation of a 'true self' as the child discovers the power of her or his own egoic desires. The mother's ability to carry off this task is rooted in biology: it is something that develops over pregnancy and is intuitive and special, qualitatively distinct from the knowledge possessed by child care experts, the naturally occurring basis for all healthy human development. Conversely, psychological problems of all kinds are 'environmental deficiency diseases', stemming from early failures in mothering.

Although, as noted above, Winnicott accepts that the newly born infant has a fragmented ego (he even allows for the existence of the id, again in contrast to Fairbairn and Guntrip), he stresses the *naturalness* of the process whereby the child's sense of integrated selfhood is formed—its requirement is simply a supportive, non-intrusive environment, and it is environmental *failure* that gives rise to internal splitting. This, in turn, represents something for Winnicott concerning the conditions for emergence of a 'self', imagined as a naturally unfolding essence in which can be found the true integrative tendency of the human subject. Interestingly, this 'self' is distinguished from the ego as whole to part: that is, the ego is an aspect of something which cannot be analysed, but only evoked as the core component of subjective life. Phillips observes:

[Winnicott] was asserting the presence of something essential about a person that was bound up with bodily aliveness, yet remained inarticulate and ultimately unknowable: perhaps like an embodied soul. 'At the centre of each person', Winnicott writes, 'is an incommunicado element, and this is sacred and most worthy of preservation' (Winnicott 1963: 187). This Self that he will describe as 'permanently non-communicating' fits uneasily, of course, with the notion of psychoanalysis as primarily an interpretive practice. (Phillips 1988: 3)

As will be seen below, the evocation of a primordially integrated self is especially contentious in the light of theories emphasising the fragmenting impact of social construction.

To complicate any simple political reading of Winnicott, however, this emphasis on a biologically programmed, natural unfolding of the infant's potentiality is nevertheless a thoroughly *social* theory, in that it is always written in terms of the self-in-relation, the infant subject existing in the context of that other subject, the mother. (Parenthetically, it should be noted that the extremely influential non-psychoanalytic theory of attachment, derived from the work of John Bowlby, shares exactly this characteristic of being a biologically oriented theory in which mentally healthy development is held to depend on good quality interpersonal experiences—see Bowlby 1969, 1973, 1980.) It is the mother's capacity to create a 'non-intrusive' interpersonal environment that determines the infant's developmental outcome; at its best, there is a kind of 'collaboration' between mother and child which promotes the psychological well-being of each of them. Phillips summarises the core notion here as follows:

> This was the conviction at the centre of Winnicott's developmental theory. It was the rapport between the mother and her infant that made instinctual satisfaction possible; previous psychoanalytic theory had assumed it was the other way round... Without this rapport between the mother and her infant... the infant experiences his desire as an overwhelming assault. The mother holds the experience to make it satisfying. Where the Id of the infant is, the mother's Ego must also be. (Phillips 1988: 100)

There are important parallels between this theory and that of Klein, but with the major difference that whereas Winnicott assumes that development is 'naturally' a creative, integrative process in which the infant's inbuilt propensities can be nurtured so that they flower into integrated selfhood, Klein sees development as a struggle to live with ambivalence, to contain conflict and make something of it.

Winnicott (1963) acknowledges the fragility of the image of perfect development that his description of good-enough mothering conjures up, and argues that it is this fragility that gives rise to a hidden aspect of the personality, a core of subjectivity held 'incommunicado' from the rest. But it is his more famous distinction between the 'true self' and 'false self' that reveals Winnicott as an exponent of the concept of fundamental psychic unity. The mother is supposed to provide her infant with the conditions under which her or his potential for selfhood can be realised. Interference with this function, for instance because of the mother's anxiety or failure to perceive the child's omnipotent desires, is experienced by the infant as an 'impingement' on the natural organisation of experience, and leads to anxiety about total disintegration. This results in a defensive hiding away of the child's spontaneous desires in the form of a secret 'true self', which avoids expression because of the danger that it will be destroyed by the inadequate environment. To enable transactions with reality a conformist 'false self' is formed, split off from the true self and protecting its integrity. The false self is inauthentic because it is built up on the pattern of the mother's desire, not the child's, hence its conformity: the child is someone else's image of her or him, acting in line with the mother's expectations and wishes so as to win her love. In Phillips' gloss:

> It is part of Winnicott's demand on the mother that she be robust; if she is in any way rejecting, the infant has to comply with her response. It is the strategies of compliance that Winnicott calls the False Self Organization. Because of this primary and enforced attentiveness to the needs of the mother, the False Self, he writes, always 'lacks something, and that something is the *essential element of creative originality*'. (Phillips 1988: 133)

Greenberg and Mitchell describe how Winnicott comes to use the false self as a single diagnostic principle, 'representing a continuum of psychopathology from psychotic states, in which the false self has collapsed, to nearly healthy states, in which the false self mediates selectively and sparingly between the true self and the outside world' (Greenberg and Mitchell 1983: 208). The true self is the essential creativity of the human subject in action, consisting of a variety of capacities such as the ability to be alone, to be in states of 'disunity' out of which new modes of experience can emerge, to live with risk and so on. The false self, on the other hand, is something close to what other psychoanalytic authors would call 'narcissism'—a defensive shutting down, organised around close scrutiny of the other and an inability to feel real.

Towards intersubjectivity

There is a striking similarity between Winnicott's account of the 'mirroring' of the child's desire by the mother and the construction of the false self, on the one hand, and Lacan's (1949) notion of the 'mirror phase' on the other. In both cases, the infant receives a kind of gift of subjectivity from the outside, from the reflection in the mirror—usually interpreted as the mother's admiring gaze. However, there is also a crucial difference in the use of these notions by the two psychoanalysts. For Lacan, there is no pre-given unity to the psyche; the 'mirror' that the child looks in gives a misleading sense of integrity; the Winnicottian 'false self' is a description of the ego as it is constructed in the mirror phase. For Winnicott, it is part of the inheritance of each individual human to become whole and unified, with the 'true self' as a bearer of the subject's authenticity, containing all her or his spontaneous desires. The mirroring function of the mother is a crucial element in this: it allows the child to experience her or his own emotional states—whether excited, distressed, erotic or aggressive—as real and acceptable, and also as communicable and comprehensible. The mother's mirroring activity thus *validates* the infant's subjectivity, supporting the emergence of a creative self in contact with the other; the false self is the product of an interference in this process. This brings into the frame a divergence of views between 'negative' theories (such as that of Lacan) that focus on the way the ideological structures of the social world operate to produce 'misperceptions' of reality (taking the mirror image for the truth), and 'positive' theories (such as Winnicott's) pursuing notions of fulfilling relationships and creative self expression even in the context of a social environment which militates against their achievement. Rustin expresses this comparison in a particularly clear way, taking as his subject Lacanian versus British Object Relations and Kleinian psychoanalysis' relationship with political thought.

> The first tradition is above all adapted to the unending investigation of the inauthentic, idealised and self-regarding aspects of human consciousness. The second tradition regards psychoanalytic investigation not only as a method of recognition of illusions and self-deceptions, but also as a source of grounded understanding of 'authentic' states of feeling and object relations, conceived as the foundation of creative forms of life. (Rustin 1995: 226)

In this context, Winnicott's interest in the necessary conditions for promotion of positive selfhood could have a benign political programme embedded in it. This can be seen in the way that some political commentators have drawn on Winnicott's ideas (often laced with attachment theory—see, for example, Kraemer and Roberts 1997) to explore ways in which the fragmenting demands of late modern society can be survived and used creatively by people. For instance, the British social theorist, Anthony Giddens (1991), has argued that the current state of modernity is one of 'risk', in which it is necessary for human subjects to have confidence in their capacity to survive if they are to forge meaningful interpersonal and social relationships. This confidence is coded as 'trust' and is derived from the early infant-caregiver relationship in much the way that Winnicott describes. Trust arises out of secure early relationships with a caregiver who can tolerate the uncertainty and ambivalence of the relationship with the infant, and it is a necessary attribute for the achievement of a coherent self capable of living in the risk environment. Elliott shows how this idea of Giddens' relates to Winnicott's notions of good enough mothering and also transitional phenomena—the 'in-between' experiences that a child has as she or he starts to postulate a separation from the mother.

> Reconceptualising the Object Relational view within a comprehensive social theory of modernity, Giddens is able to demonstrate that anxiety, trust and transitional space are fundamental psychical mechanisms which lie at the root of social interaction. Significantly, this shows that individual development and relational processes are not closed off in an asocial world (the imaginary dyad of child and mother), but are intimately bound up with general social relations. The learning of self and other in a transitional realm involves a good deal more than merely adjusting to social reality; it is actually constitutive of an emotional acceptance of the socio-symbolic world of other persons and objects. (Elliott 1994: 74)

What this implies is that the conditions of secure self-development are necessary also for the development of capacities to encounter and explore other people and social institutions, a point which has also been taken up by psychoanalytic theorists of the self and its pathologies such as Heinz Kohut and Otto Kernberg (see Frosh 1991). In

Rustin's terms, this is a 'positive' political as well as psychological programme.

Winnicott's notion of transitional space has also proved productive
for another group of theorists, calling themselves 'intersubjectivists', of
whom Jessica Benjamin is one of the most distinguished members.
'Intersubjectivity' is a term used to refer to the capacity to represent
another person as a *subject* in the strict sense of a centre of perception
and subjectivity with whom one can have a dialogue based on mutual
recognition. It is thus a step forward from the usual subject-object
dichotomy which dominates in much Western thought, including psychoanalysis. Benjamin comments:

> Subject and object, active and passive, observer and participant,
> knower and known—these reversible complementarities have
> structured the psychoanalytic relationship. The intersubjective
> perspective is concerned with how we create the third position
> that is able to break up the reversible complementarities and
> hold in tension the polarities that underly them. (Benjamin 1998:
> xiv)

As she also puts it, this is a 'subject-subject' perspective rather than
a 'subject-object' one, concentrating on the human capacity to appreci-
ate the other as both 'like' and 'other than' the self. Identification is the
psychological mechanism at the root of this capacity. In many theories,
identification is seen as a process of incorporation of otherness, a kind
of cannibalistic taking in of the other until it becomes part of the self,
no longer psychically distinct. Benjamin, however, uses as her 'point of
departure' what she calls 'Winnicott's radical rethinking of how otherness can be accepted by the self when the attempt to psychically
destroy the object is resolved through the other's survival' (Benjamin
1998: xix). Identification is consequently built out of an already-exist-
ing awareness of the other's survival *as a subject*; that is, when promoting intersubjectivity it is a loving relationship in which aspects of otherness are accepted and used by the self, without destroying the other
in the process. In Benjamin's words:

> Identificatory love is a specific formation, it is the love that wants
> to be recognised by the other as like. Identification is not merely
> a matter of incorporating the other as ideal, but of loving and

having a relationship with the person who embodies the ideal.
(Benjamin 1998: 61)

Identification can thus be seen as a form of relationship, not a way
of acting upon another; developmentally, for example, it can be a way
in which a boy aspires to be linked to his father, not to be Oedipally
rivalrous with him.

The important point about the intersubjectivist perspective is that it
builds upon Object Relations theory to address social issues through
the relational capacities of the human subject. Whereas traditional theory has been interested in the ways in which individuals incorporate
aspects of the outside world, for example, taking in maternal or pater-
nal attributes, intersubjectivism spotlights the question of *recognition,*
of appreciating, accepting and relating to others as 'like subjects'. The
self consequently can be seen to arise out of a process of recognising
the intentionality and agency (what Benjamin calls the 'authorship') of
the loved other and identifying with this. This idea moves psychoanalytic theory away from its tendency to see social life as a struggle
between individuals and towards a vision of the bridging of differences. Returning to Winnicott, it also re-establishes the mother (or
more general 'other') not just as a passive support for the infant, a mere
reflecting mirror, but as an active agent or author, exploring the infant's
incipient self and in so doing communicating the significance and centrality of the appreciation of other people's minds.

The limits of Object Relations theory as social theory

Object Relations theory makes some important contributions to
attempts to develop a psychoanalysis that deals seriously with the
impact of social factors on the development of individuals. For one
thing, it formulates its understanding of basic mental structures in
social terms: the mind consists of ego-object links which are the internalised representatives of external social relations. In this respect,
Object Relations theory is 'constructionist' in outlook, arguing that the
full personality is formed through a process of social encounter that is
more than just some inherent individuality being conditioned or otherwise influenced by the actions of other people. Rather, individuality
itself *consists of* an amalgam of personal (ego) and social (objects) components. The emphasis of these theorists on the environment is thus
not accidental: for them, there is no individual without the social, no

self without the other. Again, their formulation is strikingly different from classical psychoanalysis, even though the developmental theory of the latter also deals in detail with the experiences of the child in the context of a network of family relationships. Classical analysis takes the individual as a 'closed' system of biological drives which suffer a certain fate due to social constraints (and their own inherent contradictions); each person's internal world does not, therefore, contain anything social, even though it is affected by interpersonal events. For Object Relations theorists, on the other hand, the internal world is set into motion by sociality (maternal deprivation), and its structure and contents are the product of a collision between internal needs and real social forms.

Despite these genuine advances in psychoanalytic theory, the Object Relations position has some substantial drawbacks. These centre on the way its social vision is restricted to the mother-child network and on the notion of the basic unity of the infantile ego. There are clear conformist dangers present in Object Relations theory's romanticisation of motherhood and in its view that all psychological splits are introduced by frustrating experiences with the maternal object—for instance, that it implies a *biologically* determined mothering role which must take priority over all other aspects of a woman's life (see Riley 1983, for an account of the social policy effects of Winnicott's views). There is considerable empirical and anthropological evidence to suggest that the relationship patterns that surround early infancy are socially constructed and that infant-mother links develop gradually and often with difficulty; approaches that 'naturalise' mothering as much as Object Relations theory does neglect this data and fuel attempts to bolster traditional patterns of family life (for work 'deconstructing' mothering see, for example, Hollway and Featherstone 1997). In addition, the focus on two-person, mother-infant relations is in some ways less socially perceptive than Freud's concern with the three-person Oedipus situation. While it gives an account of the immediate interpersonal experiences of the child, it suggests that the whole of sociality can be reduced to this two-person network, failing to consider the way in which the dyad may itself be structured by something outside it—the exigencies of social structure as reflected in class, race or gender relations, for example. In the image presented by both Fairbairn and Winnicott, the external world functions only as an interference: in a perfect mothering environment, there would be but mother and babe, and nothing else. This is a conventionally asocial approach to development, suggesting that it is possible for it to occur outside society. In this respect, Object Relations theory represents only a limited advance on traditional psychology: although it extends the focus of the latter from the individual to the dyad, it goes on to treat this dyad *as if it were an individual,* suffering constraints imposed by wider society, but in no way inherently constituted by it. One of the effects of this position is to limit the scope of the theory's approach to social change. At its most extreme, it proposes that social and personal distress could be overcome if we could return to that fundamental state of human nature expressed in the new-born child's loving relationship with the mother; all would be harmonious if the world were only less frustrating. This idea leads to the proposal that complete integration and happiness is achievable through alterations in the kinds of relationships that parents form with their children, without a restructuring of society—a view opposed by many political and feminist theorists.

Notes

[1] This chapter is extracted from S. Frosh, *The Politics of Psychoanalysis* London: Macmillan, 1999

[2] The term 'object relations theory' can be quite loosely applied to indicate any approach which focuses on the relationships between the developing ego and the 'objects' (people or parts of people) with whom it comes into contact. Here it is being used specifically to refer to the work of Fairbairn, Guntrip and Winnicott; while Klein certainly dealt with ego-object relations, her approach was significantly different from those of these theorists. In fact, as noted in my *For and Against Psychoanalysis* (Frosh 1997: 19-20), 'in recent years all the mainstream psychoanalytic schools have turned their attention to what is best termed "intersubjectivity"—the ways in which mental representations of relationships are formed and the effects these have on the development and actual social relationships of individuals. Although substantial variations in terminology and emphasis still apply, there is far more overlap amongst the mainstream proponents of psychoanalysis than at any time in the post-Freudian period. For instance, Contemporary Freudians and Kleinians differ considerably on the centrality they accord to early fantasy life, to unconscious emotions and to cognitions, with Freudians being willing to credit the ego with more capacity for imagination and control than do Kleinians, who in turn remain more wedded to a vision of the infant mind as one already full of complex emotions and fantasy states. Yet, proponents of both approaches can be found who are concerned with the ways infants form mental representations of their own functioning and of other people, and of how this can be understood in terms of creative interplays between autochthonous elements of the mind, early experiences, and unconscious impulses. Indeed, it is fairly hard to find any contemporary psychoanalyst who does not accord central significance to object relationships, even if they differ on many other aspects of theory (such as the place of drives or the order of developmental accomplishments) or practice (such as the way interpretations should be phrased, or the use of the negative transference)'.

Section Three

SELF PSYCHOLOGY AND ITS RELATION TO ART

Robert Royston

Introduction

Heinz Kohut's Self Psychology is at the very least a new theoretical and clinical approach to the difficult problem of narcissism. This chapter differentiates Kohut's approach from the classical concepts of narcissism and from the ideas of Klein and the Object Relations School in psychoanalysis, but also offers a critique of Self Psychology.

Kohut's contribution to the elusive problem of the self is not, however, relevant only to psychoanalysis, but to social science as well, as its concepts may be applied to a range of different subjects. This chapter, for example, suggests how it may be applied to the field of art and intellectual creativity, and comments on the conflict between the idea of the self as a social construct and of the self as *sui generis*.

Each era in the short history of psychoanalysis has its characteristic patient. In Freud's time, the iconic patient was the hysteric. In the late twentieth century the central patient became the narcissistic character, in whom the self is regarded as over-luxuriant, arrogant and ruthless. In between these two phases British psychoanalysis was preoccupied with what came to be called the schizoid condition, and it was through the exploration of this newly-recognised pathology that the concept of the self, up until then vague, began to develop in analytic theory.

Since the schizoid condition is characterised by a sense of personal alienation, psychoanalysis can be said to have discovered the self through becoming aware of its absence. The schizoid patient, although to all appearances normal, functional and often symptom-free, described a teasing sense of unreality, states of emotional impoverishment and alienation from the body. The British Object Relations school, which founded much of its basic theory on a study of this condition, sharpened the focus on the psychoanalytic concept of the self, a concept which later grew into a central preoccupation in American Self Psychology, which offers a different and forgiving perspective on narcissism.

The self in the schizoid condition

The schizoid patient, as described by the original theorists of the British Object Relations school, Fairbairn, Guntrip and Winnicott, was emotionally flat and unspontaneous. While possibly intellectually developed, the person was so emotionally suppressed that Freud's concept of defence did not seem relevant.

In Freud, the ego, a system of defensive mechanisms, mediated the relationship between the subject's drives and the outside world. Freud here was talking about a person seen as a complete being who was nevertheless flawed. In a sector of the neurotic psyche, the ego had failed to harness and sublimate drive energy and a product of that failure was a symptom, such as a phobic state or an obsessional ritual. But in the schizoid condition, the patient's whole mode of being was a defence, and to such a degree that it became feasible to say that the self was absent from the person.

An indication of the absence of self was the patient's compliance. Presenting problems were often vague and initial work often appeared encouraging. This was deceptive, however, because the patient had intuited the analyst's agenda and produced the required material, or was simply going through the motions of analysis like an automaton, working hard but without animation. Personal desire, opinion, opposition and emotion were absent. However, if emotion was a requirement, and particularly if a hysterical feature was present, the patient would generate a show of hyper-emotionality. But all of this lacked the depth and urgency of a real analytical encounter.

Here was a striking picture of the self's absence, particularly if the self is conceived of as personal will or spontaneous desire, or if it is conceived of as opposition to an encroaching other, or as personal style, or a sense of personal agency. Was the patient the cause of things? He did not feel so, but was reactive. Had he brought himself to analysis? No: analysis had happened to him, or someone else had suggested it. He continued to come to sessions out of duty or because of the implacable demands of mindless routine. Routine and dutiful application replaced the capriciousness, the stubbornness, selfishness and generosity of the human will. Initiative, freedom and choice were absent. Paradoxically, while hyper-alert to the needs of the other person, the schizoid patient simultaneously felt divorced from society. Guntrip (1968) described how this alienation from the group could give the schizoid character a lucidity of mind and an insightful observer role in life.

The subjective experiences of the schizoid character were various. Complaints ranged from a sense of aridity or emptiness to experiences of painful unreality and worrying detachment from the world, as though the subject was imprisoned behind glass or floating outside the body. Patients complained of a lack of emotional contact with others and appeared to dread dependency, and to find occasional fleeting moments of contact with others intolerably painful. There was an all-pervasive loneliness, and a fear, in some, of psychotic regression.

Analytic work with schizoid or compliant patients moved away from traditional areas, such as the Oedipus complex and analysis of drives and the super-ego. Work came to be focused on a search for the absent part, for the emotional and alive area of the person, 'the self'. Causes were identified—the deprived child abandons ties with and needs for others. Childhood dependency had been too painful, objects too disappointing or unreliable and this had caused a retreat from feelings into a schizoid world. Rather than abide in unsatisfied need, the child closed the emotional wellsprings of life, and seceded from human relationships into rigid self sufficiency. Only superficial contact and behaviour was allowed to endure.

The analytic objective with such patients developed into the search for what came to be called the self, or the true self. This self was conceptualised as emotionally charged, in pain, deprived, needy and frightened, and by Winnicott as creative, spontaneous and playful. For him the discovery and emergence of the self was not the discovery of trauma so much as the discovery of joy.

The self in Object Relations psychology

The British Object Relations school used the word 'self' freely. But often this use was negative—there was a preoccupation with the self's absence. But what precisely was meant by the term self? In Winnicott (1958), the self is a state of mind. The self is the person who does not comply slavishly with the requirement of the impinging other, who is not taken over by a false self.

To Winnicott (1965), the false self was a functional but uncreative and emotionally dead psychological prosthetic, which came into being when the child's mother pushed for quick and inappropriate acquisition of skills and independence in infancy. The true self is facilitated by a caring and attuned mother who tolerates and enjoys the child's phase-appropriate sense of omnipotence, who shows the child its own self by reactive and appreciative facial expression. She does not impinge so the primal self is able to thrive according to its inherent nature, which is to be free, playful and creative. The self is emergent, surging forward from within, but only if the environment is benign.

When, in therapy, the patient is able to forget about the analyst's needs and to free associate without regard for anything but the pleasure of free expression, then the self is said to have been reached.

The self in classical analysis

Up until the early beginnings of the Object Relations school, 'self' was used only casually and could mean a number of things, such as the ego, or the whole person, or the person as active agent. The ego in classical psychoanalysis, of course, is a set of mental mechanisms that come into operation to mediate between the drives, which seek immediate gratification, and the punitive outside world. The Freudian ego is described as functioning automatically, outside the conscious control of the subject. Such an entity cannot be the 'self'.

The Freudian concept of libido as described in *Three Essays on the Theory of Sexuality* (1905), is closer to an acceptable description of the self. It is true that libido is a blind force. In its original form, libido seeks nothing but its own satisfaction, and having found a satisfying object becomes attached to it, seeking it again with growing recognition. Nevertheless there is a self-seeking quality, an animation, an imperiousness and an urgency in libido that appears closer to a concept of selfhood, and is, in fact, just what the schizoid character was later said to lack.

That granted, libido in Freud signally lacks qualities appropriate to the concept of selfhood. Descriptions of it can put one in mind of the homunculus, the little person inside a larger person, operating independently. All of this, too, is part of the essential atomism of Freudian psychology—the person is a bundle of different things, of drives and mechanisms, which in the development process in childhood become fused together into something of a unity. This human being, though, cannot be said to be an amalgam, a type of new metal, because within the mind various parts, each with its own character, continue to operate as units. Unity, or integration, is said to occur when these different entities work together harmoniously, when id, ego, the prohibitive super-ego, the ego ideal and so on cooperate. Neurosis in this view is the outcome of internal conflict.

To point to one of the component entities and call it the self is to exclude the others. To point to the whole person and say that it is this elusive entity, the self, is to give substance to an abstraction. 'The whole person' is simply a name given to a collection of entities. It does not in itself exist, just as 'life' does not exist as a separate entity among other entities, such as the breakfast table, history and the west wind.

Nevertheless, Freud's model of the mind was written as a science, with emphasis on precision and theory building. It would be unfair to this model, which continues to underlie all later psychoanalytic developments, to accuse it of denying the self. It is better to say, agreeing with Treurniet (1980), that classical theory took the existence of the self for granted and concentrated its attention appropriately on psychodynamic processes.

Classical analysis and the narcissistic patient

Narcissism in classical analysis is opposed to object love, and is an over-investment of the self with the libido. The subject is his own love object and the self becomes over-valued. Correspondingly the object or other person is devalued. In the consulting room, a welter of intensely difficult clinical problems are thought to develop from this.

The narcissistic patient is said to treat the therapist as a thing to be exploited. There is an envious unwillingness to acknowledge the therapist as a contributor to the well-being of the subject, and as a result the therapist often feels frustrated and undermined. Interpretations may be blocked, accepted but rapidly forgotten, or appropriated. In the latter case a patient may respond tangentially to a comment offered by the therapist and then repeat the comment but in a slightly modified form. The modification as well as the delayed uptake sever the connection between the contributor and the recipient, so that in the patient's subjective world she is the sole generator of good things, unreliant on people outside, whom she may treat with coldness and contempt.

In other words, the patient subjectively wipes out the other person as a separate mind. She appears to feel particular antipathy towards the therapist when the latter is experienced as helpful and creative. However, this antipathy, and the aggression which accompanies it, is usually not visible on the surface of the interaction, but takes place inwardly, in the patient's mind, which functions independently in its own dissociated kingdom. Here the helpful therapist is destroyed by the patient with great ease and power. For example, interpretations may be reduced in the patient's mind to clichés, or treated, not as analytical comments, but distorted into advice, injunction or complaint, which are lower-order phenomena. This subversion of the other person may take a concrete form, when, for instance, the patient visits the toilet after a session which he has experienced as helpful. Thus in a type of symbolic act, the session's curative potential is excreted because it derives from the other and not from the self.

These and other narcissistic phenomena are seen in psychoanalysis as a major obstacle to therapeutic progress; this is particularly so since psychoanalysis itself and its *modus vivendi* can be anathema to the patient, who appears to derive increased strength and stability from paralysing the therapeutic encounter. Epic therapy becomes a real possibility here, with the treatment secretly functioning not as analysis but as a type of pathological support system.

All of this is traditionally viewed as the product of the infant's failure to progress from self love to love of another, but is also seen by some, particularly Kleinians, in sinister terms (Rosenfeld 1964). In the clinical agenda of some Kleinians, narcissism can only be successfully analysed when it becomes ego dystonic, that is, when the patient starts to understand its noxious effects on her relationships, feeling states and even on her relationship with herself. After this has occurred the patient may typically dream of gangs or criminals and thugs. This shows that insight into narcissism has occurred. It has been recognised by the patient as inimical to personal well-being.

In Klein, rather more than in Freud, the person is conceived of as a collection of parts. Some of these parts may be called a self, and a picture can sometimes be glimpsed of the patient as an enclosed world peopled by inter-acting sub-selves. This vision of interacting selves in an internal world is also visible in the work of Fairbairn, one of the most important founders of British Object Relations theory, and a major contributor to the understanding of the schizoid condition. Fairbairn (1943) however asserted the prior existence of a self. A whole person or self existed at birth. What might later be seen as a collection of fragments or interacting sub-selves was, for Fairbairn, the result of damaging experiences with caretakers. In some important ways the work of Fairbairn in the area of the self is close to the later Self Psychology of Kohut.

Self Psychology

Self Psychology is a formulation about the genesis and treatment of narcissism, one that is at odds with the prevailing negative assessment of the condition. Narcissism, for decades a vexing and central clinical problem, is presented in Kohut's psychology of the self as a less malign and more treatable phenomenon.

In Kohut (1971, 1977), as in Winnicott, it is possible to say that the self is a state of mind, one characterised by a realistically buoyant self-regard, by passionate aims. ambitions, values and ideals. These all give meaning and vibrancy to life. The properly functioning self generates creativity and emotionally charged ideas. However, the self of Kohut is more complex in its functioning, its development and its analytical treatment than the innocent, nascent self of Winnicott.

Narcissism for Kohut is not a failure to disinvest the self of subjective value and transfer love to another, but instead is an attempt by the developing child to cope with a lost state of bliss and harmony. Most psychoanalytical perspectives begin with a view similar to this—that there is a type of oceanic oneness at birth that is disrupted and proceeds to disintegrate as the self differentiates from the object[1] and the surrounding world. This process is healthy but painful. In Kohut, the infant attempts to compensate for the lost state of bliss and perfection by lodging perfection in the self. The result of this is a huge over-estimation of the self's value, attractiveness and capability. Paradoxically, the infant cannot maintain this grandiose state of mind unaided by an attentive parent who sensitively and dotingly mirrors back an image which confirms the infant's greatness. Alternatively the infant may attempt to secure the lost blissful condition by storing it up in the object. A parent is idealised and the child wishes to feel close to and merged with the ideal outside figure and in this way takes back into the self the state of perfection.

In an infantile form, this idealisation of self and other are attractive and innocent and call eloquently for an appropriate response from adults. The child is exhibitionistic and demands attention and admiration, or blindly disregards the flaws in the idealised parent, believing him capable of effortless feats. However, similar characteristics in an adult, unmodified by the developmental process, usually appear in a different light, as crude, demanding, manipulative or, sometimes, charismatic.

In a child all of this is normal, and during the developmental process these narcissistic states are ameliorated and gradually lose their crude character, becoming realistic and translating into balanced self-esteem, as well as into aims and ambitions, ideals and moral principles. This development, however, requires the loving and natural responses of parental figures. That supplied, infantile narcissism also develops into a type of psychic envelope which produces stable and healthy mental states: stability of mood, coherence and integration.

Vital to the modification of primitive narcissism is the willingness of parents to be ruthlessly used by the child. They are there to serve the child's narcissistic purposes and be available to fulfill the role of admiring mirror, and must be able to allow themselves to be admired and idealised. Inevitably good parents not only succeed in this task, but also fail at times. The failures are as important as the successes because each time there is a failure the child internalises value previously invested in the object.

The parent used ruthlessly is termed in Self Psychology, a 'selfobject'.[2] This is an important term. A selfobject is a figure who is used by the child for its own purposes. There is no regard for the feelings and needs of the object, who is at first experienced simply as a function of the self.

Traditional analysis has been concerned about the manifold misuses of the analyst and the therapeutic process by the narcissistic patient. These, Self Psychology asserts, are the products of crude unmodified infantile narcissism. If the analyst confronts narcissistic phenomena by implying that narcissism is bad and its underlying causes should be analysed, then the patient will feel criticised and the treatment relationship will become embattled. One reason for this is the paradoxical vulnerability of even the most extravagant narcissistic personalities. While such a character feels grandiose, lovable, and uniquely wonderful, he or she may wither in response to comments or attitudes other people might disregard. Narcissism then is an exaggerated valuation of the self beneath which lies a morbid sensitivity.

A brief vignette may illustrate some of these themes. A female patient in her mid-twenties entered therapy in crisis, fearful that a full-scale mental breakdown was imminent. She had been struggling for many months against desperately painful experiences she could barely describe, even to herself. A type of agitated depression was present, along with periods of free-floating anxiety, but the most worrying symptom, to her, was a feeling that she was coming apart, or her world was. Nothing was right, everything was out of joint. This state, exacerbated by insomnia, could not go on, and had become utterly intolerable. Several previous experiences of similar distress had eventually faded, but this one seemed to be increasing.

The patient described the onset of her problems. She had been working in New York with an older man she hugely admired, and who had a high reputation in their shared field. He was charismatic and called forth from people unusual levels of commitment and motivation towards the moral cause to which his life was devoted.

My patient felt that she was his most valued protégé. There was real evidence that he was preparing her for a position at the top of the organisation. However, he quite abruptly appeared to lose interest in her, although this may well have been the result of mounting professional and domestic difficulties. Nevertheless, my patient described how she realised one afternoon that a decision had taken place in her mind without any conscious thought process behind it: she would resign immediately, return to London and seek a completely different professional interest. This appeared inevitable to her, and simple.

On her return, the dreaded intolerable state, which she had hoped never to experience again, set in, together with a confusion about her aims, ambitions and professional plans. She had several brief sexually intense affairs with people she at first found compelling but then rejected as boring and invasive.

This clinical extract shows the power of an idealised selfobject to bring emotional stability, cohesion and a high degree of positive self-regard into a vulnerable, unintegrated personality. Through her connection with the charismatic boss my patient acquired a high-toned concept of her worth, which in its turn brought idealistic passion, ambition and motivation, as well as creativity. The boss was her selfobject, and psychodynamically his main role was to function as an essential but inwardly missing part of her self. Her close work and special relationship with the boss brought her into touch with her own grandiosity, narcissistically invested in an external figure. And the strange suddenness of her disinvestment from him shows how the selfobject is not treated as a full person, but simply as a source of much needed self-regard. The boss briefly failed to fulfill his narcissistic role and upon that instant almost ceased to exist for the formerly dedicated protégé.

The therapeutic relationship began uncomfortably for me, with the patient praising my wonderful interpretations. She appeared genuine-

ly stunned by my brilliance, which made me feel conspicuous and fool-
ish. In addition, the disintegrated and agitated state was instantly
replaced. She felt restored to blooming mental health and wholeness,
hurled herself into a new job, gained new admiring friends, was seen
as beautiful and charismatic, developed her creative sideline interest in
which she appeared genuinely talented.

These sudden developments put me on analytical hyper-alert.
Traditionally the therapist is at pains to interpret the patient's idealisa-
tions as defensive, and to treat sudden recovery as flight into health,
and exaggerated well-being as manic. What lies behind these defences,
this overvaluation of the therapist? These are the insistent questions
from traditional analysis, and the usual answer is: idealisation hides
hatred or fear of the therapist who, if the truth be told, is actually experienced as toxic; so, peel away the idealising defence and reveal a
depriving or invading object persecuting a depressed, anxious self.
Analytical comments along lines such as these fell flat, however, with
the patient off-handedly saying my remarks evoked empty disinterest,
she didn't know where I was coming from or even care—everything
had gone flat and she was thinking of quitting.

Self Psychology recommends empathy both as an analytical mode
and an intellectual instrument, and criticises traditional psychoanalysis for introducing a value-laden Western ethic and scientific mode into
clinical work. According to this mode the narcissistic woman patient
above may be seen by the therapist as exterior, as a field to be studied
and explored by an objective agent, the therapist. From this perspective the ethic of truth-at-all-cost might naturally be introduced: the
patient, in other words, should be confronted with her own real nature.
In other words, she must be told certain things: that she denies the
independent existence of the other person, particularly when that person comes up with an idea that does not tune in with her thinking, she
egocentrically overvalues herself and is guilty of the sin of pride, and
she is her own worst enemy. Therapy with narcissistic patients con-
ducted along these lines will, according to Self Psychology, become
embattled and the patient will feel criticised and attacked.

Empathy is an altogether different mode, and emphasises the type
of attunement and emotional closeness the narcissistic patient requires.
Objectively, then, my initial interpretations in the case above were far
from brilliant, but empathy and clinical tact urged compliance with the
patient's over-valuation. She and I were a continuum; I was a projection of her unintegrated grandiose sense of self. My mistake in stray-

ing into the customary interpretive mode was analysed as distressingly unattuned, and a recreation of events with the New York boss and with parental figures, an unattunement which could lead to painful experiences of isolation, boredom and disintegration. The initial atmosphere of warmth was soon recreated.

Of course empathy is a *sine qua non* in psychoanalysis. Self Psychology did not invent it. However, Kohut's empathic mode goes further than the common usage meaning of the term. It is a type of merger of the therapist in the self of the patient. This results in a subordination of the interpretive mode to the requirements of the patient's sensitivity. Mainstream psychoanalysis has much to gain from Self Psychology here, particularly in the treatment of narcissism. An interpretive mode which is not attuned to the exquisitely delicate state of the self will be experienced by the patient as a critical attack and a moral rejection, not only of the patient's narcissism, but of the core self. Such was the case with the idealising patient above.

A question emerges, however: how does the narcissistic transference help the patient and might it not make her dependent forever on an external person? What is the analytical mode of cure as conceived by Kohut's Self Psychology?

Modes of cure in Self Psychology

Kohut likened the successful analytical process in the treatment of narcissistic disturbances to the mourning process as described by Freud (1917). In mourning, the bereaved identifies with the person she has lost and takes an image of that person into the self. In narcissistic disturbances the therapist, inevitably, fails in his attention to empathic closeness and mirroring and makes comments that are out of tune with the patient's needs, either failing to accept the role of idealised parental object, as in the case above, or by failing to act as a mirror to the patient's grandiosity.

Every time this happens the patient, momentarily disillusioned, draws some of the grandiosity invested in the other person back into the self. This process parallels the child's healthy development in a family where parents enjoy the exhibitionistic grandiosity of the child, but also inevitably fail in their role as selfobjects. Every time they do so, the child compensates by establishing some small aspect of the selfobject or mirroring object inside the self.

As this process proceeds, in childhood or in therapy, the crude narcissism of early childhood is modified and integrated into the whole personality. Here, in a new ameliorated form it contributes increasingly realistic self-esteem, as well as a feeling that can, I think, very aptly be described as selfhood. The person feels inwardly alive. Her projects are invested with meaning and passion. Energy and aliveness lend vibrancy and tone her ideals and her system of values. There are things to strive towards, fight for, enjoy, admire. Within obvious limitations she feels she is the free agent of her actions: the self, in other words, is causal and experienced as such, and this experience of agency in its turn tones up the feeling of aliveness.

Put this way, Self Psychology itself sounds idealised in its vision of narcissistic cure. However, this is not the case. Kohut was well aware of the limitations of analytic success. He was also aware that life simply does not allow even the healthiest of people a seamless experience of selfhood and emotional aliveness. His concept of cure acknowledges that every self is fed by, in fact actually requires, a milieu in which achievements and talents are explicitly valued by others. Such a milieu feeds creativity. He saw an analysis as successful if in the course of it the patient developed a creative talent or professional skill which helped supply narcissistic energy to the self. Traditional psychoanalysis would see this as only a partial success, because it leaves the patient dependent on an external source for something which should come from the internal world.

Here Kohut's concept of the self and of creativity differs from Winnicott's. In the latter's view, creativity issues from a pure source of selfhood uncolonised by an impinging other. Creativity is free, playful and primal, and the polar opposite of the compliant false self which is constellated around the needs of other people. In Kohut creativity issues from a self which the subject values and invests in, largely thanks to prior investment by admiring others. For Kohut, however, creativity is also an instrument which supplies this self with vitally needed admiration, so that in a sense the self is dependent on its own creativity.

The ideal analytic outcome, of course, is a patient who has internalised the functions of the selfobject. Such a person, possessing a diminished need for praise and recognition, would withstand attacks on the self and its products. However an analysis might be judged a success if this did not occur, but if instead the work had generated a form of creativity which worked to supply narcissistic investment from an outside source.

An example of such a source is creativity in the more limited sense, the creation of an artistic or intellectual product. The study of intellectual creativity demonstrates one application of Self Psychology outside the clinical arena. What follows is just such an application—an exploration of creativity which draws on the insights of Self Psychology and examines the creative struggle in the light of the artist's narcissistic needs.

Self Psychology and creativity

Creativity is especially valued by society and the artist in all fields is considered particularly fascinating. Novels, sculptures and painting are the subject of intense public attention, but so are the lives of the artists. Successful creative people are taken, without the requirement of evidence, to be particularly worthy of attention.

The creative life, however, is a difficult one and a huge effort of will, or rather a drive amounting to obsession, is required for success at the highest level or for the full expression of a talent. Yeats' comment that either the life or the writing can be perfected, not both, is testimony to the exacting nature of the artistic project, but also demonstrates the artist's crucial obsession with perfection.

From the perspective of Self Psychology, creativity can be seen as bound up with a type of psychological struggle. It is as though there is an engine room in the core of the self that ceaselessly motivates the artist towards production and expression and success. It is not that the work has to be enjoyed. Joseph Conrad, after all, hated the act of writing. Enjoyment is an irrelevant consideration. It is hard to imagine Dostoevsky enjoying writing between bouts of crippling epilepsy. However the work has to be done, and not simply because creditors are knocking at the door, but because of an implacable internal agenda, and even in the most difficult circumstances there are rich emotional rewards to be had.

The artist though is uniquely vulnerable to narcissistic damage. The work, if it is good, has to be original, and that means it must be mined from the depths of personal experience, transmuted through difficult mental processes and through an exacting craft into eloquence. Completed, it must have power. It must move the viewer or reader, appeal intellectually, stir mysterious responses, engage at an emotional level. However, it is true to say that while society values creativity above most other forms of human endeavor, it is also guiltlessly cruel, mocking and envious in the field of art. As a result of these factors the artist is uniquely vulnerable to narcissistic damage. The drive for perfection is huge; the rewards in terms of public esteem are huge; but huge too is the artist's self exposure. Criticism is capable of wounding the most vulnerable core of the artist's self, particularly as critical reports are often delivered with flair and read with relish by the community at large.

What is the motivating energy that flows into creativity?

Employing the perspective of Self Psychology, one may argue that art arises from, but also transcends, psychological damage. It is an example of Kohut's compensatory structure. The self is originally damaged by caretakers in childhood who withheld admiration, and failed to respond to and transmute the child's archaic narcissistic needs. They did not support, when it was appropriate to do so, the child's wish to experience herself as the centre of an admiring universe, and neither was she allowed to enjoy a limitless sense of personal confidence, capability and power. Caretakers instead were neglectful, unempathic, distracted, or quite probably actively devalued and psychologically attacked the child.

Consequently, the artist seals off the world of objects, that is of real people, as dangerous and unrewarding. There is a retreat into a world of creativity, the silent room of the writer. Here, with luck, the mind may work with unfettered freedom, in a world free of narcissistically disappointing or attacking objects. The creative products are the mirror in which the writer or thinker or artist sees a reflection of the self as valued; she is original, admirable, powerful, in control and safe. Outside the room or studio, dimly intuited, is a waiting world, ready with supplies of admiration. Many writers describe the process as soothing, as generating a feeling of being unified and enveloped.

On the other hand, the act of creation may be difficult and painful, or blocked. When the writer takes a step out of the narcissistic world of creativity and looks with a critical eye at what has been written, an agitation may set in. Is the writing as good as she felt it to be yesterday? It isn't perfect. Crude, unprocessed phrases stand out with shameful and embarrassing clarity and must be obsessively worked over again and again. The book will never be finished. Even when it is published and in the shops she will want to rewrite sections of it.

For the writer who works easily and is soothed by the work, the unempathic outside world is held at bay. For those who find the work torture, the shadow of the narcissistically rejecting and attacking caretakers is ever present and has to be fought in the act of writing, not afterwards, in the act of self criticism.

The elements of Kohut's vision of the mind in its struggle to preserve and nurture the self are clearly visible in the creative process. But what of writers, thinkers and artists themselves, and what of their lives?

The lives of some writers

Narcissism is a need for esteem. It is often associated with a callous use of other people, because the other is treated as a selfobject which exists to gratify narcissism; the other is not experienced as an emotional being with a capacity for pain. This can make the narcissistic person appear cold and cruel at times, though within the selfobject relationship they may be warm and beguiling and loving.

Jean Jacques Rousseau was such a character, and it can be strongly argued that narcissism, his and that of other writers, is important for creative success. His *Confessions* is a touching work in which the author describes his failings, sexual peccadilloes and minor perversions. A picture is created of an ingenuous, humble and morally brave man, for whom confession is an act of intimacy. The reader is drawn to empathise, forgive and admire an all too human creature. It is a frank and poignant work, and also seductive. Rousseau ingenuously puts himself at the mercy of the reader's benign and caring judgment, having first primed that judgment to proclaim his childlike innocence. Throughout all this, the writing is beautiful, radiant with a type of inspiring lucidity.

Elsewhere Rousseau wrote fulsomely about his capacity to love: 'The person who can love me as I can love is still to be born'. He also wrote: 'No one ever had more talent for loving'. 'I would leave this life with apprehension if I knew a better man than me'. 'Show me a better man than me, a heart more loving, more tender, more sensitive...' And, 'if there were a single enlightened government in Europe, it would have erected statues to me'.

In writing *the Confessions* Rousseau wished to exonerate himself. One of the pillars of his abiding reputation is a body of theory about the correct upbringing and treatment of children. From his contribution emanated a romantic tradition which stressed nature and the natural man, and saw urban sophistication as a corrupter of original innocence. In educational theory his ideas are faintly echoed by Winnicott. Education should not be drummed into the child. Instead the child's spontaneous natural enthusiasm and curiosity should be drawn towards education. This theme ran through several of his major works.

Of himself and his care for children, he wrote, 'Never, for a single moment in his life, could Jean Jacques have been a man without feeling, without compassion or an unnatural father'.

In reality, Rousseau was father to five children. He abandoned each of them immediately after birth, without even knowing their sex, at the door of the Hôpital des Enfants-trouvés in Paris. At the foundling hospital two thirds of babies died in their first year and most of the rest before the age of seven. The small remainder invariably became paupers and beggars.

Burke wrote of Rousseau, 'Vanity was the vice he possessed to a degree little short of madness'. Rousseau adopted eccentric clothing, usually a type of caftan, and wore it in England at the Drury Lane Theatre. Here, we are told, he was so eager to receive the plaudits of the crowd that Mrs. Garrick had to hang onto his robe to prevent him falling out of the box into the auditorium.

In Rousseau one can see the workings of narcissism, and can see too the powerful narcissistic urge that flowed into an important body of work.

Tolstoy

Like Rousseau, Leo Tolstoy, the humanitarian author of *War and Peace* and *Anna Karenin*, wrote resoundingly in his own praise. 'I have not yet met a single man who was morally as good as I'. However Tolstoy, like Rousseau, could treat people without regard for their well-being. Expansive and noble feeling-states and concepts concerned and uplifted him, but people in his life were useful and discardable. He wrote that he was attracted to the good and ready to sacrifice everything to it. He wrote that he felt 'immeasurable grandeur' in his own soul. Tolstoy inherited estates and sold most of them to pay his vast gambling debts. He borrowed huge sums from friends and relations and many debts went unpaid. He appeared to be addicted to sex. In his diaries he claims to be maddened by and almost dying of sexual desire, yet he writes disparagingly of women and does not hesitate to blame them for his own lusts. Girls were evil temptresses. He wrote in his diary after a visit to a brothel: 'Disgusting. Girls. Stupid music, girls, heat, cigarette smoke, girls girls girls'.

Turgenyev wrote of him: 'Drinking bouts, gypsies, cards all night long, and then he sleeps like the dead until two in the afternoon'.

He eventually married an eighteen-year-old daughter of a doctor, Sonia Behrs. Sonia, after years of observing Tolstoy's behaviour towards his own family and others close to him, anticipated the famous thought of Dostoevsky's elder, Father Zossima, in *The Brothers Karamazov*. She observed that Tolstoy was a great lover of mankind, but to those close to him he was incapable of love. She wrote in a letter to him '...we simple mortals are neither able nor wish to distort our feelings or to justify our lack of love for *a person* by professing some love or other *for the whole world*'.

But the 'immeasurable grandeur' Tolstoy felt in his soul was real. It was from that source, a type of grandiosity, a huge inflated feeling, a sense of personal greatness, that his panoramic study of war came, as well as his characters, Anna, Vronsky, Levin. And one may offer the idea that it was the grandiosity of Tolstoy's experience of his self or soul that gave him the motivation to write, and that writing sustained that grandiosity. After all, his life outside writing, his 'girls' and cards and gypsies all night and his gambling, suggests a disintegrated narcissism that addictively sought external agents to produce a sense of wholeness, cohesion and emotional stability.

Criticisms of Self Psychology

Self Psychology, like Object Relations psychology, places the individual in a social world. As in the view of Fairbairn, the child in Kohut is healthy or otherwise because of the behaviour of caretakers. But does Self Psychology take full account of the process of internalisation? According to this process as described by Fairbairn, a damaging caretaker is introjected by the child. This means that a part of the person will take over the forms of behaviour displayed by the caretaker. This behaviour will be applied in some way to the self, so that it almost becomes possible to speak of a parent inside the self, abusing the self, criticising the self.

Many patients have been narcissistically damaged not merely by a parent's failure to take on the role of admiring mirror or idealised object. Caretakers have actively undermined and criticised the child, and established an internal image of the self as bad, shameful and impotent. This sometimes results in narcissistic depletion, where a person is deprived of self-regard, feels worthless and is filled with shame and self-conscious embarrassment. They become compliant because of an expectation that others will treat them in the same way as their original objects did. Other patients might be narcissistically inflated as a defence against an underlying state of worthlessness and demoralisation.

In order to treat such conditions, it may be argued, one must understand that narcissistic mirroring in the transference is not enough. Before the narcissistic transferences can occur the internalised persecuting object must be identified and analysed. The patient must extrude this object through transference analysis, reconstruction of childhood events and working through. If this does not happen, then Self Psychology may function as a trauma bypass.

The self as aliveness and the self as identity

It may be argued from a social science standpoint that the self is a social construct. A boy, for example, is exposed to subtle cues and persuasions and to behavioural affirmations and disaffirmations. This process pushes him in a socially sanctioned direction, and he becomes an approved standard model male. His gender self is constructed from without. Self Psychology, however, has a different definition of the self. A person's identity might conform to society's model. A man might do all the 'right' male things and display recognisable gender attitudes, but feel bored, dead and meaningless. Another, similar, male may feel that his life and attitudes are charged with energy, are spontaneous, and creative. In this second person, the self is alive. The self is therefore deeper than identity, and is an attitude engendered by admiring good caretakers, and not a social construct. This position, I think, does not argue with social science, but is simply Self Psychology's different definition of the self, one which rewards both close attention and wide application.

Notes

[1] *Object*: in this chapter when this term is used in the theoretical sense adopted by Kohut, it denotes a caretaker in childhood who satisfied the child's libidinal needs and was internalised. The object may be external (a need satisfying other person), or internal (a part of the psyche which takes in character from, or behaves like, an object in the external world).

[2] *Selfobject*: this term is used by Kohut to denote a person who is used to feed the subject's narcissistic needs. A selfobject may be an admiring mirror to the self, or a person who is idealised and identified with. A selfobject is treated as a resource, without reference to his or her feelings. Caretakers in childhood are the original selfobjects. In Kohut's earlier work, the word is hyphenated.

JOINING, EXPERIENCING, AND INDIVIDUATING: EGO AND SELF IN THE GROUP

Shmuel Erlich

Introduction

The aim of this paper is to examine the relevance of two central psychoanalytic concepts—'ego' and 'self'—to the processes and functioning of groups. This effort may be regarded as continuing an earlier attempt to apply the concept of an 'ego' to family dynamics and growth (Klein and Erlich 1976). Broadly speaking, manifestations of substructures of the individual psyche in the group (ego, id, super-ego) have been broached exclusively from the perspective of the individual intrapsychic structure and its vicissitudes in the group setting (see especially Foulkes 1964: 108-119, also Yalom 1970). My argument, however, is that these concepts are Janusian, possessing two faces: one appears when viewed from the group perspective, the other from the individual's psychodynamic standpoint. I shall provide a brief and focused review of some of the underpinnings of the concepts of ego and self in psychoanalytic writings, from Freud onwards. I will present the thesis that even though 'ego' and 'self' constitute an individuated pole, one opposed to 'group', they also make up, are inseparable from, and in need of the group for attaining their potential.

On the other hand, a group may also be viewed as possessing the character and quality of an ego or a self, albeit at a new level of conceptualisation, i.e. as an organismic entity in its own right. I will further focus on the differences between ego and self as representing an essentially *different experience* of an individual subject's relatedness to its object. This differentiation provides a better understanding of ego and self in the group. I will suggest that, in my view, this understanding can be gained through the experiential modalities of 'being' and 'doing'. These experiences are connected mainly to the dimension of fusion vs. separateness of self and object. This distinction also accounts for the atmosphere that prevails in the Work Group as contrasted with a Basic Assumption Group. In groups with a well defined primary task and a strong connection to a definite product or outcome, the 'doing' modality typically prevails, and along with it, the ego and its functions predominate. Groups in which the primary task is existential, centreing on experiencing the 'here and now', rather than an instrumental or productive goal, are groups in which the 'being' modality prevails. In such groups, the focus shifts to the self, its experiences of fusion and continuous existence, and to related emotional issues and needs. While these two modalities define an experiential range, the pertinent question might be which modality is dominant at a particular moment in the group, and whether and how it is relevant and appropriate to the task.

Theoretical considerations

Development takes place at the point where 'I' and 'Group' not only come in contact, but are also intertwined, interlocked and inseparable. The psychoanalytic perspective on individual growth and development consists, as it were, of two 'complementary series'. When viewed from the perspective of external, 'actual' (interpersonal) object relations, development evolves along a dimension of increasing complexity—from a 'group', or social unit, of one—to a dyad, then to a triad, and eventually to membership in increasingly multiple and complex social groupings. When viewed from the perspective of 'internal' (intrapsychic) object relations, however, development seems to proceed from an undifferentiated merger in a larger-than-self 'group' (the dyad of mother-infant, the family system) towards an increasingly refined differentiation and definition of an individuated sense of self and 'I-ness'.

Freud was acutely aware of the significance of the interconnection between the psychology of the individual and the group. His sensitivity to this issue is reflected in the fact that his essay on *Group Psychology and the Analysis of the Ego* (1921) was written between two momentous revisions of his theoretical views, the dual instinct theory in *Beyond the Pleasure Principle* (1920a), and the structural model introduced in *The Ego and the Id* (1923). The work on group psychology anticipated the structural model of the ego, and relied on the theory of narcissism (Freud 1914). These ideas can be seen as laying down the foundations for later work on the self (e.g. Kohut 1971, 1977). Thus the study of the individual ego and the self is intertwined with group psychology.

Prior to 1923, Freud's consistent use of 'ego' was in the sense of 'the person as subject', who acts, thinks, feels and experiences the gamut of human activity. In this usage, ego connotes agency and it is both a function of consciousness and an inextricable component of it. Within Freud's topographical model, even though no 'ego' as such is delineated, the ego can be construed as being present as an active agency, coterminous with rationality and consciousness. The structural model takes into account the fact that the ego, as it tries to mediate between the instinctual id/super-ego and external reality, is itself, to a considerable degree, beyond consciousness and rationality. It stresses the inherent ability of the ego to withstand peremptoriness and introduce delay, and thus to allow for discrimination and choice, in contradistinction to the rest of the psychic system's inability to introduce and tolerate delay. The new ego-psychology (Hartmann 1950), however, transformed the ego into a systemic concept, exerting its influence through various psychological functions and processes. Conceiving of the ego as made up of interactive and integrative forces shifted the focus from personal desire, intense passion and bloody gore to the more 'refined' level of quasi-impersonal power struggles, reminiscent of dynamics within giant corporations.

Bridging the gap between the phenomenological-experiential and instrumental-functional points of view was rendered nearly impossible with the ego defined as a psychic system in charge of adaptive functions, and the self, in turn, merely a specific object-representation within the psychic apparatus (Hartmann 1950). The problem was further confounded through its entanglement with the essentially energic or quantitative issue of narcissism.

Kohut's (1971, 1977) work led the way to a rejection of the psychoanalytic psychology of ego vs. instinctual drives. A new construct, the 'Self', was designated to take hegemony as a psychological, non-drive-related superstructure. Emphasis shifted accordingly from a focus on conflict and adaptation, to need fulfilment and the provision of adequate supplies. The developmental and psychopathological focus also moved, from an emphasis on conflict in symptom formation, to issues of atrophy and arrest, dissociation and fragmentation of the Self.

Tensions between systemic and experiential models are inherent and ubiquitous. Systemic concepts lead to concern with efficiency and maintenance, with control, regulation and adaptation, and with the relationship between input and output. These in turn depend on a variety of further concepts, such as: *energy* to fuel the system; *boundaries* to delineate it from its environment and increase efficiency; a *primary task* that defines the work to be done; and *input-output* flow, which defines the relationship of the system to its environment. At the group level, these functions become manifest as *leadership, author-*

ity and *responsibility* for task definition and implementation. Experiential concepts and considerations, on the other hand, allocate centre stage to feelings, to needs and their satisfaction, fulfilment, or frustration. The absence or dearth of appropriate need-satisfying responsiveness can cause delay or arrest in the internal coherence that is formed out of the infinite series of satisfactions and frustrations of such needs.

Four levels of relationship between group and individual

I will now delineate four levels of discourse discernible in the relationship between the group and the individual. The four levels are distinct from one another, and require different levels of abstraction and conceptualisation. I also suggest different names or designations for each level (summation, consummation, organismic, and systemic) in an attempt to capture the intrinsic quality each one postulates.

1. Personal or intra-personal — 'Summation'

This level is best represented by Freud's account of group psychology (1921). Here group processes are understood in terms of individual psychodynamics. Conceptualisation remains entirely at the level of the individual group member, and explains his group behaviour in terms of mechanisms and processes derived from and representative of individual metapsychology. Group phenomena are regarded as quantitative, multiple and additive, i.e., as the *summation* of individual intrapsychic processes across the members of the group.

2. Interpersonal — 'Consummation'

Here the emphasis shifts to the encounter between individual intrapsychic dynamics and the group frame, as well as encounters among group members. The question asked is—what develops, or is barred from developing, as a result of this encounter? The encounter proceeds through interactions among different and distinct individual needs and regulatory patterns, in a continuous process of mutual stimulation and responsiveness. This process enables individual members to attain their ultimate, best and fullest self-expression through the group frame and process.

Comparing these two levels of thinking about group and individual processes, it seems that, at the first level, little or nothing is added to the individual and what is already in him; hence only *summation*, or the adding up of what different individuals contain and contribute, is indicated and possible. At the second level, however, something new is definitely added to the individual by and from his encounter with the group, which goes beyond what he personally contains and brings to it. It is only within, and by means of, this group/social framework that the individual can develop, express, and hence also perfect, his inherent potential. I therefore call this level *'consummation'*, suggesting that it implicitly harbours the notion of an ultimate or perfectible development, which is crucial in bringing potential trends to their fullest expression.

3. Supra-personal—'Organismic'

At this level we encounter for the first time such concepts as 'the group-as-a-whole' and 'the group mind'. The group is here conceived as a unit, existing at a new level of observation and conceptualisation, even if some of the concepts may still be borrowed from individual models (a prime example of this theorising is Bion [1961]). An added facet is that the group develops along stages that parallel individual stages of development. This level therefore represents a major shift in focus and understanding. The group is no longer viewed through its individual components, but as an 'organism'—an entity in its own right, possessing dynamics, structures and development independent of and reaching beyond the individuals who make it up.

4. Inter-group and inter-organisational—'Systemic'

At this level, the focus shifts to relationships between groups or the sub-groups of a system, as well as between different organisations and social systems. Here understanding is based largely on systems theory and approach. To the extent that the focus is on the individual, he is viewed as a representative of the group for which he stands. In turn, the manner in which he is treated represents relatedness to this entire group. In a sense, this level is the obverse of the level of summation. At the systemic level the individual does not count as such, but is perceived and understood through the group process, just as the group at the level of summation was regarded as a function of the individuals who make it up.

Discussion: Ego and Self at each level

The special place accorded to ego and self is maintained and safe-guarded throughout these four levels. The *intrapersonal* level is obvi-ously focused on and stresses individual makeup and behaviour: the individual person's unique traits, personality, conflicts, object rela-tions, and so on. In Freud's aforementioned essay (1921), the central explanation for the individual's propensity to regression and losing his identity in the crowd, is framed in terms of the ego-ideal, and the indi-vidual's allowing the leader to replace his own ego-ideal. In a much later development of this theme, Saravay (1975) accounts in a similar way for the same phenomenon. He employs, however, not the ego-ideal, a pre-structural concept, but the structural model itself. He con-siders individual readiness to enter into 'regression and the merging of his self with the crowd' to be based upon regression of the ego. This ego-regression causes a temporary loss of differentiation between ego and superego, and regression in the ego-function of object relations. This accounts for the decline in adequate reality testing, and the impul-siveness and moral weakness so typical of individuals in large groups.

It is the second, or *interpersonal* level, which is so familiar to us from both neo-Freudian and post-Freudian psychoanalysis. At this level, individual object relations provide the key for understanding what transpires within, around and between individuals in groups and social situations. Furthermore, the focus upon object relations is not merely, as in the previous level, an adaptive-realistic ego function whose task is to satisfy instinctual wishes. Winnicott, Fairbairn and Guntrip, as well as Erikson, Kohut and Sullivan, each in his own way, view the drive towards relatedness and relationships with others as man's primary motivation. Human living in organised social entities derives directly from this need and motive. The group reflects the vicissitudes of this primary need, enables it to come to expression, and safeguards and enhances its development throughout the life cycle.

If the level of *'summation'* can be said to belong to the ego, the level of *'consummation'* is dominated by the self. Object relations between the individual and those close to him, emotional ties of envy and jeal-ousy, love and hate, intimacy and alienation, closeness and distance, all call for a subjective perspective that emphasises the experiential moment over those of drive, conflict, reality, and their adaptive objective resolution. The emphasis thus shifts from ego to self; and it is the self, as we have already seen, that provides the experiential-subjective counterpoint to the ego's adaptive-objective vantage point.

Credits for the third, *supra-individual* level, are mostly reserved for Bion (1961). Bion sees the group as a new and emergent level. The group-as-a-whole is perceived at a deeply unconscious level as a maternal entity. As such, it evokes in the individual primordial struggles: wishes for fusion and merger as against separateness and loneliness; powerful experiences of satisfaction, nurturing and frustration; acute ambivalence—emotional (love/hate) and defensive (splitting and projective identification); and tensions between engulfment and estrangement. Taking part in the group is therefore bound to arouse primal and primitive ambivalence, anxiety and regression in its members.

The ambivalence, and acute anxiety associated with it, evoked within the group stems from the arousal of anxieties and defence mechanisms typical of the paranoid-schizoid position, namely splitting and projective identification. Group members serve as containers, ready to absorb and take in from each other the split-off parts of themselves. A common matrix develops, which is essentially covert and implicit, nonverbal, heavily symbolic and unconscious. This common matrix gives rise to the shared fantasy of the 'group-as-a-whole', the group Gestalt, or the group as an entity with its own mentality and existence. Finally, differentiation of functions and roles and induction into such roles take place, and the unique group culture evolves (Wells 1985).

At this *'organismic'* level it is clearly the group, and not the individual, which is regarded as an entity or a 'self', as is also reflected in the interpretative stance towards it. As group facilitator, leader, consultant or therapist, Bion's approach does not treat the individual as such. The selfhood he relates to is that of the group, not the individual. Individuals are, of course, related to, but as representing the commonly shared fantasy or dominant projective identification of the moment. It is within this group-as-unity, or 'Group Self', that Bion differentiated the Work Group from the Basic Assumption Group, in a way very reminiscent of the distinction I drew above between ego and self: 'Every group', Bion asserts, 'however casual, meets *to "do"* something... Since this activity is geared to a task, it is related to reality, its methods are rational, and, therefore, in however embryonic a form, scientific. *Its characteristics are similar to those attributed by Freud*

(1911) to the ego' (Bion 1961: 129, my emphasis). In a similar vein, Margaret Rioch writes, 'The work group constantly tests its conclusions in a scientific spirit. It seeks for knowledge, learns from experience, and constantly questions how it may best achieve its goal. It is clearly conscious of the passage of time and of the processes of learning and development. *It has a parallel in the individual with the ego in Freud's sense,* in the rational and mature person' (Rioch 1975: 23, my emphasis).

Interestingly, the parallel between the Basic Assumption Group and the id, which is equally indicated, seems never to have been made as clearly and forcefully as that between the Work Group and the ego. The equation of Basic Assumption with the id seems nonetheless to be strongly suggested by Bion when he states that participation in this (i.e. Basic Assumption) behaviour 'requires no training, experience, or mental development. It is instantaneous, inevitable, and instinctive' (Bion 1961: 128).

To review the ground covered so far: in post-1923 psychoanalytic theory, the ego is a systemic concept, emphasising functional and adaptive aspects, such as efficacy and utility, force and work, capacities, abilities and mental functions. The ego's *primary* (though not sole) discourse strives to be within the rational, objective and scientific world. The self, on the other hand, is primarily experiential, and related to *needs* that must be met and fulfilled to ensure its continued growth and development. The self is subjective and strives towards subjectivity. When related to the realm of the group, the implications of these concepts vary with the different levels of group process under discussion and observation. At the *intrapersonal* level the emphasis is on the ego and its functioning. The *interpersonal* level involves the self in relationship with others within the group, an encounter crucial for an experiencing human subject. Finally, at the *supra-individual* and *organismic* levels, the individuated ego/self are no longer viable entities. By means of projective identification they are constitutive of the group-as-a-whole, while through a conceptual shift they now inform us about the nature and state of this new entity. At this level of group discourse the ego/self is transformed into a *'group ego'*, as in the Work Group; or a *'group self'*, with which the individual merges, and which may, in turn, become a vehicle for the *'group id'*, as in the Basic Assumption Group.

An important dimension through all this is that of *merger vs. separateness*, around which the relationship between the individual and the group unfolds. The implication and meaning of the term *'individual'* is of 'a single human being, as opposed to Society, the Family, etc'. (Oxford English Dictionary); that is, the individual is defined by standing *apart* from the group. The word *'group'*, on the other hand, derives from roots having to do with knots and clusters: 'The etymological sense would appear to be "lump" or "mass"' (Oxford English Dictionary).

'Group' thus implies the binding of individuals into a larger mass or whole. Such binding immediately raises the question of *boundaries*. The maintenance and regulation of boundaries is one of the main functions of the ego. Boundaries set an individual apart from all others and guarantee his uniqueness and separateness. However, boundaries are also points of contact between disparate entities. This indeed is why object relations are such a central function of the ego.

Why is it that group processes give rise to regressive pulls and involve mental and psychological exertion? The process of one's *entry* into a group requires a measure of self-surrender, of giving up portions of the ego/self and projecting them (largely through projective identification) into the group-as-a-whole, or specific individuals in it. This psychological work is very demanding in terms of both the efforts exerted and the emotions invested. It requires overcoming and yielding some of the narcissistic aspects of the cohesion and fullness of the self, as well as some of the integrity of the ego, such as goal-directedness, control and boundaries. When the individual ego succeeds in finding and defining its place in society, via identity formation and investment in a specific social role, it is usually supported, reinforced and rewarded from within and without. This is indeed what happens in the Work Group: the task and character of this group are clearly defined. To the extent that the individual ego is also well defined and integrated, it finds its place readily in the group and joins by way of identifying with the task and its links with one's own identity. In groups which do not have a specific goal of producing something beyond themselves and where the primary task is not clearly defined (good examples of this are therapeutic groups, or small or large study groups), there is a powerful pull to focus on experience in the here-and-now. Under these conditions, it is the self that becomes the focus, while the ego recedes into the background. This renders structured functioning, mediated usually through one's work identity, difficult, irrelevant or impossible. Further corollaries of this experience include varying degrees of blurring of boundaries, loss of good reality testing, diminished orientation in time and space, confusion around the nature of the primary task, and the ascendance of Basic Assumptions.

Self and ego as Being and Doing

Without changing the characterisations of ego and self we arrived at, we may be able to account for their different and complementary nature from a perspective I have pursued in another context. Similarly to and following Winnicott's (1971) formulations, I have developed a conceptual framework in which the dimensions of 'being' and 'doing' form parallel and complementary tracks through which experience is processed and organised. I have termed these experiential modalities *Being* and *Doing* (Erlich and Blatt 1985; Erlich 1988, 1990, 1991, 1993, 1998). These modalities refer firstly and mostly to *the experience of subject and object*, which together comprise the range of object relations.

There are significant differences in the way the experience of subject and object is processed through these two modalities. In the *Doing* modality, subject and object are experienced as separate and distinct, and hence in a functional or instrumental relationship with each other: as acting, activated or being acted upon, as active or passive, etc. Time is experienced as chronological, dividable and realistic, as are all other components of good reality testing. Thinking is of the secondary process type and accordingly emphasises objective scientific aims and methods. The overall tendency and orientation is one of efficiency of function, of task and accomplishment, and of goal-directedness. Boundaries are clearly of vital importance in this modality: the distinctiveness of self and object finds expression in the clarity and strength of the boundaries that set them apart. The modality of *Doing* may bring to mind Foulkes' notion of 'ego training in action' (Foulkes 1964), but it categorically and essentially differs from it. Foulkes refers to action and interaction within the therapeutic scene, while the emphasis here is on the nature of the *experience of oneself and the object* by the experiencing subject.

In the modality of *Being*, on the other hand, subject and object are experienced as fused and merged, without clear boundaries, limitations of time and space or similar demands that stem from and are associated with the *Doing* modality. Boundaries exist only insofar as they encompass and contain both subject and object, suspended in fusion and unity, and allow and maintain the ongoing continuity of this experience. Thinking is typically of the primary process kind, and thus not geared towards reality testing, precision or objectivity. On the contrary, the central tendency in the modality of *Being* is towards subjectivity. The *Being* modality allows and enables the subject to fully experience him- or herself as ongoing and existing, in unity with the object.

Two further points must be added to this phenomenological account. Developmentally, it is my hypothesis that both the *Being* and *Doing* modalities exist from the onset of life. There is increasing evidence that the newborn infant is equipped and functions from the start with an acute, sharply differentiated capacity for reality assessment, based on his *separateness* from his mother; but also with a capacity for *fusion* and *merger* with her (Stern 1985). The mother, too, functions in both modalities, but her maternal ability, her 'primary maternal preoccupation', to quote Winnicott once more, is expressed in her capacity to adapt herself flexibly to the modality the infant is in or requires at the given moment.

The second addition is a functional consideration: both these experiential modalities exist and function contiguously and in parallel; with few exceptions, however, only one of them will gain ascendancy at any given moment in time.

How do these modalities add to our understanding of ego and self? From the experiential point of view, the ego represents the subject's experience of himself in the *Doing* modality. The experience of subjectivity momentarily recedes into the background, and the focus is on functional goals of doing, and the ways and means for their attainment. In other words, the experience centres on the practicality and efficiency aspects of functioning based on objective criteria. The primary focus is on the task and carrying it out efficiently and successfully, not on the 'I' engaged in it. Indeed, the experience of 'I' all but dissolves as it is taken up and absorbed (by identification) in the execution and attainment of the task or goal. The experience of the subject in the *Being* modality, on the other hand, centres on the fused existence of self and other and the quality of this togetherness, placing selfhood in the focus of experience. This experience of self becomes an existential centre that subject and other strive to attain and maintain. This experience is assisted and supported, among other things, by primary thought processes, which are not geared towards coping with external reality but towards the subjective experience of the self.

Since these two modalities function simultaneously and in parallel, it is no wonder that we meet with both ego and self in the group. In the group, as in the individual, different experiential states and stages arise and alternate; sometimes the *Doing* mode is dominant, while at other times *Being* gains the ascendancy. The Work Group, for example, is a clear and definitive exemplar of the *ego/Doing* modality at its best, and is in need of this modality in order to carry out its task and complete its work. For the Work Group, any deviation towards focusing on the self might well be considered regressive and hindering. What happens, though, when the primary task of the group is not 'to do' or produce something, but 'to be' and to observe what happens within this being? This may well be experienced as difficult and confusing, as the group struggles with this unconventional, unstructured and seemingly undefined task. Under such circumstances Bion's Basic Assumptions readily become manifest, if only to provide the group with fantasy or illusory foci for something to do.

It is worthwhile remembering that the state of *Being* is often experienced as dangerously regressive, and hence feared and rejected, by members and representatives of western industrialised society and culture. It is also significant that every one of the Basic Assumptions involves a relatedness between the 'group-self' and an object, whether out of the wish to merge or pair with it, or to fight and flee from it. Basic Assumptions Dependency and Pairing strive for fusion with the good object, while Fight-Flight represents an escape from merger with the bad object and the need to split it off, externalise and project it. In the Work Group, on the other hand, the relatedness is abstract, and takes place in relation to the task. It is the task and the goals it presents that are related to, with questions around issues of efficiency, cost, investment, reality assessment, and so forth.

Some clinical illustrations

Being as a central issue is exemplified by psychotherapy and encounter groups, and by Small and Large Study Groups in the Bion-inspired parts of (Tavistock) Group Relations Conferences. In the latter model (Miller 1989), opportunities are provided for studying, through one's own experience, what happens, as it happens, at the personal, interpersonal, group, inter-group and organisational levels. I would like to focus briefly on the Large Group process and examine it because of its unique features.

The Large Group exhibits many of the processes described, yet in a more complex and stormy fashion. This is caused by the Large Group frequently splitting itself into several smaller subgroups where group processes are proceeding simultaneously. The Large Group is frequently described as more of a mob or a crowd, where pulls towards regression are much stronger than in the small group. It may also be the case, however, that the stronger regressive pull in the Large Group stems from despair and resignation, not unlike those observed by Spitz in institutionalised infants; that is, members may despair of ever reaching a common goal or task and carrying it through. The goal of becoming a work group is even less attainable in the Large Group and it is much more difficult to control, lead and maintain on task. The threat in the Large Group is thus precisely to the ego, and indeed it is experienced as a powerful and dangerous threat to one's identity, which is in danger of being lost (Turquet 1975). One possible outcome of this is that participants may prefer 'to be with themselves', in order to maintain their differentiation, preserve the integrity of their ego boundaries, and not be swept along in what may become a dangerous and uncontrolled regression.

Two brief vignettes may help to illustrate this. In the first, a woman member of a Large Group, who hitherto had not opened her mouth, made the following statement: 'I am experiencing a lot of difficulty with eye-contact in this group'. One of the group consultants, interpreting this statement in terms of the group's primary task, said, 'I take this to mean that people are having a great deal of difficulty with "I-contact" in this group'. By this he meant that there was indeed some difficulty in relating with others in the group, but beyond that, an even greater wish for, as well as difficulty in, remaining in contact with the self, creating a conflict around investing in the group.

The second example is a vignette that took place in a closing plenary session, in which the task was to allow participants to look at their experiences during the course of the conference. A female member of the group sitting in the front row confronted the staff seated opposite her with the accusation that they did not sufficiently allow for reality. 'After all', she exclaimed heatedly and angrily, 'there is also reality'! Shortly after her vehement discharge and venting of feelings, this woman suddenly stood up, in the midst of something else, and announced she could no longer continue to be in the session. She was preoccupied with a female member who was absent. She felt acutely concerned and worried about her, because 'there was also reality', and she was therefore going to leave the room in order to find her. As she was about to step out, several members interceded and informed her that the woman she was so worried about was fine, and was in fact seated right behind her. The woman sat down stunned, was silent for the next fifteen minutes, with tears streaming quietly down her cheeks.

These vignettes demonstrate rather dramatically the difficulty in maintaining good contact with one's self and ego in a group, and especially in a Large Group, in which direct face-to-face communication is difficult or impossible. The last woman spoke in the name of the ego, the objectively and realistically attuned part of herself. She made an effort to maintain her hold on her ego and her identity, which was one of a professional helper and saviour. This also came through in her aggressive attack on the staff for, in her view, not doing enough of this, as well as in her attempt to lead the group towards a better-defined and structured task. In other words, she uncompromisingly wished to maintain her hold on the modality of *Doing* and the dominance of the ego, as a defence and protest against the modality of *Being*. It seems that she had some difficulty in being in the *Being* mode and in touch with her self. At the same time, and quite paradoxically, her efforts to maintain the *Doing* modality and focus on 'reality' were unsuccessful not only because they were defensive, but because they were, in the final analysis, inappropriate to the task of the group. Her 'reality testing' eventually confronted her with the limits and shortcomings of such reality testing, that it is not responsive and hence not adaptive to the situation. She was unable to perceive what was literally behind her. The tears and unhappiness she then experienced may reflect the emotional price that accompanied this difficult piece of personal learning.

Conclusion

In conclusion, we may say that the psychodynamic and intrinsically 'individual' concepts of ego and self are interwoven with group phenomena at a number of levels. There are levels at which 'egos' and 'selves' are what make up the group, and yet are in need of the group for attaining their fullest potential. There are other levels, in which the group receives the character and imprimatur of an ego/self, albeit at a new level of conceptualisation, as an entity in its own right.

Understanding ego and self as representing different experiences of the subject's relatedness to his object, through the experiential modalities of *Being* and *Doing*, enables a better understanding of the ego and the self in the group. In turn, these explanatory concepts help us account more fully for the different atmosphere that prevails in the Work Group as compared to the Basic Assumption Group. Although there are certainly numerous factors at work, the experiences in question are mainly connected to the dimension of *merger vs. separateness* of subject and object. In groups where the primary task is well defined and connected to a definite product or outcome, the *Doing* modality usually prevails, and along with it the ego and its functions are dominant. In groups where the primary task is not productive but existential, centreing on experience in the 'here and now', the *Being* modality prevails. With the *Being* mode in ascendance, the focus shifts to the self and its experience. We are then more in tune with introspection, with wishes (e.g. for fusion and for continuous existence) and their frustration, and with related emotional issues (e.g. self-worth and self-acceptance).

It is appropriate to regard these two experiential modalities as defining an experiential range or continuum. The questions remain: which of the two modalities dominates the group at a particular moment, and whether and to what extent is this relevant and appropriate to the task at hand? For the practicing clinician, these are far from esoteric or irrelevant considerations. Since the concepts of ego and self represent well defined and different universes of discourse, to employ these terms will often guide the clinician into adopting one particular frame of reference, to the detriment and exclusion of another. My emphasis on the experiential dimensions is actually intended to prevent him falling into such traps. The clinician can relay on his own subjective experience as a guide, in conjunction with such considerations of the setting that are relevant, such as the nature of the task at hand and the goal that is pursued. This is especially pertinent where groups, rather than individuals, are concerned. Attending to the task and its definition, and at the same time to the prevailing experiential mode, yields a much more reliable understanding of the group and/or the individual, and can inform us as to whether it is the ego or the self that is in focus.

THE SEARCH FOR 'SELF' AND 'OTHER' IN THERAPEUTIC COMMUNITIES

Tom Ryan

As is true with most psychoanalytic theoretical and clinical concepts, a multitude of differences and disagreements regarding the meaning of the concept of the self exist not only between the various schools of psychoanalysis but also within the so-called homogenous orientations. Although the concept of the self remains a central theoretical and clinical idea within psychoanalysis it continues to elude any clear understanding. For example, definitions of the self range from thinking of it as an idea or set of ideas; as a structure; something that is experienced,;something that takes actions, or the sum total of one's unique life history (Shane and Shane 1980). This lack of clarity and consensus surrounding the understanding of the idea of self is further compounded by the tendency of many psychoanalytic writers towards reification of ideas and in Gregory Bateson's terms mistake the map for the territory (Bateson 1972). The self as a concept or organising principle easily slips into the idea of the self being considered as something substantive, an entity existing in the space of the mind, rather than as a 'technical way of thinking about people or a way people think about themselves' (Schafer 1976: 189).

In this chapter I am going to explore some of the contributions to the debate about what the self is. I will particularly focus on those authors who have criticised the prevalent tendency within psychoanalytic theorising towards a reification of the self. I will argue that instead of talking of a 'self' we should be thinking in terms of 'selving' as a continuous, dynamic, inter-subjective process out of which a sense of self emerges (Fast 1998). I am particularly interested in the ways individuals develop, change, maintain or preserve their 'sense of self' through their relationship with others. Laing's idea of 'induction'—those 'techniques' or 'interpersonal actions' through which people manoeuvre others into feeling, thinking and behaving as they require—is a significant part of all relating and is crucial in understanding the ways in which a sense of self forms and develops through interactional processes (Laing 1969). I will also explore how these dynamics become enacted in the specific setting of a therapeutic community. The family-like structure of a therapeutic community offers a unique opportunity to observe (and participate in) the means by which residents attempt to induce others, through various relational strategies, to collude with their definitions, conscious or unconscious, of their selves.

Singular self or multiple selves

The failure to distinguish between a subjective self (a sense of self) and the self as a theoretical concept inevitably leads to gross epistemological problems. As Schafer puts it, 'self and identity are not names of identifiable homogeneous or monolithic entities; they are classes of self-representations that exist only in the vocabulary of the observer. The self-representations in this class are maintained unconsciously... and many remain forever uncoordinated, if not contradictory' (Schafer 1976: 189).

These epistemological problems could be more easily avoided by following William James' proposal, made as early as 1892, that a distinction be made between the self as subject (the self as I) and self as object (the self as me) (James 1892). The self as object refers to the self as observed in self-observation. The self as 'I' is a subjective, dynamic self. It is the observer in the observed and includes the ways we think, feel, perceive, remember, and imagine. James, and more recently Kegan and Fast, strongly argue that by focussing on the subjective or 'I-self', we can avoid the temptation, in part created by our language, to consider the self as a thing that acts (Kegan 1982, Fast 1998). They propose that it is our very actions which include our thinking, feeling and willing, that constitute the subjective self. As Fast urges, 'We must learn to think of ourselves not having a self, but of doing self things or, for lack of a more suitable word, perhaps of "selving"' (Fast 1998: 7).

Any discussion of the subjective self must account for the paradoxical experience of change and continuity, multiplicity and singularity that are an inextricable part of a sense of self. The subjective self is experienced as having a sense of continuity, a recognisable pattern of thoughts, behaviour and ways of relating that constitutes a unique self. As I will discuss later, this subjective experience of self as singular and continuous is illusory but necessary as it provides an important adaptive function. According to Stephen Mitchell, psychoanalysis conceptualises the self in two broadly different and contradictory ways: the self as singular and layered, which is grounded in a spatial metaphor, and the self as multiple and discontinuous, which is grounded in a temporal metaphor (Mitchell 1993). The model of the self as singular and layered stems from our strong sense of a continuous I over time. Despite an experience of variability of a sense of self within different relational context or changeable subjective states, such as mood swings or emotional variability, we continue to have a sense of a constant, enduring identity. We all have our own inimical ways of organising and presenting ourselves, what Donald Spence calls 'our personal signature', which are always identifiable as belonging to us (Spence 1982).

The major proponent of the self as integral and continuous within psychoanalysis has been Kohut (Kohut 1997). Within Self Psychology primary importance has been assigned to the idea that individuals organise and maintain an integrated sense of self. It is impossible to connect to other human beings, Kohut believes, without first being centred in our own subjectivity. The task of the therapist in the Self Psychology tradition is to 'locate' this self-expressive pattern and through the 'empathic attitude' mirror and confirm the patient's true subjectivity.

Thinking of the self as singular and continuous primarily stems from Freud's conceptualising of the mind as a psychic structure. Although many analytic thinkers have pointed out that the psychic structure is not something substantive, but refers to recurring patterns of experience over time, many still theorise the self in these terms. However, it is important to note that the idea of a fixed and singular self is ethnocentric and is in stark contrast to non-western cultures, where the subjective experience of individuals is of 'no-I-ness'. Clifford Geertz firmly states:

The western conception of the person as a bounded, unique, more or less integrated motivational and cognitive universe, a dynamic center of awareness, emotion, judgement, and action organized into a distinctive whole and set contractively both against other such wholes and against a social and natural background is, however incorrigible it may seem to us, a rather peculiar idea within the context of the world's cultures (Geertz 1973: 59).

The idea of the self as multiple and discontinuous within psychoanalysis is central to object relations theory. Stephen Mitchell suggests that the self began to be conceived of as multiple when various analytic thinkers began to, 'conceive of the id as involving a way of being, a sense of self, a person in relation to other persons, bringing it much closer in nature to Freud's portrayal of the ego and superego. (Melanie Klein, Fairbairn, Edith Jacobson, Loewald, Lacan, Otto Kernberg—all in their own ways and in their own language portray the id as a person or collection of persons in passionate relationship to other persons or parts of persons)' (Mitchell 1993: 104). Within these formulations the sense of self becomes inextricably linked to a relational context. It is only through our interactions and relationships with significant others that we learn to become a person. Within the object relational model the idea of self is, 'a manifold organisation of self, patterned around different self and object images and representations, derived from differing relational contexts. We are all composites of overlapping multiple organisations and perspectives, and our experience is smoothed over by an illusory sense of continuity' (Mitchell 1993: 104).

Coming from an another orientation, Harry Stack Sullivan also emphasised the illusory nature of a continuous, singular self. He believed this to be in strong contrast to how we actually behave with other people. We never act, according to Sullivan, singularly but always in relation to another. Individuals can behave very differently with different people at different times or even differently within a continuous relationship at other times. What appears to be a constant and unique individuality is the 'mother of all illusions' disguising the reality that we are different people at different times. This multiple, discontinuous, relational view of self is usually outside of our awareness (Sullivan 1950).

Despite the illusory nature of a singular and constant self, it also appears to be a necessary illusion. Without a sense of a constant and continuous self we would have no way to organise and prioritise our ways of being in the world. We would become completely immobilised by an ever-changing experience of ourselves. Like those who suffer from multiple personalities, we would be unintegrated and fragmented. 'What may have begun as an illusion', Mitchell states, 'often becomes an actual guide to living by virtue of our necessary belief in it' (Mitchell 1993: 111). In a similar vein, Nancy Chodorow suggests that it is the understanding of our particular feelings that gives 'coherence, continuity, and meaning to the self...' but this 'coherence', she insists, is not fixed or unchanging, but 'is consistent with and even requires, multiple, shifting senses of self and identity' (Chodorow 1999: 40). A too rigid or fixed sense of self leads to stagnation and a barren sense of self. In contrast a lack of any sense of continuity or coherence of a sense of self will lead to fragmentation. For an individual to experience some sense of centrality or coherence of self, a finely balanced, dynamic interplay must exist between these two modes of experiences.

Daniel Stern also offers a relational view of self. He admits that there is no clear understanding of the self but it nonetheless acknowledges that it is a firm subjective reality. Our sense of self, according to Stern, 'provides a basic organising perspective for all interpersonal events'. He vaguely defines this self as: 'the agent of action, the experiencer of feelings, the maker of intentions, the architect of plans, the transposer of experience into language, the communicator and sharer of personal knowledge' (Stern 1985: 5).

Although not in the exact form as just stated, he further asserts that some sense of an emerging self, what he terms the core self, exists very early on in infancy well before self-awareness and language. The infant's sense of self may in some fundamental way include some

> sense of agency... the sense of physical cohesion... the sense of
> continuity... the sense of affectivity... the sense of a subjective self
> that can achieve intersubjectivity with another... the sense of
> transmitting meaning... In short, these senses of self make up the
> foundation for the subjective experience of social development,
> normal and abnormal. (Stern 1985: 7-8)

Later, with the onset of language and self reflection, this fundamental core self further develops and transforms into new experiences.

Although most people would agree with Stern's idea that the sense of self is observable after the presence of language and self-reflective awareness, many disagree with his claim that an infant experiences a sense of self, even at the primitive level suggested by Stern. For example, the philosopher, Marcia Cavell accuses Stern of adultomorphising the infant, attributing adult experiences and capabilities to the neonate (Cavell 1993: 108-109). She strongly reasons that, unlike an adult, an infant is neither capable of self-awareness nor possesses the necessary capacity for conceptualising or for transmitting meaning, which are the very foundation to having any sense of self. She concurs with Litchenberg's view that, 'If we define "empathy" as entering into the state of mind of another person, then an adult has a very difficult, almost impossible, task to empathise with the infant. As an adult, in the very attempt to enter the infant's state of mind, we use, at least in part, an adult symbolic mode of cognition; that is, to the extent that we put thoughts in the head of the baby in order to understand him or her, we miss the nonsymbolic nature of the infant's state of mind' (Litchenberg 1983: 173). In other words it is only through the acquisition of language, a necessary condition, that these capacities for self-reflection and self-reference are present and a sense of self becomes a possibility.

A more contemporary, dynamic view of self is offered by Irene Fast, who asserts that it is not the self that is engaged in action but that the actions themselves constitute the self. For Fast, interactions take precedence over representations and sense perceptions. She argues that, 'Our inner worlds are our ways of selving, of making meaning of events perceptually, emotionally, cognitively, or motorically' (Fast 1998: 112). Following the work of Kegan, she emphasises that we should conceive of the self as an activity not as an entity (Kegan 1982).

Fast proposes two criteria that are necessary for identifying activities as self: presence of 'personal agency' and the 'individual's sense of "I"'. However, the presence of personal agency (purposive behaviour), may not necessarily be accompanied by a subjective sense of self. This 'sense of I-ness' depends inextricably on the degree of integration of what Fast calls 'I-schemes' into 'complex and layered networks whose self and nonself aspects are differentiated'. Like Stern's conception of protonarrative envelopes, Fast defines I-schemes as patterns or templates that develop from the infant's interactions with their world and become the foundation for future interactions.

Our sense of I-ness or agency is directly affected by the degree to which I-scheme constellations are integrated. The greater the integration the stronger the sense of centrality of self. A failure of integration may lead to a fragile or fixed sense of self. The goal of psychoanalytic therapy for Fast is the, 'transformation of that which has been experienced as an impersonal occurrence into experience that has a quality of I-ness'.

Harold Searles has written extensively about the ways in which this 'fine balance' of a sense of self can be undermined and sometimes totally damaged. In his intriguing paper 'The Effort to Drive the Other Person Crazy—An Element in the Aetiology and Psychotherapy of Schizophrenia', Searles explores the types of interactional and interpersonal processes that can lead to a fixed or unintegrated sense of self. Through his therapeutic work with psychotic individuals and their parents he concluded that someone could literally be driven crazy if they were repeatedly exposed to interpersonal interactions, *'which tends to foster emotional conflict in the other person—which tends to activate various areas of his personality in opposition to one another'* (Searles 1959: 256, my italics).

Searles describes a variety of 'techniques' involved in this process of driving someone mad. For example: 1. The simultaneous or rapidly alternating, stimulation-and-frustration of sexual and other needs; 2. The request or demand of sympathy or help from a significant other, which, when offered is then rejected; 3. Relating to a person on two different and unrelated levels. For instance, speaking about an intellectual topic whilst being sexually seductive. This obviously leaves the person confused. 4. Switching from one emotional mode to another and being completely emotionally unpredictable. Searles argues that 'these techniques tend to undermine the other person's confidence in the reliability of his own emotional reactions and of his own perception of outer reality'. (Searles 1959: 260) This type of repeated interpersonal communication inevitably affects an individual's sense of separateness and continuity of self. Although Searles is primarily concerned with severely emotionally distressed individuals, his formulations also facilitate our understanding of the interactional processes involved in the formation and presentation of a 'sense of self' in emotionally less damaged individuals.

Similarly, Laing also speaks of how individuals' experience or identities can be shaped and, at times, dramatically affected by the interactional processes that occur within families. Our sense of who we are and how we relate to others is the result of a complex set of actual and fantasised ways of relating within the family. Borrowing concepts from mathematical set theory, Laing suggests that it is not objects or part objects that we internalise but different modes of relating which may in turn be mapped onto future relationships or situations. This internalised set of family relations forms a fantasised 'family' that becomes 'a medium to link its members whose links with one another may otherwise be very attenuated' (Laing 1969: 13). Laing goes so far as to say that, 'the preservation of the "family" is equated with the preservation of self and world and the dissolution of the "family" inside *another* is equated with death of self and world-collapse' (Laing 1969: 14).

Like Searles, Laing also describes various 'techniques', what he calls 'transpersonal defences', which are employed by an individual *'to regulate the inner life of the other in order to preserve his own'* (Laing: 1969: 13, my italics). Laing is more precise than Searles in his observation that it is specific interpersonal actions which tend to confuse or mystify, not just the inducing of emotional conflict, that causes an undermining of self or, in extreme situations, madness. Laing describes five types of interpersonal actions: 1. Complementary identity, where another is required to fulfil or complete a sense of self; 2. Confirmation and disconfirmation; 3. Collusion; 4. False and untenable positions; 5. Attributions and injunctions.

All of the complexity of the different levels of the interactional processes and the resulting internal confusion were originally described in Gregory Bateson's double bind theory. The double bind involves one or more individuals, where one of them is designated the victim. The victim is given a message to do something; however, on another level, a contradictory message is also communicated. A further injunction places the victim in an untenable situation by forbidding him to leave the situation by commenting on it. Bateson illustrates the workings of the double bind with the following example: a mother is visiting her son in hospital and, upon greeting him, opens her arms either to embrace him or for him to embrace her. As he comes closer, she freezes and stiffens. He stops in his tracks. She remarks, 'Don't you want to kiss your mummy'? but he remains still and silent. She then says, 'But, dear, you mustn't be afraid of your feelings' (Bateson 1956: 251).

Searles, Laing and Bateson emphasise that the 'victims' of these various interpersonal actions learn to perceive their worlds in those very same or very similar faulty perceptual and relational patterns. Inevitably, they in turn will relate and conduct themselves with others in a similar manner or attempt to induce others to collude with their sense of self as victim. Laing and Searles concur that a primary motivation behind 'driving someone crazy' is to preserve one's own very fragile sense of self or sanity. In order to control unacceptable thoughts, feelings or behaviour in oneself, one must control others to ensure that one's equilibrium will not be disturbed. For this to be effectively achieved one must act directly on the other person's experience, what Laing calls induction. Through induction, which, according to Laing, is a significant part of all relating, the other is manoeuvred into feeling, thinking and behaving as the other requires. Those on the receiving end of such 'techniques' or 'interpersonal actions' will also develop their own coping strategies. Inevitably, these may include repeating what has been done to them or inducing others to help to sustain a very delicate sense of self.

Clinical illustrations

For the major part of my professional career I have been involved with the Arbours Association which runs three long-stay residential therapeutic communities. The communities were established to provide an alternative to psychiatric care for individuals with severe emotional distress. They provide a non-institutional, psychodynamic setting where all of the residents are expected to be responsible for the daily running and maintenance of the community.

The therapeutic community is an ideal setting for observing the myriad ways that individuals act upon themselves and others in order to maintain or change their usually fragile sense of selves. As these residential communities with their lack of a hierarchical institutional structure resemble family groups, they more readily facilitate complex emotional experiences which are reminiscent of family relationships. Transference experiences in the community, unlike the two person focussed transference dynamics of the therapy consulting room, is multi-targeted, ubiquitous and interminable.

Sometimes life in the community may appear to be an emotional muddle with everyone entwined in one way or another. Group members continually perceive others in accordance with their own past experiences, fantasies, internal dramas and sense of self. Through their daily interactions with each other, all the residents to varying degrees seek out others to affirm their definitions of self. To ensure a preservation of their self view, some residents may employ various 'interpersonal actions', as discussed above, to induce others to collude with their fragile identities. Through awareness and understanding, residents may begin to disentangle themselves from what can be very constraining and distorted ways of perceiving and conducting relationships and to integrate those unacknowledged or denied aspects of themselves. In part, therapeutic effectiveness can be measured by the degree to which the participants become aware of their mapping or entanglements and how successful they are in disentangling themselves from the recurring emotional minefield.

Some residents enter the community with no clear coherent sense of self. They complain of being fragmented, confused and devoid of a firm sense of an identity. They seem to lack any sense of continuity of a self and invariably look to others to validate or provide them with an acceptable identity. Other residents portray a fixed, rigid sense of self which they fiercely attempt to preserve for fear of becoming fragmented or disintegrated. These individuals desperately try to persuade others to confirm and collude with their view of themselves, even when such a view is obviously greatly detrimental.

The following clinical examples will illustrate these different expressions of self and the various relational strategies used to induce others to collude with their definitions of their selves.

Tanya, a young woman with a history of acute psychotic episodes, experiences a lack of any cohesive sense of self. She repeatedly complains that she has no centre nor a firm sense of who she is. Frequently, she is confused, indecisive and mistrusts her own perceptions. Her relationships with others in the community are constantly strained as she desperately uses them like a mirror to reflect or affirm some fragile aspect of her self. Her relentless neediness and demands for help can be frustrating to the other residents, who feel driven to find ways to avoid her. Because of her emotional fragility and doubts about her perceptions, Tanya finds it difficult to have a sense of separateness between herself and others and inevitably becomes confused about who is doing what to whom.

She describes herself as locked into a mutually collusive relationship with her mother, who she primarily experiences as intrusive and dominating. Yet, there were times when Tanya believed that only her mother could offer the understanding and help that she needed to survive. Whenever Tanya would feel distress, she and her mother would spend hours together trying to unravel the reasons for her difficulties. This confidant scenario was continually re-enacted in the community when Tanya would implore the other residents and helpers to spend exclusive time with her to discuss her seemingly endless crisis.

At times, when Tanya was feeling anxious, her mother would accompany her to her university courses. Unfortunately, Tanya's frequent emotional crises became a primary means by which mother and daughter provided a reaffirmation of their need and love for each other. Through this relationship, Tanya became increasingly less able to think or act for herself. Yet, in ways similar to the double bind injunctions as described by Bateson, Tanya has been unable to leave the relationship. If she were to separate, she believed either her mother or she would be destroyed, but to remain means the continuation of a lack of separateness. Unable to discern what belongs to her, Tanya is unable to take any pleasure from her ambitions and achievements, such as her academic success, which in any case she believes belongs to her mother. Since being in the community Tanya has cut off all communication with her mother in an attempt to regain some sense of her separateness and individuality. Recently, Tanya has agreed to meet with her mother through some family meetings, but fears that she may again succumb to what she experiences as her very 'powerful' mother.

While in the community, Tanya has mapped various aspects of her symbiotic relationship with her mother onto her relationships in the community. For example, Tanya's recurring emotional crisis, where she becomes overwhelmed with suicidal thoughts and feelings of despair, repeats the dynamics of the mother-daughter relationship. She continually attempts to create the special, undivided attention she received from her mother with the residents and helpers in the community. The other members of the community, however, experience her endless need for care and attention as intrusive. They are usually left feeling frustrated or angry when their interventions appear not to make a difference. Unfortunately, Tanya in turn feels rejected but she remains unaware of how her intrusiveness and constant neediness create the very rejection she fears.

Slowly, Tanya is beginning to experience more of a separate sense of self, which she sometimes refers to as finding her own voice. More recently, she feels less confused, asserts herself more frequently and only exhibits slight anxiety when making decisions. Tanya's propensity for what I had referred to earlier as an illusory sense of a singular, constant self, is required and necessary in order for her to experience an I-ness that she can call her own. Otherwise, she will continue to experience herself as chaotic, confused and fragmented.

Unlike Tanya, some residents display a fixed, rigid sense of self, which they desperately attempt to maintain at all costs for fear of disintegration. For example, Joan entered the community with a sense of herself as being deprived, neglected, abused and physically unwell. Although at times she presents herself as competent, assertive and creative, she insists on promoting a less adequate view of self. She is adept at using her various somatic complaints and fears to convince others and herself of her definition of her self as needy, deprived and abused.

Joan rigorously maintains this sense of self by repeatedly retelling embellished stories of her childhood which are full of material and emotional deprivation. Whenever anyone new enters the community, Joan is certain to take them aside and recount her story as a prelude to how she expects them to perceive and relate to her. Joan desperately requires the complicity of others to preserve this fragile view of herself as a needy victim. She formed a collusive, complementary relationship with another woman resident, where each one reciprocally underpins the sense of self of the other. Together, they form a powerful force within the community to combat any attempts by others to disturb their specific identities.

Whenever Joan's equilibrium of self is challenged, she begins to experience intolerable anxiety which she desperately attempts to control at all cost. Usually, at these moments Joan becomes unwell with one or more of her numerous physical ailments. Her physical incapacity inevitably induces others to experience her as someone who is unable to cope. Reassured by the collusive validation of her identity, Joan's anxiety subsides and she can continue to maintain her usual, restricted sense of self.

To preserve her rigid sense of self, Joan must continually deceive herself and constantly induce others to mirror her view of self as needy and dependent. Although she expresses some interest in expanding her narrow view of self to include more competent aspects of herself, Joan is too fearful to step outside of her present constricted identity. Her restricted, rigid sense of self as victim enables her to avoid feeling fragmented and disintegrated.

With regard to their experience of their sense of self, Tanya and Joan are at opposite ends of a continuum. Joan desperately clings to a rigid, narrow view of a self that excludes a host of other possible ways of perceiving herself. Tanya, on the other hand, is continually in flux and lacks any sense of constancy or singularity. Both, however, require the complicity or collusion of others to maintain or preserve their usual perceptions of their selves. Thus, what becomes enacted in a therapeutic community is only a magnified view of what occurs generally. Inducing others to collude is not exclusive only to those with serious emotional distress. Whatever our emotional status, we all employ 'interpersonal techniques' to induce others to collude with and help us to maintain our illusory but necessary sense of a singular and constant sense of self. Unlike Tanya and Joan, most individuals, more or less, successfully juggle that 'fine balance' between the experience of an 'illusory' constant, continuous self and the experience of a less conscious, discontinuous, changeable self.

Conclusions

The interpersonal processes and enactments within the therapeutic community underline the complex nature of the concept of self and enhances our understanding of how an individual sense of self is conceived and preserved. From the therapeutic work in the community, it becomes clear that the self is not an entity as is frequently thought, but a complex, dynamic process of self-representations and meaning—making through what Fast describes as 'doing self things' or 'selving'. Furthermore, as evidenced by the above clinical examples, the relational nature of the sense of self becomes obvious. Our sense of self is borne out of early primary relationships and continues to be maintained, to a greater or lesser extent, by various 'relational techniques' through our on-going relationships. Finally, the illusion that the self is constant and singular is a necessary condition that enables us to act in the world with some sense of continuity and separateness. Without this sense of constancy or singularity we would become, like Tanya, fragmented and confused with no clear sense of an 'I-ness'. Yet, without a 'fine balance' between the illusory constancy and a multiple changing self, we can become stuck, as did Joan, in a rigid, deadening, restricted sense of self.

SHIFTING THE EGO TOWARDS A BODY SUBJECT

Mary Lynne Ellis

In this chapter I shall consider Freud's notion of the ego in the light of other theories of subjectivity within the field of continental philosophy, namely those of Foucault and Merleau-Ponty. The work of most British-trained psychoanalytic psychotherapists, with the exception of those trained in the Lacanian or Jungian schools, continues to be underpinned by a notion of subjectivity in which the concept of the ego is central. In this view of subjectivity, it is assumed that human beings live in a perpetual state of conflict between the id's passionate drives and the regulating function of the ego. My aim here is to consider the limitations of this view of subjectivity in theory and practice. Although there have been a number of challenges to Freud's theorising of the ego by, for example, the Object Relations schools, these have tended to revolve around questions as to when, developmentally, the ego is formed and as to whether or not 'ego strength' should be the goal of psychoanalysis. Such theorising does not extend to a more fundamental questioning of the values informing this conceptualisation of subjectivity and nor how far the notion of the 'ego' is crucial to the practice of psychoanalytic psychotherapy.

Questions regarding how we conceptualise the ego are not abstract; they matter to clinical practice because our particular notions of maturity and of 'healthy' relationships underpin our responses to our patients both consciously and unconsciously. Our formulations arise from a particular cultural and historical context and arise from within a specific tradition of Western philosophical thought. If we adhere uncritically to this tradition how can we be sufficiently sensitive to the uniqueness and diversity of our patients' experiences, particularly those of people who are not from white western backgrounds? In presenting a critical consideration of Freud's notion of the ego, my aim is to highlight the importance of a conceptualisation of subjectivity that acknowledges the social and cultural specificity of people's experiences.

Too often, such an approach to subjectivity is dismissed by psychotherapists as a 'collapse into sociology'. It is argued that the complexity of the individual is being lost, and that the 'truth' of the individual resides in the depth of an 'internal' world which is separate and distinct from the socio-cultural context. However, for those of us who work with people from a diversity of class and cultural backgrounds and with people from a range of sexual orientations, it is increasingly apparent that to disregard the social context is to be profoundly neglectful of an individual's specific experience of their own subjectivity as it appears in wishes, dreams, and fantasies. Furthermore, it is not sufficient to merely 'add on' a recognition of political and social context; how a person speaks to us in psychotherapy of their suffering and their joy, their anger and their passion is shaped and produced by the cultural context. If we do not acknowledge this we fail to recognise the complexity and richness of their struggles and conflicts.

Freud's notion of the ego[1] deserves close attention since his conceptualisations, as the pioneer of psychoanalysis, continue to influence how the ego is understood by most psychoanlytic psychotherapists today. Although Freud had the courage constantly to question and revise his theories, his tone is that of an acultural 'objectivity'. For example,he claims that his description of the ego arises from 'various facts of analytic observation' (Freud 1923: 12). However, as I shall argue, the ego is, on the contrary, a culturally specific concept which is underpinned by various intellectual traditions and socio-cultural values that Freud does not acknowledge. An examination of the concept of the ego thus offers the possibility for psychotherapists and social scientlists to consider how our theorising and practice are themselves shaped by particular values and, furthermore, to consider the limitations of a psychoanalytic theorising and practice that does not address the social context of the individual.

I will attempt to demonstrate how Freud's claims of 'objectivity' arise from the influence of Enlightenment philosophers and their view that 'science' can offer us certain knowledge about the world. I shall argue that his association of the ego with 'reason' and 'science' does not sufficiently allow for the impact of the social context on the constitution of subjectivity (Freud 1923: 25). In contrast, Foucault's account of power as producing bodies and sexualities can enable psychotherapists to be more sensitive to the multiple meanings of for example, sexuality and aggression (Foucault 1984: 105). Freud's account is also restricted by the dualistic thinking characteristic of the Cartesian tradition (Descartes 1968: 156-157). This is highlighted particularly in his account of the gendered ego where the binary oppositions of 'masculinity' and 'femininity' do not allow for the socio-cultural specificity of these terms (Freud 1923: 31-33). Moreover, his claim that the

Oedipus complex, which is central in his theorising of the ego, is universal does not allow for the diversity of sexualities and their socio-historical specificity. As Franz Fanon (Fanon 1986: 152) and Bronislaw Malinowski (in Jones 1928: 365) argue, the Oedipus complex assumes Western European patterns of familial organisation. I shall argue that Freud's notion of the ego does not sufficiently allow for cultural diversity.

In contrast to Freud's account of the ego, Merleau-Ponty theorises subjectivity as culturally and historically specific (Merleau-Ponty 1986: 189). His subject is a 'body subject', 'intentional' and embodied, oriented towards the world and he challenges the dichotomies of 'internal' and 'external' which are operative in Freud's account. I shall argue that Merleau-Ponty's view of subjectivity can contribute to the development of a psychotherapeutic approach which is truly sensitive and alive to difference and diversity.

The mechanics of the reasonable ego

Freud's failure to acknowledge that his observations are informed by a number of assumptions arising from his specific cultural and historical position is evident throughout *The Ego and the Id* (Freud 1923: 12-66). For example, he writes that 'these thoughts are linked to various facts of analytic observation' (Freud 1923: 12). He describes the ego as an observable 'entity' (Freud 1923: 23). In claiming that he is writing from a position of neutrality, that of objectivity, he does not acknowledge that 'objectivity' is *itself* culturally determined. Freud's assumption that there are objective, universal standards through which truth can be determined is in line with Enlightenment thinking. The Enlightenment was an intellectual movement that began in England in the seventeenth century and developed in France and Germany in the eighteenth century. It is informed by a view of man as rational by nature. Enlightenment philosophers view reason as crucial to the acquisition of knowledge and privilege 'science' as the ideal form of knowledge. The use of reason enables 'man' to think and act correctly, and reason is claimed by Enlightenment thinkers to be ahistorical and acultural. This view of human subjectivity continued to influence western philosophical and popular thought in Freud's time.

Freud's theorising of the ego reflects the Enlightenment's view of subjectivity. He claims that the passions of the id, which are ruled by the desire for pleasure (the 'pleasure principle') are brought under control by the ego. Although Freud refers to the ego as part of the id, he simultaneously emphasises their distinctness, claiming 'the ego represents what may be called reason and common sense, in contrast to the id, which contains the passions' (Freud 1923: 25). He describes the relation between the ego and the id as analogous to that between a rider and his horse. The rider has to control the superior power of the horse, although, in order not to be parted from his horse, he also at times has to guide the horse in the direction it wants to go. Similarly, the ego has to respond to the demands of the id as though they were its own.

In line with the Enlightenment's privileging of science, Freud also draws on analogies from anatomy and science. Fromm argues that Freud's theorising was particularly influenced by the discourse of mechanistic materialism. (Fromm 1978: 48)[2] This was based on the principle that all psychic processes can be explained and understood through knowledge of physiological processes. The effects of this view are evident in the anatomical analogies that run through Freud's account in *The Ego and the Id*. For example, Freud describes the ego as wearing a 'cap of hearing' (Freud 1923: 25), the perceptual system forming its surface 'more or less as the germinal disc rests upon the ovum' (Freud 1923: 24). It is a part of a 'mental apparatus' in which unpleasurable sensations and feelings 'exert a driving force' and seek 'discharge', enabling a lessening of tension (Freud 1923: 22). The ego 'secures a postponement of motor discharges and controls the access to motility' (Freud 1923: 55). Even where Freud introduces these descriptions as analogies the effect he conveys is that the ego and its workings are as tangible as a part of the body, a piece of the brain, rather than concepts.

Freud does not acknowledge the impact of western philosophical thought on his theorising.[3] Instead, he gathers support for this view of the human subject as torn between reason and passion from the popular view of his time: 'All this falls in line with popular distinctions which we are all familiar with' (Freud 1923: 25). He thus takes the popular distinction between reason and passion as evidence of its truth rather than as a truth designated as such by the dominant discourse of the time.

The notion of a rational subject as an ahistorical, acultural subject in Enlightenment thought has been criticised by a number of European philosophers, including Heidegger, Merleau-Ponty and Foucault. They question the notion of universal, rational, and objective standards by which goodness or truth can be determined. In their view what constitutes 'reason' is itself always historically and culturally specific and would also challenge the notion of 'passions' as alingustic and acultural. They argue for a notion of subjectivity as always shifting and contextual, historically and culturally, never fixed.

As psychotherapists working with people from a diversity of social, race and class backgrounds, a view of subjectivity as contextual can enable us to be open to more complex understandings of the specific shifting and interwoven positions taken up by our patients in different social contexts. If we adhere to Freud's Enlightenment view of what constitutes a 'mature' ego, we risk being insensitive to their particular uniqueness and differences. In the case example at the end of the chapter, I will demonstrate in more detail the crucial importance of a view of subjectivity as shifting and both socially and culturally specific to our clinical practice as psychoanalytic psychotherapists.

It could be argued that Freud's radical claims with regard to the disruptive effects of the unconscious challenge the Enlightenment view of the subject. In *The Ego and the Id* he simultaneously conveys the ego as a 'monarch' and a 'submissive slave who courts his master's love' (Freud 1923: 56). The ego is a slave to its master, the id, because its methods of taking control of the id involve disguising its conflicts with reality. Furthermore, in attaching the id's libido to itself (through identification) it assists the death instincts in the id to gain control over the libido. In so doing, it runs the risk of becoming the object of the death instincts and being destroyed. It is at risk too from the super-ego's harsh demands. The ego is thus described by Freud as 'the actual seat of anxiety' (Freud 1923: 57). This strand in Freud's account appears to challenge the notion of the rational subject of the Enlightenment. However, he does not go far enough. He argues that, ultimately, the goal of analysis is 'to enable the ego to achieve a progressive conquest of the id' (Freud 1923: 56).

Words and drives

Freud argues that there is a distinction between unconscious sensations or feelings and unconscious ideas. This reflects his assumption, derived from his understanding of scientific explanations, that there is an observable world which lies beyond language and interpretation. He argues that unconscious ideas rely on a connection to 'word-presentations', residues of memories, which are derived from the preconscious, whereas feelings are either conscious or unconscious and do not depend on transmission through 'word-presentations' even if they are connected with them (Freud 1923: 20). This distinction between unconscious feelings and sensations and unconscious ideas arises from an assumption by Freud that there is an extra-linguistic, acultural, natural world of drives or instincts which arise within us and which are then negotiated by the ego and the super-ego, subject to various defences such as resistance and repression. One of these drives is 'the uninhibited sexual instinct proper' (Freud 1923: 40).

This view of language was challenged by philosophers contemporaneous with Freud, such as Heidegger. For Heidegger, language is not a communication from the interior of one subject to the interior of another; instead, speaking occurs within a background of already shared meanings particular to a given linguistic community. Language is therefore always contextual; it is not the 'external' expression of something 'inner':

In telling, *Dasein* expresses itself not because it has, in the first instance, been encapsulated as something 'internal' over against something outside, but because as Being-in-the-world it is already 'outside' when it understands. What is expressed is precisely this Being-outside. (Heidegger 1990: 205)

The view we take of language and subjectivity is crucial to psychotherapeutic practice. For example, if we accept Freud's view that unconscious, acultural impulses become socialised through the control of the ego and the super-ego, i.e. through restriction and prohibition, we assume that there are natural impulses that can be known and universally identified as, for example, sexual or aggressive.[4] How can we 'know' these except through the medium of language, whether spoken or written? The inseparability of feelings and language is highlighted by Merleau-Ponty,[5] who was a major, although little acknowledged, influence on Foucault:

It would be legitimate to speak of 'natural signs' only if the anatomical organization of our body produced a correspondence between specific gestures and given 'states of mind'. The fact is that the behaviour associated with anger or love is not the same in a Japanese and an Occidental. Or, to be more precise, the difference of behaviour corresponds to a difference in the emotions themselves. (Merleau-Ponty 1986: 188-189)

For Merleau-Ponty there are no natural, acultural and alinguistic impulses as Freud theorises. His emphasis on the specificity of language, whether verbal or gestural, is important for practicing psychotherapists. Our medium is language yet there are few debates in the mainstream psychoanalytic world regarding the theories of language which inform our work. Merleau-Ponty's theorising highlights the importance for psychotherapists of an acute sensitivity to the specific words and gestures of our patients. Furthermore, it emphasises the dangers of assuming that there are thoughts and feelings that we can 'know' and identify 'scientifically' as anger and aggression. If we are committed to a practice which is sensitive to cultural differences it is crucial to understand, as Merleau-Ponty argues, that such thoughts and feelings are experienced and expressed in an enormous diversity of ways, depending on the particular cultural context.

Foucault[6] takes Merleau-Ponty's theorising further by arguing that, in any particular culture, certain discourses become dominant and shape our interpretations of the world. He argues against Freud's notion of repression, claiming that discourses produce sexuality in such a form that it comes to appear as natural: there are no 'natural' sexual instincts outside discourse which then undergo repression. By this he means that interpretations of the body and sexuality as natural unities are the effects of discourses; they are not factual distinctions given at the level of the body. For Foucault there is no body prior to history or discourse. In being 'totally imprinted' by history the body is saturated with and moreover, produced by historical forces. (Foucault 1984: 148)

The ego, the super-ego and power

Foucault's critique may be better understood if we compare his understanding of the operations of power within our culture with Freud's notion of the super-ego on which his formulation depends. The super-ego is a part of the ego that can also stand apart from the ego. It manifests itself as a sense of guilt since it is associated with a prohibition, moral judgments and harsh criticism (voice) derived primarily from the child's identification with the power of its father who, for Freud, holds the main seat of authority. Cultural prohibitions have a secondary influence in shaping the super-ego. The ego is constantly involved in a battle for control over the demands of the id, the natural feelings and sensations arising unconsciously from within the individ-

ual's body, while also being under threat of the restraints of the super-
ego.[7] Freud's conception of how power operates is highlighted in his
description of the ego's relation to the id as analogous with a rider trying to control his horse and also that of a 'constitutional monarch'
poised to impose his veto on any proposed parliamentary measure
(Freud 1923: 55). This view of power as imposed from above contrasts
with Foucault's view that power is not only prohibitive, it is also productive. For example, in his description of how religious confession
required the admission of forbidden sexual thoughts and practices, he
argues that paradoxically, this led to a proliferation of discourses on
sex and sexual practices. 'Power operated as a mechanism of attraction,
it drew out those peculiarities over which it kept watch... power
anchored the pleasure it uncovered' (Foucault 1984: 45). The power
that scrutinises sexualities for the purposes of restriction is thus simultaneously involved in their production.

Foucault's theorising with regard power and subjectivity offers a
solution to the problem often posed by psychoanalytic psychotherapists as to the relation between the 'internal' worlds of their patients
and the 'external' world, namely the wider socio-political context. This
problem arises from the presupposition of a clear division between
these two worlds, which as I will argue in the next section of the chapter, arises from the Cartesian heritage that structured much of Freud's
thinking. Foucault's theorising of how subjectivities and sexualities are
themselves formed through the convergence of multiple, shifting discourses which arise at a particular historical time and within a particular cultural context cuts across what are regarded as fundamental
oppositional distinctions. These oppositions, Foucault argues, are
effects of dominant discourses; they do not exist prior to these discourses. His theorising highlights for psychotherapists that our understanding of the broader socio-cultural and historical contexts of our
patients cannot be simply 'added on' to our interpretations of our
patients' unconscious and internal worlds.[8] Subjectivity is itself produced through and by the social context with its specific constellations
of social and familial relations and childrearing practices.

Cartesian dualisms

The influence of Descartes (1596-1650) can be discerned throughout
Freud's account of the ego and its workings. His theorising is premised
on dualistic distinctions between reason and passion, thinking and

feeling, culture and nature, mind and body, internal and external. These dualisms originate from Descartes' conception of the world as being divided into two distinct entities, matter and mind or spirit (these two are not differentiated). He defined matter as spatial, extended and divisible and mind as non-spatial, unextended and indivisible.[9] Although, according to Descartes, these are entirely different substances, they are nevertheless co-joined, a paradox which is not addressed by him (Descartes 1968: 156-7).

Freud's conceptualisation of the ego as having both conscious and unconscious aspects (Freud 1923: 17) appears to throw into question many of the dualisms which Freud's theorising generally relies upon. Although the ego is unconscious, it is not repressed. However, just as repressed unconscious contents do, it exerts powerful effects and requires analytic work in order for it to become conscious. Drawing on Groddeck, Freud develops this formulation further by proposing that the 'entity' which is modified by the perceptual system and begins by being pre-conscious, is the ego (Freud 1923: 23). The ego extends into the 'id' (also Groddeck's term): the ego is therefore 'that part of the id which has been modified by the direct influence of the external world' (Freud 1923: 25). In this section of *The Ego and the Id*, binary oppositional distinctions between conscious and unconscious, ego and id, internal and external, begin to dissolve. However, this leads Freud to a radical question from which he takes flight, 'When we find ourselves thus confronted by the necessity of postulating a third Ucs. which is not repressed, we must admit that the characteristic of being unconscious begins to lose significance for us' (Freud 1923: 18). The question appears to offer too much of a challenge because, as he admits, 'the property of being conscious or not is in the last resort our one beacon-light in the darkness of depth-psychology' (Freud 1923: 18).

Freud thus returns to the safety of the Cartesian tradition. His distinctions between the 'unconscious feelings' and 'drives', which arise from within an individual's body, and the external world, requiring the mediation of the ego (Freud 1923: 25); between 'unconscious feelings' and 'unconscious ideas' or 'thoughts' (Freud 1923: 20); and between the ego as 'reason' as opposed to the id with its unruly 'passions' (Freud 1971: 25) all echo Descartes' dualisms. Freud's classification of unconscious drives into opposing categories of life (Eros) and death instincts in *Beyond the Pleasure Principle* (Freud 1920a: 52-60) and further developed in *The Ego and the Id* (Freud 1923: 40-47) also presupposes such dualisms. In both these accounts Freud is explicit about his 'fundamental dualistic point of view', emphasising 'we cannot escape that view' (Freud 1923: 46).

Descartes' view that opposing substances and forces exist objectively in themselves does not take into account the effects of language in our interpretation of the world. He assumes that there is an objective world composed of two substances, which we then name through language. From a Foucauldian point of view, the binary oppositions of Descartes have continued to operate as a dominant discourse arising from a particular intellectual tradition in the West. They do not name an already existing state of things; they instead 'produce' this view of the world (Foucault 1984: 105).

Freud is unaware that Cartesian dualistic thinking informs his clinical observations (which he assumes are value-free) or that this kind of thinking arises from a particular cultural and linguistic tradition. This leads him to establish false problems and speculative solutions. For example, in presupposing a sharp polarity between love and hate, Freud is forced to solve the question of accounting for cases where it appears that one is transformed into the other without relinquishing his prior assumption. A circuitous theorising is required to explain this,[10] leading to the development of concepts such as 'sublimation' and 'desexualised ego-libido' (Freud 1923: 45-46). These in turn become established as if they are objectively observable entities or processes.

The consequences of this are highly relevant for the practice of psychotherapy. If we uncritically assume that there are oppositional entities and processes which lie outside language, we are unlikely to be sufficiently attentive to the unique, shifting, and particular relations between the conscious and unconscious aspects of our patients' experiences which are always already within language, whether visual or verbal. Indeed, for many patients, the rigid oppositionality of many of their distinctions is a major source of their distress. As the therapeutic work develops, these dualisms become less acute and possibilities for more flexible and subtle distinctions emerge.

The gendered ego

Freud's account of the gendering of the ego further reflects his dualistic thinking. He argues in *The Ego and the Id* that the ego is in danger of pathology if its identifications are 'too numerous, unduly powerful and incompatible with one another' (Freud 1923: 30). Although

Freud's account allows for a shifting and somewhat precarious path towards 'masculinity' and 'femininity', he is highly prescriptive regarding the final identification that constitutes the achievement of the 'mature' ego's masculinity or femininity. The Oedipus complex is pivotal in the negotiation of gender identifications and, for Freud, it is universal: 'every new arrival on this planet is faced with the task of mastering the Oedipus complex' (Freud 1905: 226). In the case of the boy, the threat of castration forces him to relinquish the object-cathexis of his mother and either identify with her or intensify his identification with his father. Freud is explicit as to which outcome is more 'normal', namely the latter identification: 'In this way the dissolution of the Oedipus complex would consolidate the masculinity in a boy's character' (Freud 1923: 32). For girls, the 'normal' outcome is identification with her mother. This will, according to Freud 'fix the child's feminine character' (Freud 1923: 32). For both sexes, the super-ego has a specifically masculine character, that of the father.

Freud acknowledges that there is a contradiction in his view of how masculine and feminine identifications occur (Freud 1923: 32). His first assumption is that the ego is constituted by identifications with lost objects and it thus 'contains the history of those object choices' (Freud 1923: 29). Since Freud assumes that the child's passion at the Oedipal stage is for the parent of the opposite sex, which subsequently has to be relinquished, it could be assumed that its ego identification would be with that lost parental object. Yet in his account of the dissolution of the Oedipus complex, normal resolution involves identification with the parent of the same sex. This is thus not consistent with his notion that identification is predicated on loss. Interestingly, he argues that it is more common for a girl to take up the abandoned object into her ego, identifying with her father but, he claims, this outcome depends on 'the masculinity in her disposition' (Freud 1923: 32).

Thus the gendering of the ego ultimately depends more on biology than on social or historical factors. Furthermore, he does not allow for the historical and cultural specificity of terms such as 'masculinity' and 'femininity'. He associates femininity with passivity, a weak super-ego, and sexual desire for men. Masculinity is diametrically opposed to this, reflecting the dualistic thinking which pervades Freud's thought; it is associated with activity and aggression, a strong super-ego, and sexual desire for women.

In his introduction of the notion of a 'complete Oedipus complex' (Freud 1923: 33), Freud appears to be proffering a more complex account of gender identifications. It arises from the bisexuality he considers originally present in children and subsequent ambivalent relations to the parents. In this scenario the boy, for example, has an ambivalent relation to his father and an affectionate relation to his mother and, simultaneously, 'behaves like a girl' in an affectionate relation to his father and in a hostile rivalry in relation to his mother (Freud 1923: 33). This account, while adhering to normative notions of 'masculinity' and 'femininity' allows for more diversity and does not seem to presuppose a dominance of or fixity within either gender. However, Freud goes on to elaborate how the existence of this 'complete Oedipus complex' is to be found in neurotics (Freud 1923: 33). The dissolution of the complex will result in a mother-identification and a father-identification within the ego but 'the relative intensity of the two identifications in any individual will reflect the preponderance in him of one or other of the two sexual dispositions' (Freud 1923: 34). Freud again resorts to a biological determinism in his theorising of the gendered ego.

Freud assumes that 'normal' sexual development for men and women results in heterosexuality. For example, in *The Ego and the Id*, he associates homosexuality in men with the transformation of an aggressive hostile attitude into an affectionate object-choice (Freud 1923: 37, 43). Although he makes a radical claim for an original bisexuality in babies and young children, prior to the negotiation of the Oedipus complex, he nevertheless assumes that normal resolution of this leads to heterosexuality.[11]

Freud's accounts of the vicissitudes of the path of the libido from the bisexuality of infancy, through the Oedipus complex and arriving finally at a masculine or feminine identification with a heterosexual orientation is inconsistent, since it is interwoven with a number of different and often contradictory discourses. His assumption of an original bisexuality implies a bisexuality that is already biologically given. However, the child's libido is then shaped through its social relations with its parents. Freud fails to see that these familial relations are situated within a wider context. For example, his assumption that the child's first love object in the 'pre-Oedipal' stage is the biological birthmother (as opposed to the father or other carers) reflects a biologistic view which does not take into account the wider social context and patterns of child care specific to early twentieth century Europe. The next stage, the Oedipal, involves complex struggles for the child with its desires for the parent of the opposite sex. This involves a momentous switch of affection for the girl, an affection that Freud explains through the notion of penis envy. The girl's envy for the penis as a 'superior' organ leads her to desire her father, thus precipitating her Oedipus complex. Again, there is a shift into biologism as well as a presumption of inferiority in girls and women: the girl does not biologically have a penis and, it is assumed, she cannot help perceiving this as a 'lack'. This 'lack' catapults her into a particular relation with her father, which, Freud assumes, is one of desire. His notion of penis envy arises out of a prior normative assumption that girls and boys must have a heterosexual attraction to one of their parents and the necessity of explaining how this occurs in girls. Finally, however, identification with the parent of the same sex and taking up a masculine position as a boy and a feminine position as a girl depends on 'sexual disposition'. Where does this sexual disposition arise from if children are, as Freud also claims, originally bisexual? Freud begins and ends with a biological given in his account of 'normal' development, although these 'givens' appear to contradict one another.

In Freud's account of the gendering of the ego, it is evident that he is limited by the Enlightenment view of subjectivity and its commitment to 'science' as the ideal form of knowledge. This cuts across the more radical possibilities of his theorising of bisexual possibilities and the precarious identifications taken up by the ego. 'Masculinity' and 'femininity' are achieved as final states of maturity, held as universal for men and for women. Freud's conceptions of masculinity and femininity have been the target of a number of feminist critiques since the 1970s (Chodorow 1978a, Irigaray 1985, O'Connor and Ryan 1993). Many of them have focussed on the particular restrictions that Freud's view of the mature 'feminine' ego have placed on women and argued that this arose from the particular socio-historical context in which Freud practised, namely a middle-class patriarchal European culture of the first quarter of the twentieth century. It is crucial that psychotherapists critically consider the assumptions which underpinned Freud's theories at that time and also examine how far these continue to inform their own views of 'maturity' in both men and women. It is also important to acknowledge the current socio-historical factors which shape our own critiques and developments in our own theorising. Such questioning has major implications for clinical psychotherapeutic work. If psychotherapists fail to consider them, they are unlikely to be sufficiently open to the multiplicity of interpretations of masculinity and femininity brought by their patients, some of which may be restrictive and some productive, according to the unique experience of each individual patient.

The economic ego

Freud's conceptions of familial organisation and of 'masculinity' and 'femininity' arise from a specific context, namely middle-class Vienna in the first quarter of the nineteenth century. Fromm argues that it is crucial to consider how far this economic context shaped Freud's conceptualisation of the libido (Fromm 1978: 51). He describes the ethos of European middle-class businessmen, amongst whom Freud practised, as based on a principle of scarcity and on the value of saving. According to Fromm, Freud's concept of libidinal impulses seeking discharge with the aim of easing unpleasurable tensions reflects this principle. In a context in which commodities are limited, Freud's notion of desire is thus founded on lack, rather than on abundance.

More recently, the assumption that desire arises from lack has been challenged by the feminist philosopher, Grosz, who argues for a conceptualisation of desire as productive, occurring between skin surfaces rather than arising from those zones designated by Freud as specifically erotogenic. She conceptualises desire in terms of 'proliferation' and 'intensifications', which strongly contrast with those of lack and scarcity (Grosz 1994: 81). Grosz's theorising from within a very different socio-cultural context, i.e. the 1980s and 1990s and following the impact of the second wave of twentieth century feminism, highlights the specific cultural limitations on Freud's account of the libido. Fromm's and Grosz's analysis can be further extended with regard to Freud's emphasis on the restrictive role of the ego: it has to 'hold in check' the demands of the id (Freud 1923: 25), it has to 'desexualise' or 'sublimate' the libido of the id, it is itself at risk of punishment by the super-ego (Freud 1923: 55). Its 'operations' are based on restriction, the maintenance of scarcity rather than production and expansion. Freud describes the workings of the ego as if they are objectively observable yet, as Fromm's and Grosz's claims highlight, his interpretations arise from a specific economic context.

The ethnocentric ego

Freud's theory of the ego was shaped not only by the economic context of middle-class Vienna, but also the context of white, European, Judeo-

Christian culture. Despite his position as a Jewish man at a time of increasing discrimination against Jewish people, Freud does not consider racial differences or the effects of racism in his conceptualisation of the ego in *The Ego and the Id*. (1923). Although debates in relation to Freud's conceptions of femininity were waged in the 1920s and 1930s and are often returned to by contemporary feminist scholars (Walton 1997: 223), there have been comparatively few challenges, particularly within the psychoanalytic field, to the unacknowledged racial assumptions which underpin Freud's theory of the ego. In the 1920s, Malinowski, an anthropologist, and in the 1950s, Fanon, a psychoanalyst, were among the first to challenge the institution of psychoanalysis on the grounds of its ethnocentrism. However, it is only during the past decade that an increasing number of critiques have emerged questioning the implicit association within psychoanalytic theory between psychological maturity and 'white' European subjectivity (for example, Butler 1993, Spillers 1997, Walton 1997). The paucity of critiques is undoubtedly linked to an understandable assumption by many people from both black and other ethnic minorities that psychoanalysis has nothing to offer them. Since psychoanalysis is founded upon a particular universalising conception of white European subjectivity, and since very few black people are accepted on to psychoanalytic psychotherapy trainings, doubts about its relevance to the experience of people from black and some minority ethnic backgrounds are well founded.

The focus on sexual difference in psychoanalytic theories arises from the presupposition that sexual difference is the fundamental difference between human beings, more fundamental than racial difference. Butler and Walton contest this, arguing that sexual and racial difference are instead articulated through one another and that neither difference is primary (Butler 1993: 181-182, Walton 1997: 225). According to Walton, it is assumed that the male-female binary is universal since not everyone is presumed to have been affected by a black-white binary in their development. However, as she points out, the acceptance of such a binary view does not depend on being raised in a mixed community of black and white people, although such an upbringing is more common than generally acknowledged. Racial ideologies pervade the lives of both white Americans and Europeans 'whose fantasmatic life is permeated by the Orientalist and Africanist ideologies that underwrite and justify what... had become a long and vexed history of European colonialist expansion and decline' (Walton

1997: 226). Yet, how such ideologies shaped white people's subjectivity was not recognised by psychoanalysts since 'race' was conceived of as 'blackness', as primitive and as having nothing to do with 'civilised' white subjectivity.

Malinowskis's early challenge to Freud is directed specifically at Freud's assumption that the Oedipus complex is universal. He argues that his account of it:

> [C]orresponds essentially to our patrilineal Aryan family with the developed patria potestas, buttressed by Roman law and Christian morals, and accentuated by the modern economic conditions of the well-to-do bourgeoisie. (Malinowski in Jones 1928: 365)

For Malinowski, Freud's theorising of the Oedipus complex only applies to a specific middle-class, patriarchal, Christian context with a legal system inherited from the Romans. Ironically, Malinowski's critique, while recognising that there are culturally specific forms of family organisation underpinned by particular religious or other cultural values, does not consider the implications of his own interpretation with regard to Freud's position as a Viennese Jew. Fanon also argues against the universality of the Oedipus complex, claiming that in the French Antilles, for example, no neurosis associated with the complex can be identified in ninety-seven per cent of the families (Fanon 1986: 152).

Freud's theory of the Oedipus complex is central to his account of ego development. As Malinowski and Fanon point out, it presupposes a specific configuration of familial relations and patterns of child care specific to white Western culture at the time of Freud's writing and assumed by him to be universal. Freud's failure to consider race, ethnicity, or racism with regard to the formation of the ego in his account of the ego in *The Ego and the Id* reflects his rootedness in Enlightenment thought. As I have outlined, Enlightenment thought affirms an essential unity, founded on 'reason', of all individuals beyond what are regarded as superficial cultural differences. It does not allow for the multiplicity and diversity of cultural languages, institutions and practices in which individuals are located and which shape their various intersubjective relations. These may be radically different from the white European model which Freud presupposes.

Furthermore, Freud does not recognise the extent to which his account of ego development is predicated on an excluded black 'Other' which is operative within white Western institutions, as much through an absence of black people in any given context as much as through their presence. Hammonds argues, for example, that a consequence of this is that black women's sexuality is relegated to 'the irreducibly abnormal category in which there are no distinctions between homosexual and heterosexual women' (Hammonds 1994: 138). Subjectivity is unavoidably shaped by the institutions, traditions, languages and practices of a particular culture. If these are shot through with discriminatory attitudes towards blackness, both implicit and explicit, all subjectivities will consequently be marked by these.

A consideration of how subjectivity is racialised once again raises the question of how subjectivity is shaped by the wider culture. For Freud, the child's conscience (his super-ego or ego-ideal) is constituted primarily through his relation with his father and the dissolution of the Oedipus complex. It is later influenced by the child's relations with other authority figures. In Butler's view, it is possible to extend Freud's concept of the ego-ideal with its role of regulating social norms to include that of maintaining particular cultural expectations with regard to race and gender (Butler 1993: 182-183). For example, she argues that the norm of whiteness in white culture is regulated through the ego-ideal. However, this claim fails to take into account the extent to which, from birth on, all the child's relations are informed by particular practices which are unavoidably underpinned by specific cultural values with regard to race and skin colour.

Embodied subjectivity

Butler's rewriting of Freud's concept of the super-ego hinges on its being founded on a notion of power being imposed from 'above'. As I have discussed above, Freud's account of the role of the super-ego assumes that ideas, wishes and feelings which are acultural and pre-linguistic arise from the id and are then mediated by the ego under the scrutiny of the super-ego. How do such ideas, wishes and feelings come into being except as already located within a cultural context?

In contrast to Freud, Merleau-Ponty, the French philosopher who wrote the *Phenomenology of Perception* (1945) just over twenty years after Freud's *The Ego and the Id*, does not avoid issues of race with regard to subjectivity. He argues that our embodiment itself is culturally and historically specific since, as 'intentional' subjects we are always already in the world. By 'intentional' Merleau-Ponty means that consciousness is always consciousness of the world and we are thus, as subjects, always oriented towards the world. (Merleau-Ponty 1986: xviii) His concept of embodiment challenges the Cartesian dualisms that pervade Freud's account:

> The union of soul and body is not an amalgamation between two mutually external terms, subject and object, brought about by arbitrary decree. It is enacted at every instant in the movement of existence. (Merleau-Ponty 1986: 88-89)

Just as his notion of 'embodiment' undermines dualistic distinctions between body and mind, it also challenges those between internal and external, subject and world. For Merleau-Ponty our bodies are neither simply subjects or objects, our bodies are 'our general medium for having a world' (Merleau-Ponty 1986: 146). They are open to the world and through them the world is given form and meaning. The body is a condition of the world's existence because it is through our bodies that the world appears to us. As a phenomenologist, Merleau-Ponty is concerned primarily with 'a direct description of our experience as it is', rather than a search for explanations in terms of causes (Merleau-Ponty 1986: vii). Although Merleau-Ponty is influenced by Freud, he does not make use of Freud's notion of the ego (Merleau-Ponty 1986: 157-158). His theory of embodiment challenges many of the assumptions on which Freud's conceptualisation hinges. In *The Ego and the Id* Freud makes, for him, the rare claim that 'the ego is first and foremost a bodily ego' (Freud 1923: 26). By this he means that the ego is derived from 'bodily sensations' and it is therefore a mental 'projection of a surface of the body' (Freud 1923: 26). This remains undeveloped but, as it stands, this conceptualisation appears to reflect the dualistic thought which I have identified as problematic and which Merleau-Ponty's account of 'embodiment' aims to disrupt.

Merleau-Ponty's notion of embodiment arises from his rejection of naturalism. He praises Freud for his attempt to integrate sexuality and existence in his theorising of the libido as 'what causes man to have a history', enabling individuals to establish themselves in different contexts (Merleau-Ponty 1986: 158). However, he also launches an impassioned critique against the naturalism and explanations in terms of causality which he considers restrictive in psychoanalysis:

> We refused, as we always will, to grant to that phallus which is part of the objective body, the organ of micturition and copulation, such power of causality over so many forms of behaviour... It is not the useful, functional, prosaic body which explains man; on the contrary, it is the human body which rediscovers its symbolic or poetic weight. (Merleau-Ponty 1994: 69)

Merleau-Ponty's critique of naturalism leads him to argue against Freud's universalising of the developmental stages in children's sexual development. He claims that the orifices designated by Freud as universally erotogenic represent just a few of the many possible ones current in cultures as yet unknown to us (Merleau-Ponty 1964: 101). The notion of an ego constituted through Oedipal identifications, held by Freud to be universal, is thus at great variance with Merleau-Ponty's notion of an intentional embodied subject.

The value of Merleau-Ponty's account of the subject as intentional and embodied is highlighted with regard to race and ethnicity. For Merleau-Ponty, race and cultural differences are neither naturally acquired, nor are they a result of tensions between the ego and the ego-ideal. Instead, they arise from a subject's 'style' of being in the world (Merleau-Ponty 1986: 143-144). This 'style' arises through a person's intersubjective relations and the accumulation of a background of shared meanings that become embodied. For Merleau-Ponty, listening is itself a form of embodiment such that words are 'not signs to be deciphered but "the transparent envelope" of a meaning within which (the subject) might live' (Merleau-Ponty 1986: 133). For Merleau-Ponty, to live in an intersubjective context is to live within a linguistic context of words as well as gestures. The gestures we acquire and the way we live a situation are specific to the style of our particular culture. For Merleau-Ponty, this would include class:

> The angry Japanese smiles, the westerner goes red and stamps his foot or else goes pale and hisses his words. It is not enough for two conscious subjects to have the same organs and nervous system for the same emotions to produce in both the same signs. What is important is how they use their bodies, the simultaneous patterning of body and world in emotion. (Merleau-Ponty 1986: 189)

Merleau-Ponty's account of subjectivity as intentional and embodied allows for cultural specificity and diversity to a much greater
extent than Freud's account of the 'ego'. It challenges dualistic distinctions between 'internal' and 'external' worlds and situates the subject
within a world of language, gestural and spoken, allowing for the
embodiment of different cultural meanings. Merleau-Ponty undermines naturalistic conceptions of subjectivity. He does not theorise an
'inner' world of instinctual impulses which are harnessed by the id
under the watchful eye of the super-ego. Instead, he argues that sexuality is interfused with existence and does not exist as a specific excitation that lies outside and prior to the rest of our existence. It is historically and culturally specific and cannot be adequately theorised within the limitations of universal developmental stages in which the
Oedipus complex is held to be pivotal.

How psychotherapists conceptualise subjectivity has profound consequences for their practice. Any notion of subjectivity is, as we have
seen in this discussion of Freud's and Merleau-Ponty's accounts,
underpinned by values arising from within a particular cultural context. If psychotherapists rely uncritically on Freud's notion of the ego
and the centrality of the Oedipus complex, this has consequences for
their work with homosexual patients. They will be interpreted as being
arrested in their sexual development and the possibilities for living
happily in same-sex relationships will be foreclosed by the psychotherapist. Furthermore, the psychotherapist will not be open to the
specific meanings same-sex relationships have for those patients and
how identities as 'lesbian or gay' are themselves socially and culturally specific. As I have previously argued

> In psychoanalytic theorising there is no distinction between the
> same-sex sexuality between, for example, two upper-class mar-
> ried white women such as Virginia Woolf and Vita Sackville-
> West in the twenties and that of a black working-class woman
> who identifies as a lesbian queer in the nineties. (Ellis 1997: 372)

A consideration of my work with a patient, Elaine, highlights the
limitations of adhering to Freud's Enlightenment-influenced conceptualisation of the ego and the importance of being open to differences
and the possibility of multiple identifications in relation to gender,
race, class and sexuality. Elaine was a twenty-seven-year-old mixed
race lesbian, the only child of a black Afro-Caribbean father and a

white English mother. Her father was a building labourer who had been unemployed for long periods in Elaine's childhood. Elaine wanted psychotherapy because she wanted to 'put an end to' her bouts of anxiety and depression. She had a demanding job in a lesbian and gay youth project and felt constantly under pressure: however hard she worked and however successful she was she never felt she was achieving enough. Elaine had been with her present partner, Donna, for two years.

Elaine had been unsure whether she would be able to trust me as a white psychotherapist whom she assumed was middle-class and heterosexual. She was afraid that I might see her lesbianism as a pathology and she also wondered if I could ever sufficiently understand how isolating and undermining her experiences of racism had been for her. She had been raised on a mainly white housing estate and was the only black child in her primary-school class. However, it was in her secondary school, where there were other black pupils, that she felt most taunted and exposed in the face of gangs of white girls who would threaten her and call her 'wog' and 'chocolate face'. Yet she also did not feel she really belonged with the black children, since her mother was white.

Elaine had felt unsupported by her parents in the face of this hostility and, it emerged, felt particularly abandoned by her father who had very high expectations of her. It seemed to her that he was only ever interested in whether she was getting high enough marks at school. Elaine thought now that he had been desperately anxious for her to succeed where he had not as a black immigrant in 1950s Britain. This also led him to deny and ignore her attempts to tell him about the racism to which she was subjected. Elaine described her relationship with him as being one where they were constantly 'at war' and, in her adolescence, they were constantly engaged in bitter and intense political arguments. In the therapy, an important dream revealed Elaine's unconscious longing to be closer to her father and to be accepted by him. She mentioned at this point how very painful it was to her that he would not accept her being lesbian.

As a teenager Elaine experienced two brief relationships with boys. When she was twenty, she had her first relationship with a woman. It was at this point that Elaine 'came out' as a lesbian and became very involved in black lesbian politics. Two years later, she had a short sexual relationship with a black gay man. She kept this secret from her lesbian feminist friends for fear they would think that she was not a 'proper' lesbian. It took Elaine a long time to talk about this to me in case I neatly categorised her as bisexual. She decided with the consent of her lover that she would have a one-off sexual encounter with a man in an attempt to 'sort it all out'. The encounter highlighted for her both how much she loved Donna and wanted to stay with her and also how it was possible for her to experience sexual pleasure with men. She continued to feel she was living an impossible paradox since a 'proper' lesbian was someone who had never been attracted to men. In response to my question as to why it was so important to know whether she was either lesbian or heterosexual, more memories emerged about her experiences of racism and feeling that she belonged neither to the white nor the black groups of children.

As Elaine felt increasingly confident that I was taking seriously her feelings of denigration and exclusion by both black and white people, it became possible to interpret her anxieties in the transference. She said that she often chastised herself for not 'doing therapy properly' and thought that I must really think that she was 'stupid'. She wished she knew what I expected from her. I responded to her by saying, 'So you would be able either to meet these, or do battle with me, as you did with your father. Not knowing what I expect means you have no definition and without that you feel vulnerable and stupid'.

As the work continued links emerged between Elaine's need for certainty and her wish to be a 'proper' lesbian. For Elaine, uncertainty and incompleteness in many aspects of her life were associated unconsciously with failure. She spoke at this time of her difficulties in being spontaneous and how she admired and envied people like her lover who were. For Elaine, spontaneity was associated with the risk of being 'stupid', 'silly' or 'wrong'.

Two years into the therapy, Elaine began to risk more spontaneity in her relation with me. This had started with her admission that she often thought that I saw her as 'stupid'. At this time she joined a Latin-American dance class with her lover. At first she was extremely nervous, feeling awkward and out of time. Then, suddenly, in one class she felt an enormous shift and she found she was carried by the music in time with her partner. She was also amazed at the individuality of all the women, despite the fact that they were all dancing the same dance. I acknowledged how important it was for her to discover her own spontaneity and individuality in relation to the other dancers, and how this became possible only when she stopped thinking about 'getting it right'.

In working with Elaine I did not interpret her lesbianism as being 'caused' by her feelings of disappointment in relation to her father, forcing her to identify with her father as a 'masculine' lesbian.[12] My work was not informed by Freud's notion of 'ego maturity', achieved through the working through of this relationship and the restoration of her heterosexuality. Nor did I collude with her search for her 'true' identity, whether lesbian, bisexual or heterosexual, black or white. It was important for Elaine to see that her anxiety about being a 'proper' lesbian was connected to her desperate need for certainty and perfection. This arose partly from her father's high expectations of her, stemming from his experiences as a black immigrant. It also arose from a cultural context that is saturated with fixed notions of sexual identity as well as of white subjectivity being superior.

If I had adhered to Freud's notion of the ego as acultural and ahistorical, I would not have been sensitive to the way in which her experience of her subjectivity shifted between and across a number of different positions—'black', 'mixed race', 'lesbian', 'working class' and 'heterosexual'—and was shaped both in response to and as a resistance to different forms of discrimination. It was through my reading of Foucault that I was able to be attentive to her differing experiences of her subjectivity (or subjectivities). I recognised that her own difficulty in accepting that the fluidity of her subjectivity reflected the constraints in Freud's theory of the ego as universal and heterosexual. Since she had been raised in a white European culture, her view of subjectivity was inevitably shaped by the dominant discourse of Enlightenment thought to which Freud, in his account of the ego, adhered. Merleau-Ponty's account of embodied subjectivity was crucial in enabling me to acknowledge the enormous importance to Elaine of being carried with her partner by the music. It crystallised the possibility of movement, of moving beyond the dualisms of 'inner' and 'outer', and the finding of a unique gestural language which could also be shared with others.

How the psychotherapist conceptualises 'ego maturity' will affect his/her sensitivity to the specific intersubjective worlds of both their black and their white patients and the effects of class position, gender and institutionalised racism on these worlds. For many psychoanalytic psychotherapists, such awareness in the consulting room is dismissed as 'a collapse into sociology', a failure to perceive the ego-identifications arising from early relations with parental figures, as if these figures were not themselves located within a wider cultural context. By contrast, Merleau-Ponty's account challenges these distinctions between 'internal' and 'external' worlds in the constitution of our subjectivity. It acknowledges that subjectivity is always contextual and that differences are lived and embodied through and in the world in a multiplicity of ways. If psychotherapists really attend to the details of how patients live the textures of their unique worlds, with an openness to diversity, multiplicity, complexity and contradictions, it will be evident that these cannot be contained within Freud's notion of the ego and its parental identifications.

Notes

[1] Freud's theorising of the ego underwent a number of changes. For the purposes of this chapter I will focus particularly on his later formulations as they appear in one of his later theoretical works, *The Ego and the Id* (Freud 1923).

[2] Fromm points out that one of Freud's teachers was Von Brucke, a physiologist who specialised in mechanistic materialism (Fromm 1978: 48).

[3] For example, according to Ronald Clark, Freud attended the seminars of the philosopher, Brentano. in the 1870s (Clark 1980: 22, 33-34).

[4] In *The Ego and the Id* Freud theorises the 'instincts' as divided into two classes, sexual (Eros), associated with love, and death (Thanatos), associated with hate and destructiveness (Freud 1923: 40-47).

[5] Merleau-Ponty (1907-1961) was a French philosopher who had initially been a psychologist. He became a phenomenologist who extended Husserl's phenomenology of intentional consciousness to the corporeal aspects of human existence, arguing for a notion of an embodied subject situated in concrete lived experience.

[6] Foucault (1926-1984) was concerned with analyses of the present in terms of the past. However, he challenges a notion of history which views the present as being caused by the past. For Foucault, an examination of the past highlights the contingency of what we are presented with, not the inevitability of it. One of his primary concerns is with the construction of subjectivity. He argues that concepts such as 'sexuality' or 'normality' or 'nature' are socio-historical concepts arising from the dominant discourses of a particular culture; they are not intrinsic to the subject.

[7] Jonathan Lear argues that Freud's tripartite structure of the psyche is derived from Plato. According to Lear, Plato's conception of the psyche had three parts: 'appetite' (for food and sex), 'spirit', concerned with pride, honour and anger, and 'reason', which seeks knowledge (Lear 1998: 59).

[8] In my article 'Who Speaks? Who Listens? Different Voices and Different Sexualities' (Ellis 1997: 369-383), I present two cases of a white man and a mixed race woman showing the relevance of Foucault's theorising for clinical practice.

[9] This critique is made by J. Cottingham (Honderich (ed.) 1995: 191).

[10] Freud's circuitous theorising parallels that of Descartes in his argument for the existence of God. He claims that, since we are capable of thought, we therefore exist (*Cogito ergo sum*). However, my thoughts may be distorted and I may be being deceived. Yet, if I can doubt, I must have a notion of a more perfect being than myself, namely, God. Since God is perfect,

he would not be systematically deceiving me and he gives me the ability to discern what is true and what is false (Descartes 1968: 53-132).

[11] See *Wild Desires and Mistaken Identities, Lesbianism and Psychoanalysis* (O'Connor and Ryan 1993: 268-270) for a thorough critique of the Oedipus complex in relation to the theorising of lesbian sexuality.

[12] See Freud's 'Psychogenesis of a Case of Female Homosexuality' (Freud 1920b: 145-172).

WHY I AM NEVER MYSELF: ON PRESENCE AND ABSENCE IN LACANIAN THEORY

Dany Nobus

Shelving the self

One of the main challenges for every visitor to Lacanian psychoanalysis is to make sense of his concepts. It is hardly possible to say exactly what Lacan meant by the split subject, the Other, the phallus, jouissance and the object *a*—to name but a few of his coinages—without taking account of the historical and theoretical context in which these notions appeared, and without including a panoply of other terms (desire, fantasy, the unconscious, the symbolic, the real and the imaginary), which then require clarification in their own right, *ad infinitum*. This exercise of exegesis is nonetheless valuable, if only because eventually one will at least understand what Lacan meant when he asserted that meaning (*sens*) always escapes, insofar as it flees from the cask of language (Lacan 1975 [1973]: 11). In addition, the evasiveness of meaning in Lacanian theory has not deterred some courageous scholars from compiling reader's guides (Muller and Richardson 1982), dictionaries (Evans 1996, Roudinesco and Plon 1997), and encyclopedias (Kaufmann 1993), although they may of course not have discovered the semantic problems until they had finished their projects.

For once, in agreeing to write a chapter on Lacan for this collection of papers, I was not so much faced with the onerous task of having to detail an abstract, oblique nomenclature, as with the seemingly worse assignment of having to elucidate something that is simply not there. For I wish to make clear from the outset that in my reading of the entire corpus of Lacan's oeuvre, which spans a period of almost fifty years, there is no such thing as a notion of the 'self' that can lay claim to conceptual status. Difficult as it is to explain why Lacan had recourse to some of the terms mentioned above, and to understand what they were supposed to convey, the problem posed by questions as to why he did *not* entertain a panoply of popular psychoanalytic notions (character, insight, attachment, individuation and, indeed, the self) seems almost insuperable, that is to say insoluble on the grounds that Lacan did not always justify his repudiation of certain terms.

To the best of my knowledge, the only time Lacan lent himself to a critique of the 'self' was in his seminar 'The Psychoanalytic Act' (Lacan 1967-68), during a discussion of Winnicott's influential studies on psychoanalysis and child development. Addressing Winnicott's core antagonism between the true and the false self, Lacan contended, 'Who does not see, when we already possess within analytic theory the *Real Ich*, the *Lust Ich*, the ego and the id, all those references that are sufficiently articulated to define our field, that the addition of the self, as it is avowed within the text with false and true, represents nothing but the truth? And who does not see either that there is no other true self behind this situation than Mr Winnicott himself, who posits himself there as the presence of the truth' (Lacan 1967-68: lecture of 6 December 1967).[1]

Stripped from its Winnicottian skin, the self received a much more vehement blow in Lacan's subsequent lecture, 'If there is anything the analytic experience reminds us of, it is that if this expression "self-cause" (*cause de soi*) means something, it is precisely to indicate to us that the self (*le soi*) or what is called as such—in other words the subject to which everyone has to accede, since even in some Anglo-Saxon field where it can be said that people understand nothing at all about these questions the word self had to emerge—adapts itself to nothing in analytic theory, nothing corresponds to it' (Lacan 1967-68: lecture of 10 January 1967).

Lacan's *coup de grâce* came in June 1969, in his summary of 'The Psychoanalytic Act', 'It is certainly not excluded for confessions to be articulated there (in the parodic Church of psychoanalysis) that are worth collecting. Such as this forgery which is pronounced "the self", perhaps the first [forgery] of this standing to escape the list of morphemes that is made into a taboo because they are Freud's... Nevertheless, once launched this "self"—the theme proliferates, and in the direction of the auspices under which it was born—will be the loss of the psychoanalyst, disqualified by it. The cult element of its profession is, as in other cases, the sign of being unequal to the act'(Lacan 1984 [1969]: 20-21).

However obscure the rationale behind these assertions may be, their tenor cannot be misjudged. Lacan was adamant that the self should never have been introduced within psychoanalytic theory, and that its propagation could damage the foundations of clinical practice. In the light of Lacan's unambiguous stance, it is all the more remarkable that many a commentator on his work has turned a blind eye to his refutations, acting as if even the most controversial psychoanalyst of the post-war period had *also* arrived at an elaborate theory of the self. Despite its absence from the Lacanian conceptual corpus, and despite his explicit rejection of the term, Lacanian theory has indeed on numerous occasions been coerced into accepting the self. For many a researcher it has been unthinkable for Lacan *not* to think about and contribute to a psychoanalytic account of the self. And although it is only fair to say that the aforementioned quotations are not easily accessible, buried as some of them are in unedited and unpublished French transcripts, the eagerness with which Anglo-American authors have read the concept of the self into Lacanian texts, which do not contain any trace of it, invites some reflection in its own right.

Before unearthing Lacan's motives for discrediting the self, and facing the epistemological issues presented above, it is therefore worthwhile to examine some of these sources according to which Lacan *does* have a theory of the self. Hence, instead of trying to answer the question as to the absence of the self in Lacanian theory directly, I shall approximate it through a critical investigation of views endorsing the 'Lacanian self'. In most cases, these views rely on the ostensible compatibility between the self and other Lacanian concepts; in some instances they are rooted in some observed parallels between Lacanian psychoanalysis and Kohut's self-psychology (Kohut 1971, 1977, 1984).

Sources of the Lacanian self

The first Anglo-American text ostensibly attuning Lacan's work to the reign of the self was Anthony Wilden's *The Language of the Self* (1968b), which was published—a sublime irony—shortly after Lacan's fulmination against the self in 'The Psychoanalytic Act'. A young American philosopher with a special interest in French psychoanalysis, Wilden had been designated as Lacan's guide and interpreter during the Baltimore conference on structuralism in the autumn of 1966 (Roudinesco 1990 [1986], Lacan 1970 [1966]). Alongside the translation and annotation of Lacan's 'Rome Discourse' (1977b [1953]), he subsequently wrote a book-length study of the psychoanalyst's trajectory for his PhD thesis (Wilden 1968a). *The Language of the Self* was based on this thesis.

Wilden's book played a pivotal part in the dissemination of Lacan's ideas within the Anglo-American world, yet it cannot be held responsible for the infiltration of the self within Lacanian theory, since Wilden did not produce a sustained argument about the 'Lacanian self'. The contents of Wilden's volume should not be judged by the nature of its flag, which probably explains why it was later reprinted with a different title (Lacan 1981[1953]). In choosing to situate Lacan's work within the broad intellectual configurations of the self, without strictly identifying it with these traditions, Wilden (his supervisors and/or publishers) simply exhibited an allegiance to a prevalent paradigm within the Anglo-American social sciences, through which Lacan's contributions were presumably more likely to gain acceptance amongst scholars and practising therapists alike.

Employing the notion 'self' as the obvious translation for the German word *Selbst* in Hegel's *Phänomenologie des Geistes* (1952 [1807], 1977 [1807]), and its French equivalent *soi*, Wilden approached Lacan's terminology in *'Le stade du miroir'* (1966a [1949]) and the *'Discours de Rome'* (1966b [1953]) with exemplary caution, leaving some of the key terms untranslated and pointing towards the underlying conceptual crux in his annotations. Justifying his decision to maintain Lacan's original distinction between 'ego', 'moi' and 'je' in the 'Rome Discourse', Wilden noted, 'The words "ego", "moi", and "je" are left as in the French. The ambiguity of Freud's use of the term *das Ich* is well known, but Lacan's concept of the *moi* is essentially that of the *Idealich* or the *Ichideal*... At the same time, Lacan's use of *moi* shares the *Ich's* sense of "self," (*Selbstgefühl*) as Freud sometimes employs it, especially in the earlier works' (Lacan 1981 [1953]: 101). No prodigious acumen is required to observe that Wilden was at great pains to find his route in an ocean of four languages—French (*je, moi*), German (*Ich*), Anglo-Latin (*ego*) and English (*self*)—and that his remarks did not always contribute to a better understanding of the terms' connotations. Demonstrating his precision, yet complicating the picture further, he elsewhere rendered *moi* in a passage from Lévi-Strauss's 'Introduction à l'œuvre de Marcel Mauss' (1950) as 'self', whilst maintaining the reference to the French term (Lacan 1981 [1953]: 256) and whilst Lévi-Strauss had acknowledged the Lacanian locus of the notion *moi*.

Since Wilden's seminal translation of the 'Rome Discourse' and his probing interrogation of Lacanian theory, new English translations of Lacan's texts have appeared and the secondary literature has acquired massive proportions. Many of these translations are less meticulous than Wilden's, to the extent that those responsible have often imposed a standard psychoanalytic vocabulary onto the Lacanian corpus without pondering over semantic nuances and without including the original French terms. The best-known example of such normalizing practice concerns the translations of Lacan's essay *'Le stade du miroir'* (1966a [1949]), which are also particularly relevant for pinpointing the sources of the Lacanian self. Around the time of Wilden's *The Language of the Self*, an English translation of *'Le stade du miroir'* by Jean Roussel appeared in 'New Left Review' under the title 'The Mirror-phase' (Lacan 1968 [1949]). Like Wilden, Roussel not only grappled with the complexity of Lacan's grammar, but also with the excess of technical terms. Merely with reference to the psychic functions and structures involved during the child's mirror-stage experience, Lacan utilised some fifteen different terms in the space of barely ten pages: *je, sujet, être, moi, individu, homme, organisme, identité, conscience, je-idéal, ça, je-spéculaire, je-social, personnalité, imago,* and *corps*. On the whole, Roussel translated Lacan's cornucopia of terms accurately and consistently, with one notable exception: wherever Lacan used *moi*, he endorsed the lingua franca and opted for 'ego' instead of the perfectly adequate yet psychoanalytically uncommon 'me'.

Most of Lacan's subsequent English translators have taken this equivalence between *moi* and 'ego' for granted, despite its resulting in the disappearance of important textual differentiations. For example, in the widely referenced English translation of Lacan's 'Rome Discourse' by Alan Sheridan, the unglossed substitution of 'ego' for *moi* deprives the reader of the opportunity to discover Lacan's simultaneous usage of *moi* and 'ego' as non-interchangeable concepts—sometimes in one and the same paragraph—and introduces a series of peculiar incongruities. Consider the following fragment from the 'Rome Discourse', in which Lacan reiterated the gist of his article on 'The Mirror Stage' (1977a [1949]):

> If the subject did not rediscover in a regression—often pushed right back to the 'mirror stage'—the enclosure of a stage in which his ego contains its imaginary exploits, there would hardly be any assignable limits to the credulity to which he must succumb in that situation. And this is what makes our responsibility so formidable when, along with the mythical manipulations of our doctrine, we bring him one more opportunity to alienate himself, in the decomposed trinity of the ego, the superego, and the id, for example. (Lacan 1977b [1953]: 70-71)

Some dubious choices of words aside, the major flaw of this passage relates to the fact that in the first sentence Lacan wrote *moi* instead of 'ego', and that he explicitly separated *moi* from 'ego' in the second sentence, the latter term belonging to an 'alienating conceptual trinity'.

Lacan never intended his *moi* to be the equivalent of the 'ego' as it had been described within the Anglo-American appropriations of Freudian theory, and more particularly within the then dominant ego psychology paradigm of psychoanalysis spearheaded by Heinz Hartmann. In Hartmann's account of mental life, the ego is an 'organ of adaptation' which possesses a conflict-free sphere, that develops to a large extent autonomously under the influence of learning and maturation, and which analysts may embrace as their ally during psychoanalytic treatment (Hartmann 1958 [1939], 1964 [1950]). During the early 1950s Lacan debunked every single aspect of Hartmann's depiction of the ego, arguing that it did not tally with Freud's conception of the *Ich* (Lacan 1988a [1953-54]: 24-25), and that Freud had never considered a conflict-free zone, much less the autonomous development of the *Ich's* functions (Lacan 1988b[1954-55]: 11-12). Since this is the general tone of Lacan's discussion, why would he model the *moi* on the characteristics of the 'ego'? Why would he first dismantle the central value of a popular psychoanalytic concept and then re-introduce it through the back door under a different guise? From 'The Mirror Stage' (1977a [1949]) onwards, Lacan emphasised the dialectical origin and permanently conflictual status of the *moi*, whilst vehemently disputing its role as the analyst's clinical companion. By rendering Lacan's *moi* as 'ego', the singularity of his notion thus vanishes and a central part of his argument is being reabsorbed by the hegemonic discourse of the psychoanalytic establishment.

If Lacan's translators are to some degree accountable for the proliferation of psychoanalytic materials on his 'theory of the ego', they cannot be charged with fostering the mirage of the Lacanian self. To the best of my knowledge, within the entire body of Lacan's texts available in English (Nobus 2000: 214-224) *moi* has been rendered as 'self' on only two occasions, at a point when the practice of translating *moi* as 'ego' must have left the translators agape. At the start of his first public seminar on 'Freud's Papers on Technique', Lacan gauged Otto Fenichel's ideas on the ego in 'Problems of Psychoanalytic Technique' (1941), telling his audience that '[t]he issue is knowing whether the meaning of the ego exceeds the self [*moi*]' (Lacan 1988a [1953-54]:16). Here, 'self' is clearly a desperate move to ensure that Lacan's phrase makes sense, yet it is a rather extraordinary option in light of the fact that John Forrester knew very well that 'self' is the standard translation for *soi* (Lacan 1988a [1953-54]: 135) and that he had a good alternative in the word 'me'. In addition to this passage in Lacan's *Seminar I*, there is an interesting paragraph in his *Seminar VII* (Lacan 1992 [1959-60]) where Lacan broached the etymology of the French word *même*, which can mean 'self', as in *moi-même* (myself), or 'same', as in *la même chose* (the same thing). Lacan pointed out that *même* derives phonetically from the Latin *metipsemus*, which refers to 'that which is most myself in myself, that which is at the heart of myself, and beyond me [*moi*], insofar as the self [*moi*] stops at the level of those walls to which one can apply a label' (Lacan 1992 [1959-60]: 198). When translating this fragment, Dennis Porter must have realised that Lacan's remarks on the origin of the French colloquialism *moi-même*, which has a perfect equivalent in the English 'myself', did not warrant the replacement of *moi* by the technical term 'ego'. Yet his decision to render *moi* as 'me' and 'self' in the space of one sentence makes the argument completely nonsensical. For Lacan's whole point is that the *même* (self) in *moi-même* (myself) is superfluous inasmuch as beyond the *moi* (me) there is nothing but a void: 'What in French (but also in English) at least serves to designate the notion of self or same (*même*), then, is this interior or emptiness, and I don't know if it belongs to me or to nobody' (Lacan 1992 [1959-60]: 198). In other words, it is not the self (*même*), but the me (*moi*) which functions as a psychic wall to which labels can be attached; the interior, core self behind the wall of the me only exists as a central abyss.

Unlike Lacan's translators, his Anglo-American interpreters have been relentless in reading the self into his theory. As mentioned previously, the sources fall into two broad categories: those in which the self is held to be synonymous with one of the concepts Lacan used to capture the psychic structure, and those in which the theoretical congruities between Lacanian psychoanalysis and Kohut's Self Psychology purportedly justify the creation of a 'Lacanian self'. Within the first category, an additional distinction can be made between authors who promote the self as a conceptual alternative to the Lacanian ego (*moi*), and those who consider the self to be on a par with the Lacanian subject (*sujet*). I will briefly exemplify the accounts within each of these categories, demonstrating how they have contributed to the spurious advancement of the Lacanian self.

The equivalence of the self and the ego in Lacanian theory, and more specifically in Lacan's representation of the mirror-stage, has been defended by numerous scholars in a plethora of papers and books. For the sake of brevity, I will restrict myself to two examples from the works of well-respected academics. In *The Self and its Pleasures*, Carolyn J. Dean contended that Lacan's conception of the mirror-stage revolutionised the existing psychoanalytic interpretations of the emergence of the ego, including those championed by Freud, owing to its emphasis on the determining factor of misrecognition:

> The infant's 'self', or ego, is thus not innate but constructed...
> through its identification with an other, in this case, through the
> reified gaze in whose reflection it... misrecognizes its self. It is
> this misrecognition (the taking of itself for a unified entity) that
> constitutes identity, this fantasy of wholeness that constitutes the
> reality of selfhood, this self-alienation that, paradoxically, consti-
> tutes the self. (Dean 1992: 50-51)

Whereas the inverted commas at the beginning of this citation convey a sense of inadequacy in the translation of ego as self, the rest of the paragraph takes away every remaining doubt about the centrality of the self in Lacan's description of the mirror-stage. Of course, if there is one term which did not feature within the intricate jungle of different notions Lacan presented in his mirror-stage paper it is the self (*soi*), yet Dean did not seem to be bothered by this.

A similar perspective on Lacan's mirror-stage paper has been offered by Anthony Elliott in his much acclaimed *Social Theory and Psychoanalysis in Transition*. Glossing Lacan's concept of the imaginary, Elliott claimed:

> It is a realm of being in which the division between subject and
> object does not exist. In fact Lacan claims that from this imagi-
> nary merging of self and other it is possible to redramatize the
> genesis of the ego. Concerning this emergence of the self, Lacan
> contends that narcissistic identifications enable the formation of
> selfhood, that a primordial alienation characterizes the subjec-
> tive process, and that 'lack' structures all self-other relations.
> (Elliott 1992: 125)

Elliott's explanation is at once more sophisticated and less accurate than Dean's. Apart from equating the self and the ego, he extrapolated the meaning of the Lacanian self to incorporate what he denoted as 'the subjective process', whose action stands in opposition to that of the object and the other. Nonetheless, he was as confident as Dean in his interpretation of Lacan's mirror-stage as the paradigmatic experience for the social construction of the self.

Both authors not only take the ego to be the equivalent of Lacan's *moi*, they also crucially fail to acknowledge that the self had originally been introduced into psychoanalytic theory in contradistinction to the ego. In his seminal 1950 paper on ego psychology, Hartmann put the necessity for such a conceptual separation high on the agenda, 'In analysis a clear distinction between the terms ego, self, and personality is not always made. But a differentiation of these concepts is essential if we try to look consistently at the problems in the light of Freud's structural psychology' (Hartmann 1964 [1950]: 127). Hartmann believed that in Freud's 1923 structural theory (Freud 1923)—the second topography consisting of the psychic components of the id, ego and superego—the ego was regularly utilised with reference to the person(ality), and not as the name of a psychic substructure. Hartmann agreed to maintain the term ego as the designation of a specific mental organisation, proposing the new term self as a more appropriate typification for those instances in which the ego represents the whole person, as when the relationship with external objects is at stake. Therefore, the 'opposite of object cathexis is not ego cathexis, but cathexis of one's own person, that is, self-cathexis; in speaking of self-cathexis we do not imply whether this cathexis is situated in the id, ego, or superego. This formulation takes into account that we actually do find "narcissism" in all these psychic systems; but in all of these cases there is opposition to (and reciprocity with) object cathexis' (Hartmann 1964 [1950]: 127).

In aligning the self with the ego in their accounts of Lacan's mirror-stage, Dean and Elliott thus commit a dual error. First of all they assume that Lacan's paper deals with the imaginary constitution, or rather construction of the ego, in the accepted ego psychology meaning of the term as the organising system in the mind and the hallmark of one's identity. In fact, Lacan explicitly repudiated the reduction of any of his notions, and especially the me (*moi*), to this synthesizing function, since he did not consider such a conflict-free component to be operative in a consistent fashion. Secondly, they rely on the identity of the ego and the self, through which they betray not so much the Lacanian spirit as the ego psychology constellation under which the self was born.

Other researchers have rediscovered the self in Lacan's notion of the (split) subject. Instead of an imaginary construct, the Lacanian self accordingly functions as an unstable, decentred agency whose features are determined by the linguistic flow of signifiers. This symbolic Lacanian self has gained ascendancy as a staple of postmodernist feminist writing on (gendered) subjectivity. This does not imply that all feminist authors are ready to endorse Lacanian psychoanalysis. Applauding Lacan's critique of the integrated individual and his concurrent insistence on subjective fragmentation, feminist theorists such as Flax (1990) and Chodorow (1978a, 1994) have argued that the Lacanian self surreptitiously reinvokes the traditional dominance of masculinity, since it derives its existence from a symbolic order whose cornerstone is the quintessentially male signifier of the phallus. Or, as Flax put it, 'Despite his heroic self-image as a brave Nietzschean negator of bourgeois culture, elucidating our primal alienation and fractured selves, Lacan replicates rather than dismantles a dominant strain of modern Western thought extending from Descartes through Sartre... An incomplete and stereotypically masculine form of self is posited as the unalterable linchpin in the chain of signifiers said to constitute culture' (Flax 1990: 107).

The topic of this paper does not allow for an extensive discussion of the extent to which these critical assessments of the Lacanian self are valid. Suffice it to say that the feminists' critique of Lacan is not an artefact of their prior substitution of the self for the subject, and needs to be situated within the broader context of their long-standing 'struggle with psychoanalysis' (Buhle 1998). Exchanging the subject for the self is not a precondition for challenging Lacan's ideas on subjectivity from a feminist point of view. The introduction of the Lacanian self stands quite apart from the feminist portrayal of his work as a well-disguised campaign for the subsistence of patriarchal values, and corresponds to a different need. Unfortunately, few authors have acknowledged that the self does not belong to the same semantic tradition as the subject, and even fewer have reflected upon the reasons behind the conceptual replacement. One of the exceptions is Jessica Benjamin, who conceded that it is important to 'retain some notion of the subject as a self, a historical being that preserves its history in the unconsciousness, whatever scepticism we allow about reaching the truth of that history' (Benjamin 1995: 13). I will return to Benjamin's point further in my text, when charting the possible motives for the Lacanian self.

In what is meant to be a definitive statement on the nature of the Lacanian self, Socor (1997) has recently combined the two previous approaches—the self as ego, and the self as subject—with a panoply of supplementary glosses. Without blushing, Socor distinguished between not less than eight 'central organizing principles of the Lacanian self'. In succession, the Lacanian self is (i) an imaginary self; (ii) a presocial entity; (iii) a case of mistaken identity; (iv) an alienated self; (v) a divided subject; (vi) an (unconsciously) spoken self; (vii) a located self able to recognise itself; and (viii) the recognition of the self as absence (Socor 1997: 198-199.) It is rather shocking to observe that the writer of a book on presence and absence in psychoanalysis seems to have an extraordinary talent for transforming a radical conceptual absence into a pervasive presence. Contrary to one of her organising principles of the Lacanian self, Socor evidently refused to recognise the self as an absence: all the notions which Lacan had conjured up, although perhaps not always as rigorously as one would have wanted, in his paper on the mirror-stage (1977a [1949]), and much more, were harmoniously corralled into the catch-all term of the self.

As stated above, there is a second category of sources on the Lacanian self, which take their bearings from a perceived congruence between Lacanian psychoanalysis and Kohut's Self Psychology. This correspondence may surprise, since Kohut's viewpoints on psychic functioning and the premises of psychoanalytic practice are in many respects the opposite of Lacan's. Whereas Kohut (1978 [1959]) emphasised his view that analysts should never underestimate the power of empathy and introspection, Lacan was adamant that explaining and understanding, in whatever form, are anathema to proper psychoanalytic interpretation (Lacan 1988a [1953-54]: 73; 1993 [1955-56]: 22; 1994 [1956-57]: 341). Whereas Kohutian therapy seeks the reconstitution of the functioning self (Kohut 1977: 209), Lacanian psychoanalysis is geared towards subjective destitution (Lacan 1995 [1967]: 8). And whereas language, fantasy, desire and enjoyment (*jouissance*) are the structuring components of the human mind in Lacanian theory (Lacan 1998 [1957-58]: 261-317), Kohut's model of the psychic personality hinges on narcissism, idealised parental imagos, frustration, skills, talents, and self-esteem (Kohut 1984).

Despite these key incompatibilities, especially highlighted by Lacanians (Laurent and Schneiderman 1977, Cottet 1985), Lacan and Kohut have also been painted as kindred spirits partly because of their common defiance of the psychoanalytic establishment. Presumably this explains why Lacanians have continued to express an interest in Kohut's work (Miller 1987, NN 1996). In a new critical reading of Kohut's case of Mr. Z (Kohut 1990 [1979]), John P. Muller expertly summarised the principal points of convergence between the Lacanian and the Kohutian approach:

> Not only did their lives overlap, both dying in 1981, but their work too, shows remarkable correspondences, at least at first glance. Both were practising analysts who drew upon their own experience to offer a reformist critique of mainstream psychoanalysis, especially of ego psychology. Both criticize making the ego the criterion for truth and reality, Kohut by focusing on a comprehensive notion of 'self' and Lacan by elaborating the 'subject of the unconscious'. Both men emphasize disintegration anxiety and put mirroring phenomena in the forefront... Both challenge the accepted notion of the patient's 'resistance' and instead stress the clinical importance of recognition. Both criticize the kind of training provided by psychoanalytic institutes... In their overall characterization of contemporary existence, both Kohut and Lacan use the figure of 'tragic man'. Finally, although both openly operated from a reformist position, each stressed his proper orthodoxy. (Muller 1996: 135-136)

At once detailed and comprehensive, Muller's survey shows that Lacan and Kohut have indeed more in common that one is led to believe on the basis of a mere comparison of their terminology. Yet Muller is not only accurate in his presentation of the similarities, he is also careful not to conflate Kohut's self and Lacan's subject (of the unconscious), thus avoiding the conceptual trap in which many an Anglo-American commentator on Lacanian psychoanalysis has fallen. To give but one recent example, in a wide-ranging study of the history of psychoanalysis on both sides of the Atlantic, Schwartz has taken the vehement critique of ego psychology in both Lacan's and Kohut's intellectual trajectories as a sufficient argument in support of the exchangeability of the self and the subject. According to Schwartz, '[t]he self in Anglophone psychoanalysis was the missing subject that Lacan made the centrepiece of his system in France' (Schwartz 1999: 259). Of course, the Kohutian self is as much affected by a split as the Lacanian subject—if not more, since Kohut at one stage theorised the self as split off vertically *and* horizontally from the disavowed and unconscious contents of the personality respectively. (Kohut 1971, Siegel 1996: 86-103) However, unlike the Lacanian split subject, which signals the very absence of mental control on the level of the unconscious, the Kohutian self is characterised by cohesion, strength and harmony, and operates alternatively as a centre of initiative, a recipient of impressions, and a spatially cohesive and temporally continuous structure (Kohut 1984: 99).

Now that the various sources of the Lacanian self have been mapped, it is time to investigate the motives from which they derive their vigour. Who or what is responsible for the erroneous discovery of this prodigy? Why have so many authors—historians, feminists, literary scholars and psychoanalysts alike—contributed to the creation and maintenance of a conceptual illusion? And why have such divergent Lacanian notions as the me (*moi*) and the subject collapsed so swiftly into an idea that is as pragmatically encompassing as it is semantically empty? Alongside these pressing issues, I shall also attempt to answer the question as to why Lacan repudiated the self, thus addressing the topic of this essay more directly.

The salvos of the self

The proliferation of the self in contemporary interpretations of Lacanian theory could first of all be explained with reference to the ubiquity of the notion in the Anglo-Saxon world, not only as a technical term or a smidgen of disciplinary jargon, but also as a word in everyday language. As Spruiell has noted: '*Self* is a necessary word, used every day, a noun related to the pronouns, employed most often as an adjective and as a prefix. It cannot be avoided in ordinary discourse, not even by psychoanalysts or philosophers' (Spruiell 1995: 421).

It is difficult to disagree with this statement, inasmuch as the word 'self' is indeed so prominent in the English language that it would definitely be odd if somebody never used it in colloquial conversation, whatever his or her socioeconomic status, religion, education and profession. However, as Spruiell pointed out, 'self' is in most cases used as an adjective and a prefix, and examples are provided in every English dictionary, ranging from self-abuse to self-will. Its use as a noun is much less common, and some sociolinguists might even feel inclined to argue that the extent to which 'self' appears as a noun in somebody's discourse counts as a marker, i.e. reveals something about his or her social background and professional activities. Put differently, whereas the self as an adjective or prefix is so customary that it only becomes conspicuous when someone does *not* use it, its substantiation is noticeable in itself and immediately situates someone's discourse within a specific sociocultural framework. Even if the person in question knows nothing about the psychology of William James, the symbolic interactionism of George Herbert Mead, or the self-psychology of Heinz Kohut, his or her employment of 'the self' as a synonym for social identity, human agency, consciousness or personality betrays the discourse's allegiance, implicitly or explicitly, to one or more of these intellectual "sources of the self"' (Taylor 1989).

Claiming that the Lacanian self originates in a linguistic inevitability surely needs to be put into the right perspective. Whilst Anglo-American professionals cannot really avoid using 'self' as an adjective or prefix, much less as a pronoun—just as much as Lacan himself (sic) could not always refrain from using *soi* in this way—they can surely prevent themselves from utilising it as a noun, especially when they belong to the psychoanalytic profession, where the significance of the self has probably been more debated than anywhere else (Levin 1969, Mitterauer and Pritz 1978, Spruiell 1981, Blum 1982, Rangell 1982). Thus, the emergence of the Lacanian self in the professional literature must be accounted for by other than purely linguistic turns.

Does it stem from profound ignorance? Isn't the substitution of the self for the Lacanian me (via the ego) and/or the subject in many academic texts an indication of the fact that their authors not only lack knowledge of Lacan's conceptual apparatus, but also of divergent theoretical strands in the history of psychoanalysis? Is the mistake simply due to intellectual blindness, a not uncommon disease amongst researchers who have been working too long within the narrow confines of one theoretical paradigm? Aren't the specialists, or rather the over-specialised authorities in the field, also those who are most ignorant of the broader context, and therefore most likely to make errors of judgement?

From this angle, it is interesting to observe that the Lacanian self has been recognised by both psychoanalysts and 'lay-people', Object Relations theorists as well as Lacanians, feminists and mainstream authors alike. Indeed, despite the connotations of the concept that they so ardently seek to defend, the 'Selvation' army does not really have a distinct identity. Relying on the above principle that degrees of ignorance increase with levels of specialisation, it is maybe not surprising that some orthodox Lacanians have equalled—with some reservations, I have to admit—the subject, the ego and the self (Ragland-Sullivan 1986: 1-67), or have argued that one 'should resist translating *moi* as "self" or "identity"' (Ragland 1995: 9) only to retain subsequently the notion of the self between inverted commas (Ragland 1995: 12). Yet, still in line with the above principle, it is perhaps more surprising that less dogmatic psychoanalytic psychotherapists such as Joseph Schwartz (who is actually a physicist turned psychotherapist turned historian), also shamelessly align the Lacanian subject with the Kohutian self (Schwartz 1999: 258-259). If it is true that ignorance follows in the footsteps of the accumulation of specialised knowledge, and those who have not committed themselves to one particular discipline or action plan—feminist literary scholars with an interest in psychoanalysis such as Gallop (1982), or sociologists working on the history of psychology and psychiatry such as Rose (1996)—have also conjured up the Lacanian self, the conclusion is that ignorance cannot explain the notion's inception and dissemination. Furthermore, multidisciplinary scholars have been much more influential than sectarian psychoanalysts in promoting the Lacanian self, so the counter-argument that the ignorant intimates may still be responsible for the notion's popularity really does not hold.

Over and above the linguistic and epistemological motives, I wish to entertain what I believe to be a much more powerful ideological dynamic behind the redemption of the Lacanian self. Traditionally, the term self has always been associated with ideas of identity, individuality, autonomy, personal liberty, freedom of choice, and consciousness. Long before social scientists started to conceptualise the self at the end of the nineteenth century, the western world was infatuated with these ideas, not only in the realms of moral philosophy, ethics and political science (Taylor 1989), but also in medicine and within general healing practices (Porter 1997: 7). Now, with the advent of the modern risk society (Beck 1992), and its associated feelings of ontological insecurity and existential anxiety, individuality has become so problematic that people are in need of rebuilding a healthy 'self-identity' (Giddens 1991). It is no longer sufficient for people to have a self; they need to be capable of experiencing this self as belonging to themselves, as being one and the same, and as offering a solid basis for building their personal future in a world characterised by socioeconomic globalisation and individual fragmentation.

When Hartmann and some of his European colleagues arrived as refugees in the United States during the late 1930s and early 1940s, they particularly welcomed an already existing tendency towards the integration of psychoanalysis and psychology, which entailed a more sustained emphasis on the ego as the seat of personal autonomy and psychic integrity (Hale 1995: 231-244). Like so many other immigrants, Hartmann *cum sui* must have felt shattered by the experiences of the Second World War. Thus promotion of ego psychology and its therapeutic goals of individuation and re-adaptation was perfectly suited to alleviate the worries of everyday life, both personal ones and those stemming from the environment into which they had just settled. Although the self was originally introduced into psychoanalytic theory to solve a conceptual problem in Freud's explanation of narcissism, it simultaneously constituted the intellectual backdrop against which new identities, liberties and autonomies could be manufactured (Freud 1914a, Hartmann 1964 [1950]: 127-128).

In my view, the re-emergence of the self into the Anglo-American appropriations of Lacanian theory also bears witness to a fundamental longing for the maintenance of psychic mastery—a craving which is as private as it is political, as personal as it is ideological. Of course, this yearning is less instilled by the ravages of an international conflict, but it is being fuelled continuously by the perceived elusiveness of our virtual society, the assumed disintegration of important moral values such as friendship and trust, and ever more strenuous professional requirements of quality, performance and flexibility. What the 'Lacanian self' reflects is a deeply felt need to uphold a sense of personal conscious control, a feeling that human beings can and must play an active part in the shaping of their own destinies. Psychoanalysts are as susceptible to these issues as the average citizen, as is exemplified by the above quoted passage from Benjamin (1995). Although Benjamin is not at all sure that it is possible to reveal the truth of a historically continuous self, she nonetheless believes that the self should be safeguarded from the ethereal dimension of postmodern subjectivity.

Lacan, for his part, never considered the self to be a valuable notion for psychoanalysis. In Lacan's view, all the aforementioned connotations of the self should be exposed as neurotic illusions, and the degree to which human beings are convinced that they possess a strong identity is more indicative of psychosis than anything else. During the early 1950s, Lacan even went so far as to say that the strong personality which ego psychologists were so keen to (re)build in their clients is not much different from the unshakeable identity of the psychotic. He substantiated his point with one of Lichtenberg's famous aphorisms, 'A madman who imagines himself a prince differs from the prince who is in fact a prince only because the former is a negative prince, while the latter is a negative madman. Considered without their sign, they are alike' (Lacan 1977b [1953]: 109, note 52).

In Lacanian theory, neither the me nor the (split) subject are indebted to the arena of the self. On the one hand, the me 'is structured exactly like a symptom... it is only a privileged symptom, the human symptom *par excellence*, the mental illness of man' (Lacan 1988a [1953-54]: 16). On the other hand, the me has no depth, since it encompasses a series of imaginary identifications which revolve around the initial identification with the equal other in the mirror. In reference to Freud (1923: 29-30), Lacan contended that the me is a mental component that 'is constructed like an onion, one could peel it and discover the successive identifications which have constituted it' (Lacan 1988a [1953-54]: 171). But behind all these identifications there is no essential core, no central nucleus, no anchored true identity. The me does not operate as part of a larger 'self', nor does it shield a hidden self. It is but a surface or wall behind which there is nothing to be found.

The Lacanian (split) subject of the unconscious is even less tributary to the self than the Lacanian notion of the me. Whatever the term 'subject' may suggest, the subject of the unconscious is basically an absence, through which Lacan endeavoured to grasp the lack of subjective control somebody has over his or her unconscious thought processes. The subject of the unconscious represents the absent knower behind the unconscious knowledge, as a result of which there is no such thing as a unitary, self-fulfilled subject (Lacan 1977c [1960]: 293-295). Therefore, I (as a subject) can in principle never be or coincide with myself, unless the subject of the unconscious is cancelled out, all nonsense disappears, and psychosis looms on the horizon again. I cannot prove to myself that I am (Lacan 1977c [1960]: 317), and it is even less possible to say 'I am the one who am', which would probably bring me close to God, were it not for the fact that this God, who 'affirms himself as identical to Being leads to a pure absurdity' (Lacan 1990 [1963]: 85).

In conclusion, within Lacan's theory of psychoanalysis the me has all the qualities of a flat screen and the subject of the unconscious all the characteristics of an absence. When the me is replaced by the self, an illusory whole (the person) is substituted for an imaginary part (the

me)—in a process that could be designated as an inverted metonymy—
and depth is substituted for surface. When the self replaces the subject
of the unconscious, something missing in the body of Lacan's theory
comes to occupy the place of what is missing, of the central lack, in his
conception of the mind. In this way, a conceptual lack (the self) paradoxically covers up and gives presence to a fundamental psychic lack,
which represents the desubjectified influence of the unconscious. In
other words, the 'Selvation army' transforms the conceptual presence
and mental absence of the Lacanian subject into the conceptual absence
and mental presence of the Lacanian self; a conceptual absence (the
self) thus serves as the basis for endowing a mental absence (the subject) with new presence. Lacan's conflictual model of the mind consequently appears with a new consistent selvage, which not only protects
the many loose ends of his account against too much ravelling, but also
satisfies the contemporary needs for individuality and autonomy.
Whatever the merits of this adventure, if Lacanian theory is worth sal-
vaging the selvages of the self will have to be dissolved.

Note

[1] All translations of texts for which there is no published English version are my own.

'THAT'S JUST NOT ME AT ALL'—THE DIFFERING SELVES OF POST-STRUCTURALISM AND PSYCHOANALYSIS

Colleen Heenan

Freud's idea that the self was an unknown quantity posed an episte-mological challenge to a society characterised by humanist beliefs of humans as rational, aware beings who knew about and were in charge of their thoughts and actions. However, while Freud proposed devel-oping a 'science of the mental unconscious' (Freud 1916-17), postmod-ern and post-structural thinking critiques many psychoanalytic truths and structures central to psychotherapy. While some would argue that postmodern and psychoanalytic theory are antithetical (Rose 1990), others such as Flax (1990, 1993) not only suggest compatibility between some concepts but also that each have something to learn from the other.

In this chapter, I suggest there is much to gain from exploring the sometimes overlapping, yet often contradictory concerns of post-struc-turalism and psychoanalysis with understanding the 'self' and the con-struction of meaning. Deconstructing clinical material facilitates awareness of the discursive process of psychotherapy, wherein the clinician is inevitably bound by the historical, cultural and gendered specificities of its practices (Rose 1990, Parker 1997). Rather than revealing truths hidden within the psyche, I suggest the practitioner *constructs* notions of the self. However, while advocating the impor-tance of understanding how the self is socially constituted, I do not abandon a belief in the existence of unconscious processes. Moreover, I part company with the post-structuralist notion that, because the self is constructed through language, it is lacking in agency, arguing that understanding agency requires using concepts from both psychoana-lytic and post-structural thinking. While stating that a post-structural-ist perspective is essential in critiquing psychoanalysis, I suggest retaining some aspects of a psychoanalytic notion of self. However, I would align myself with writers such as Flax (1990, 1993) who distin-guish between a 'core' self and a 'true' self. Flax also makes clear the gender biases inherent within both these traditions.

First, I briefly outline some key ideas within postmodernist and post-structuralist thinking. Next, I make use of excerpts from a psy-chodynamic psychotherapy group for women with eating disorders, in order to demonstrate the potentials of taking a discursive perspective into the clinic room. I offer a strategic deconstructive reading of the text, indicating the epistemological shift required by the clinician in adopting a post-structuralist perspective, examining subjectivities as both discursive and psychodynamic constitutions. I then augment the reading by returning to ideas from psychoanalytic theory, introducing the possibility of combining both perspectives. Finally, I review the complexities and tensions that arise in attempting to amalgamate these apparently incompatible points of view.

While taking a critical stance towards psychoanalysis, I write as a clinician committed to its principles and practice. Both my academic and clinical work has been influenced by both mainstream feminist thinking (see Tong 1989, Butler and Scott 1992), as well as feminist Object Relations theory (Chodorow, 1978a; Benjamin, 1998). My interest in postmodern and post-structural thinking arose from my struggles as a feminist psychotherapist working in a women's therapy service, where I had developed models of therapeutic eating disorder work, incorporating both psychoanalytic and feminist beliefs. I felt disturbed by the ways in which, while psychoanalytic theory had much to offer in terms of understanding both the complexities and fixedness of eating disorders (Farrell, 1995), it continually disregarded the impact of the *social* construction of femininity on unconscious processes. While feminist Object Relations theory offered incisive accounts of the particular cultural and historical constructions of gender subsumed within psychoanalytic portrayals of femininity and masculinity, it failed to fully address the contradictions inherent within its adherence to psychoanalytic notions that the self is *revealed* through clinical material. In summary, both theoretical groups position themselves as capable of exposing truths, rather than as participants in constructions of reality.

Postmodern? Post-structural? Post-what?

This first section briefly introduces readers to some of the concepts central to my discursive critique of psychotherapy. I focus on ideas of the 'self' and of 'truth', as well as language constructing agency. While arguing that psychoanalysis is a discursive project, I suggest there are points of mutual concern between psychoanalysis and postmodernism which can be exploited for the benefit of clinical thinking. This selective exposition of theoretical issues leads to a demonstration of how therapeutic material can be read from a discursive perspective.

*Post*modernist and *post*-structuralist thinking critique core ideas from modernism and structuralism (Hollinger 1994).[1] For instance, the modernist meta-narrative of knowledge and rationality as essential to the attainment of freedom, is embodied by humanist philosophy, which regards the 'self' as a subject of substance, with definable properties. The modern self is seen as a conscious agent, simultaneously an experiencing subject, an 'I', as well as being an object of study. Central to humanist beliefs is the idea that the human subject can produce and elaborate a self in response to its cultural, economic and political context. While the self responds, it also interacts with, and resists its surroundings, through 'free will', or the development of an autonomous ego (Frosh 1991). Thus, while the self develops socially, it also contains an individual 'real' self that, it is believed, can be known about through the application of scientific principles. Accordingly, social sciences such as psychology were developed in order to understand, control and predict human behaviour. Thus, the modern self, 'can be thought of as a psychological structure that contains within it the various processes of mental life; it is implicit in this idea that there is something organised, stable and central about the self, that selfhood comprises a core element of each individual's personality and subjective existence' (Frosh 1991: 2). In contrast, *post*modern perspectives reject 'grand narratives', essentialism and universalism, shifting to local and specific knowledge, in addition to regarding subjectivities as positioned by particularities, as opposed to individual selves. A further difference is postmodernism's disbelief in the idea that explanations for surface events can be found in underlying causes.

Structuralism refers to both a meta-theory and a methodology which is also anti-humanist in its rejection of the agentic subject, and anti-empiricist in its rejection of *observation* as capable of revealing truth (Morrow and Brown 1994). As well as critiquing modernist beliefs, implicit within structuralist thinking is the idea that meaning is both produced from *within* language and fixed by it (Weedon 1987). However, *post*-structuralism challenges the idea that language *fixes* meaning. While meaning is regarded as *constructed* in and through language, at the same time it is contextual and temporary, thus rejecting modernist beliefs in the self as agentic and containing meaning. For instance, Harré (1989) suggests modernist notions of the self are constructed out of *grammatical* reflectiveness. His idea of the 'grammatical self' proposes that individuals come to believe they exist, due to mistaking the *function* of the indexical labels, 'I' and 'me', with the *objects* to which they refer. This conflation is further exacerbated because of the ability to position the self—or for the self to be positioned—as a speaking subject, through taking up 'I' as an *indication* of agency, choice and responsibility.

This 'turn to language', as Parker describes it (1992: xii), introduces further concepts, those of 'discourse' and 'discourse analysis'. The following quote indicates the complexity of these ideas:

> [D]iscourse and discourse analysis is three-dimensional. Any discursive 'event' (i.e. any instance of discourse) is seen as being simultaneously a piece of text, an instance of discursive practice, and an instance of social practice. The 'text' dimension attends to language analysis of texts. The 'discursive practice' dimension, like 'interaction' in the 'text-and-interaction' view of discourse, specifies the nature of the processes of text production and interpretation, for example, which types of discourse (including 'discourses' in the more social-theoretical sense) are drawn upon and how they are combined. The 'social practice' dimension attends to issues of concern in social analysis such as the institutional and organizational circumstances of the discursive event and how that shapes the nature of the discursive practice, and the constitutive/constructive effects of discourse referred to above. (Fairclough, 1992: 4)

Discourse analysts aim to 'facilitate a historical account of psychological knowledge, mount a critique of psychological practice by challenging its truth claims, and require a transformation of our notions of what a good methodology should be like' (Burman and Parker 1993: 9). Embedded within this deconstructive stance is not only a concern with how people use language to construct notions of selves, but how the very notion of a 'self' has come to be constructed. Discourse analysts use the term 'subject', instead of 'self', in order to make clear their 'theoretical approaches which emphasise the way in which the social domain constitutes subjects rather than the other way round' (Henriques et al. 1984: 2). Interest in 'subjectivity' delineates an interest in 'individuality and self-awareness—the condition of being a subject—but understand in this usage that subjects are dynamic and multiple, always positioned in relation to discourses and practices and produced by these—the condition of being a subject' (Henriques et al. 1984: 3). Thus, there is a concern with ways in which people are discursively positioned not only by language but also within wider social discourses. Discourse analysis takes place at both a micro and macro level, 'cover[ing] all forms of spoken interaction, formal and informal, and written texts of all kinds' (Potter and Wetherell 1987: 7), from 'shared patterns of meanings and contrasting ways of speaking', to 'ideological dilemmas' (Billig, in Burman and Parker 1993: 2).

Central to the discourse analytic approach I adopt in the next section are ideas from the postmodern philosopher Michel Foucault (1961, 1972, 1978a, 1978b). Foucault's notion of discourse refers to 'domains of knowledge' (Fairclough 1992: 39), offering an analysis of both how discourses construct society, and how discourses are articulated, through social, or discursive practices. Moreover, the Foucauldian subject is not an agentic 'author of his own story', but is constituted, or *positioned* by his discursive activities or 'statements' such as hypothesising or teaching. Positioning is historically specific as it is constrained by what is discursively available. The question here becomes, 'What position must be occupied by the individual in order to be a subject'? (Fairclough 1992: 44). By asking the question, 'Which social conditions give rise to or make available, particular discourses'? (Burman and Parker, 1993: 3), studies of the individual are not regarded as 'true', only historically and culturally *possible*. Thus, we might ask what made it possible to develop particular notions of the psychoanalysis self.

Foucault suggested that the population of modern societies is managed by means of 'bio-power' (1978a). Techniques of 'bio-power' instil 'self discipline', as opposed to acting as forceful, external oppressions. Practices of 'confession' such as psychotherapy become the sites for moral cleansing and forgiveness. In presenting Foucault's theories on bio-power, Fairclough says, 'If the examination is the technique of objectifying people, the confession is the technique of subjectifying them' (Fairclough 1992: 53).

Psychotherapy and discourse

Foucauldian theorists such as Rose argue that psychotherapy is simply one more technology of subjectivity, constituting *therapeutic* selves, wherein everyday experiences are regarded as 'exemplary and exceptional' (Rose 1990: 244). For the therapeutic self, work is not an exchange of labour for cash rewards but a matter of fulfilment and identity; mundane experiences become 'life events' which are regarded as psychologically meaningful; experiences of life and death become 'part of the work of life itself' (Rose 1990: 245) and interactions become potentially meaningful 'relationships' of varying degrees. Rose argues that the production of selves as psychologically significant constructs and legitimises opportunities for therapeutic intervention.

However, some postmodernists and post-structuralists regard the potential of psychoanalytic theory as residing in its challenge to the notion of the self as unitary and rational (Henriques et al. 1984; Frosh 1987; Flax 1990). 'This is one of the sources of the subversive impact of psychoanalysis: it overturns the western view that the distinguishing mark of humanity is reason and rationality' (Frosh, 1987: 25). Flax delights in the *ambiguities* of Freud's theory, pointing out how his structural model highlights 'heterogeneity, flux and alterity. The distinctions between inner and outer determinants of experience break down' (Flax 1990: 60). Even psychoanalysts such as Ogden remind the reader that the very notion of psychodynamics presupposes that the self is not a static but *dynamic* concept. He suggests psychoanalysis replaces the term 'self' with 'subject' in order to convey its dynamic, reflexive, and semantic state:

> Analysis is not simply a method of uncovering the hidden; it is more importantly a process of *creating* the analytic subject who had not previously existed. For example, the analysand's history is not uncovered, it is *created* in the transference-countertransference and is perpetually in a state of flux as the intersubjectivity of the analytic process evolves and is interpreted by analyst and analysand... In this way, the analytic subject is *created* by, and exists in an ever-evolving state in the dynamic intersubjectivity of the analytic process: the subject of psychoanalysis takes shape in the interpretive space *between* analyst and analysand. (Ogden 1994: 47, my italics)

However, while the psychoanalytic subject is 'always becoming', the frameworks used in psychoanalysis do, in spite of their inconsistencies, seem to carry the weight and authority of truth. The dynamic formulation constructs and constrains a prescribed range of possibilities, a formulation which involves a linear notion of development, thus fixing, for instance, gender 'identity' as primary and thus determining (Butler 1990). Although Ogden (1994) suggests that Freud's use of a linear model reflects his epistemological difficulty in conveying his more dynamic ideas, and that Klein's notion of 'positions' grasps this indeterminacy much better, Flax (1990, 1993) argues that Freud was also committed to Enlightenment models of empiricism and the 'self' as generating meaning. So, while conflicts could not be escaped, change *in the self* could occur through change in the structure of unconscious processes.

In many ways, psychoanalytic theory constructs its therapeutic subject in a similar way to the fragmented, shifting, multiple subject posited in postmodern and post-structuralist strands of thought. As Ogden noted, meanings are temporary constructions and language is the medium for constructing the subject. Frosh reminds us Freud believed that '[l]anguage both expresses the symbolism of the unconscious and is the means of unravelling it. It therefore embodies subjective experience but also provides a route to the source of that experience—the *construction of subjectivity itself'* (Frosh 1989: 136, my italics). And so, we turn to therapeutic text.

From theory to practice

In this section I demonstrate how a discursive analysis of clinical material differs from a psychoanalytic reading. Using two brief clinical extracts, I show the practitioner the usefulness of taking a discursive stance. However, I return to a psychoanalytic perspective, ending with a combined analysis of text. Both perspectives have something to offer clinicians and academics. I then finish the chapter with further discussion of the merits and tensions in adopting a discursive framework for exploring psychoanalysis.

The following extracts come from a project in which I acted as both therapist and researcher. Running a short-term (20 session) feminist psychodynamic eating disorders therapy group for women, I taped and transcribed both clinical and supervisory sessions. I then reflexively analysed selected extracts from the transcripts from a feminist Foucauldian perspective, exploring ideas from postmodern and post-structural thinking; in particular, how psychotherapy (and clinical supervision) is a discursive process, in which 'selves' are not discovered, but constructed. It also appeared evident that there are unconscious aspects of the 'self'. In this chapter, my analyses of the extracts are selective and strategic.

'Putting on a face'

In the following text the group members discuss some of the complex ways in which they negotiate aspects of their selves:

Helen:[2] 'That's like me. I mean I wouldn't use exactly the same words. I asked you about that last week (?) but the person, I mean, that people like—that's not me. That's just not me at all'.

Laura: 'It's just a face'.

Helen: 'Mmm'.

Tina: 'Do other people have that external face'?

(?)[3]: 'Yes, mmm'.

Maureen: 'Nobody that knows me, knows anything about this. They think I'm very outgoing and very, always got something funny to say and always the one-liners. They've no idea really, what's underneath. It's a, it's a defence mechanism that you just present'.

Lyndsay: 'It's like a front that you put up, so that nobody can get past'.

(?) : 'Yes, mmm'.

Lyndsay: 'Somebody said that to me the other day, oh, "You're really, really lucky, you've got a good family" and which is true. "You've got everything going for you, like". If you knew, you wouldn't say that. But, it's because I don't let them, you know. I put this front up that everything's all right and carefree, you know. And they don't know, you just get on with things and inside, you know, bits of you are dying and...'

(?): 'Mmm'

Lyndsay: 'You know, I thought "I just wish you knew". But then, by the same token, they only know if you let them know and it's—you, you can't let them know'.

Within a psychoanalytic discourse, interpreting this material encourages us to focus on the speakers' words as revealing the intricacies of their individual conflicts. The way in which they describe these struggles might lead us to adopt an Object Relations framework (Greenberg and Mitchell 1983), turning to ideas from Fairbairn with respect to the apparently persecutory nature of their internal objects. Lyndsay's evocative description of how 'bits of you are dying' might also direct us towards Winnicott's 'false self', in order to better understand the relation between her psychic and physical starvation. Moreover, given the way in which participants so readily identified with each others' talk about 'that external face', one might want to understand this as aspects of a group phenomenon (Foulkes 1975). One could go on exploring psychoanalytic themes, using language and other processes, as mediums for developing insights into unconscious processes. As the therapist, my interest is in getting as 'true' a psychodynamic account as is possible, making use of my theoretical understanding of the content and process of therapy, in order to offer accurate hypotheses about cause and effect. The better we are all able to understand the individual and the group, the more trusting the emotional atmosphere, then the more likely it is the members will be able to resolve their difficult relationships with food, body size and shape and to change themselves. However, here I want to take a deconstructive stance not simply towards the clinical material, but also towards the situation that made it possible for it to occur.

Taking a discursive approach to this material means approaching these women's 'talk' as ways in which they construct, rather than reveal themselves. As Harré put it, '[t]o be a self is not to be a certain kind of being, but to be in possession of a certain kind of theory' (in Burr 1995: 125). In the previous section, I noted how language constructs through drawing on discourses. A Foucauldian perspective suggests there are discourses 'at work' on this piece of clinical material, both *in* and *on* the text (Parker 1992). In turn, discourse and discursive practices make particular narratives available for use, by particular groups. Given that this is a group of women and that it is women who mainly present with eating disorders, one of the discourses 'at work' on the text would be that of gender. However, in reading the text from a feminist perspective, we would need to ask questions about the subject position of women, or the constraining effect of the gendered discourses at work in the text. For instance, 'How are women positioned by discourses about food, body size and shape'? For example, in contemporary western society, there are particular moral, medical and consumerist discourses about the amount or type of food it is appropriate for women to eat, and the appropriateness, healthiness and appeal of particular body sizes and shapes or lifestyles. These discourses draw on, as well as compete with each other, the effect of which is to make available *certain* subject positions for participants to take up. In deconstructing these, feminist theorists have made clear the gendered discourses which are interwoven within these, constraining as well as constructing notions of, for example, femininity or sexuality, notions which contribute to subjectivity.

Returning to the above piece of text in the context of understanding gendered subjectivities, we might want to re-think how these *women* use the particular 'defence mechanism' of 'putting on a face'. In everyday 'feminine' talk, we might understand this to refer to the way many women apply 'makeup' to their faces, on a daily basis. This ritual could be said to be a gendered enactment of Foucault's (1978a) 'discursive panopticon' (Bartky 1988, Smith 1988). This term refers to the way in which, through the private and public 'disciplinary project[s] of femininity' (Bartky, 1988: 71), women are not only constantly observed but also learn to observe themselves and others without apparent coercion. Moreover, the insidiousness of this discipline is that it provides the means for a sense of accomplishment, of being in control, of identity. For women, an acceptable 'public self' needs to be presented; it seems that the 'private self' requires a cover. But are these 'external faces' solely performative?

A further discourse which appears to be 'at work' on the text is that of psychoanalysis. The women's notions of selves draw on psychoanalytic repertoires of selves as 'public' and 'private', 'active' and 'passive', selves which can be 'split'; ways of knowing about the self which have come to be regarded as 'common sense' (Rose, 1990; Parker, 1997). At one level, it does seem that there is, for these women, an agentic self who can 'put on an external face'. As soon as Helen starts to talk about 'that person whom people like', as not being her (although she is referring to herself), the others appear to immediately understand what she is saying, and offer their 'hidden faces' for examination. Not surprisingly, given the strength of modernist and psychoanalytic discourses of uniqueness and privacy, at least one woman (Tina) is surprised to find that she is not alone in 'putting on a face'. The ability of these 'external faces' to speak and act *for* the individual women suggests conscious intention or agency and Maureen indicates that 'it's a defence mechanism'. The 'face' functions to protect both themselves and others from their 'inner' selves, whatever these may be. Both Maureen and

Lyndsay make it clear that 'it' is the eating disorder, which 'nobody that knows me, knows anything about'. At the same time, Lyndsay also seems to equate the eating disorder with 'the bits of her dying inside'. However, the 'external face' appears to be entrapping, 'bits of Lyndsay are *dying* inside'. She is ambivalent about letting others know about her *dying* self—her thinness isn't acute enough to warrant another's immediate concern—but is also unable to speak through the front: 'you *can't* let them know'.

This metaphor of the 'external face' illustrates some of the similarities between Foucault's notion of discourse, and the notion of defence mechanisms in psychoanalysis; the ability to talk *about* defences can invoke a sense of agency (Harré, in Burr, 1995). However, at the same time, the defences are acting upon the person, constituting them, or 'talking' for them. While they can seem to be *conscious* choices— 'putting up a front'—this particular defence (not just of 'putting on a face', but of eating disorders) does not appear to be one chosen through 'free will', but arises out of contemporary western discourses about femininity and appearance. The defence thus subjectifies the women, both in constituting and in tying them to identities. Here, I think the unconscious processes of splitting and projection, and of Winnicott's 'false' self, are more apt than Foucault in explaining the tenacity of an 'external face', behind which 'bits are dying'. There is an internal life and death battle. The battle is partly to find what's 'behind the face', but also to find the appropriate *words* requires articulation. This not only constructs but also makes the self public; speaking the words belies the self on a number of levels.

Finally, we could briefly inquire what social conditions make it possible for me to both run a therapy group for, and carry out a research project on, a group of women patients. Further, how am I able to speak about them with authority, from my position as a therapist and as a researcher, as an identifiable 'group'? How is it that they have apparently willingly taken up positions as clients? Here, it could be understood that therapy is the 'confessional', promising salvation through self-awareness (Rose, 1990). The women can reveal their problems, be absolved of blame, and become 'better' women; that is, without eating disorders but with rational insight. Adopting the position of 'eating disordered therapy patients' perpetuates the notion that the cause of their problems is in them—an individual pathology. Moreover, my position as a therapist also contributes to reproducing and thus maintaining this notion. As such, while I might argue that a *feminist* psychoanalytic understanding of the gendered and socially constructed nature of eating disorders may better grasp the complexities and tensions of the discourses 'at work' on women, at the same time, psychological accounts could be read as perpetuating the 'depoliticising' of feminism, by focusing on individuals, as opposed to societal change (Kitzinger and Perkins 1993).

Articulating the self involves constructing an agentic self. However, in the next extract it becomes clear that agency requires some formed sense of self as a sexed and gendered person.

'I don't feel like I'm anything'

While some of the women could 'put on a face', in the following extract Laura struggles with her identity. She talks about her very difficult relationship with her parents:

> *Laura*: They'd had two girls already and he wanted you know, the last one to be a boy but he wasn't so he tried to turn *me* into one and he *nearly succeeded* and that's what I feel like now. *I don't feel like I'm anything*. I don't feel like I'm a boy or a girl or a woman or a man or anything. *I feel nothing. I'll never get married* 'cause I don't, I don't feel nothing. I don't feel nothing for nobody, except my dad, that's it. I feel nothing for nobody. I *think* I love my mum but not like my dad. I *don't respect my* mum. I'm not sure I really like her but I love her—I think 'cause she's my mum.[4]

Within a psychoanalytic discourse, Laura's talk about herself reveals a fundamental concern, an uncertainty as to whether or not she has a 'self'. Further, she makes it clear that having a sense of self requires being *gendered*. We might want to turn again to Winnicott's 'true' and 'false' self, and wonder whether Laura has had to sacrifice gender identity in order to defend herself against her father's disappointment. While she states, 'I don't feel like I'm anything', earlier on, she refers to herself as 'he' (in saying that her father wanted 'the last one to be a boy but *he* wasn't', she is referring to herself). Moreover, Laura seems to be unable to risk allowing herself to experience any emotions—she repeats a number of times, 'I feel *nothing*', and *'nothing for nobody'*—unless they are feelings about her *father*. Her lack of respect for her mother may indicate some dis-identification with her as a woman—one who is unable to produce the boy that her father desired.

Given the context of the eating disorder group, it is crucial to consider the function of Laura's differing ways of eating (ranging from starvation to compulsive eating), and differing body sizes (from very under- to very over-weight). Within a feminist Object Relations discourse, they could be regarded as a means of resisting her father's ongoing assault on her developmental and sexed self. She attempts to resist definition through her body, defying its need for food, or filling it with more than it can cope with. However, this gendered resistance comes by *joining in* on the attack on her body/self. She starves her body in an attempt to deny her existence as a woman, then fills her body until it becomes further distorted and swollen, going back and forth between the two extremes. However, it is difficult to regard Laura as having taken control of her life through her eating disorders—even the disorder resists definition.

At one level she *has* taken control, in that she can get her father to stop interfering with her life by stirring up his concern about her very being. If she loses enough weight to warrant hospitalisation, he becomes gentle and encouraging and stops making inordinate demands on her. If she puts on a great deal of weight, he regards her as useless and weak, just like her mother. But it seems that where her actual father leaves off, Laura's 'internal' father takes over, berating her, condemning her, withholding from her, or stuffing her with garbage. Every sign of independent life inside her terrifies her, setting up a punitive, sabotaging dynamic which to her can feel like a welcome relief from independent thoughts and feelings that threaten her attachment to him. However, it isn't clear whether or not the body/self she tries to control is *really* her, or is an embodiment of an internal, demanding and punitive 'mother-object'. Like her father, she treats her woman's body like an 'object' to be manipulated, yet like him, she cannot completely control it, or her. Who or what part of her 'self' is 'in charge' at any one time? Even opting for hospitalisation involves deferring to an external authority.

If we read Laura's clinical material within a discursive framework as 'text', we might see this as another example of how psychoanalytic discourses about identity have entered everyday talk. Further, this extract also exemplifies how this discourse draws on and conflates prevailing discourses and social practices about identity and 'normal' sexual orientation. Thus, Laura presupposes that whatever sex she is, she will be heterosexual, and will get married. Further, the text indicates how therapeutic talk about the 'self' draws on modernist notions of coherency, which in turn includes sexual categorisation. Laura seems to be arguing that to relate to both herself and to others, she needs to belong to a sexual category and belong to some developmental stage— 'boy or girl, woman or man'. Moreover, unless she *is* sexed—'a boy or a girl or a woman or a man', she not only does not 'feel like I'm anything', she feels *nothing*; in addition she feels 'nothing for nobody'. Thus, 'knowing oneself' or relating to others, appears to require knowing one's sex.

Within a post-structuralist perspective, the fact that her father's efforts have left Laura undefined may give cause for celebration, a chance to 'play' with either sex or aspects of gender (Butler, 1993). However, returning to psychoanalytic discourse, Laura's fundamental uncertainty about her identity gives cause for concern. She seems to be a person *desperate* to be discursively constituted—if not, she does not seem to exist. As Flax points out, while Winnicott's notion of 'true' and 'false' selves conjures up images of some underlying self which the practice of psychotherapy will excavate, 'performing the self' requires the ability to suspend certainty (Flax 1990). In turn, this requires some sense of stability, if not coherence about identity, whether one is a therapeutic patient or an academic philosopher. Indeed, while being positioned as a patient may invite particular readings of text which are imbued with discourses about normality and abnormality, as the therapist reading this text and interacting with Laura, I have concerns— and ethical responsibilities—about her ability to 'play' with identity. Like her, I *am* concerned with coherency, albeit a coherency in which she is neither 'positioned' by her father's ideas about identity, nor my own. As such, both Laura and I have a different project in mind than that of either postmodernists or post-structuralists.

In this section, I have taken up the notion of selves as discursively constituted subjectivities, but ones that can also be understood through invoking psychoanalytic discourses. The women seem to have few means to resist how they are positioned through their appearances. Indeed, even the apparently agentic act of 'putting on a face' comes to constitute them in gendered ways, as do their eating disorders. Each acts upon their bodies as means to simultaneously access and transform their 'selves'.

The differing projects of psychoanalysis, postmodernism and post-structural-ism

A discursive analysis of psychotherapy text offers a particular challenge to the therapist. The guidelines for 'reading' the text differ from that of psychoanalytic discourse. However, while this may be of theoretical or political interest to some readers, the practitioner may be forgiven for wondering how this may benefit the patient. My suggestion is that reading therapeutic text from a discursive perspective makes *public* the *private* world of psychotherapy (Heenan 1998). This enables not just the practitioner, but also the patient, to reflect on the various discourses which *position* and thus constrain both psychoanalytic and feminist notions of 'selves'. 'Truths' about the self are not lying inside, waiting to be 'discovered'; instead, they are constructed and reproduced between patient and therapist. While this perspective has been taken up from psychoanalysts working within an intersubjective framework (Ogden 1994, Stolorow et al. 1993), it needs to be understood that psychotherapeutic discourse is also constrained by its historical, social, psychodynamic and gendered discourses. As such, it is not just the *dynamic* process which occurs between the practitioner and patient which *creates* the 'analytic third' (Ogden 1994) but the *discursive* process which *constructs*. The practitioner needs to bear in mind the kind of self which they are constructing *with* the patient, not in terms of theoretical consistency but by considering how they are positioning the patient.

In this final section I briefly review some of the contributions which postmodern and post-structural ideas can make to psychotherapy, while also arguing for the need not to be constrained by these discourses. Two key ideas have come to be associated with postmodern and post-structural thinking—a rejection of the belief in, and possibility of knowing about, coherent, rational selves, plus the suggestion that the self is socially constructed through language and discursive practices. I continue to argue that a more inclusive reading of text requires encompassing a psychoanalytic theory of unconscious processes. In order to demonstrate this, I look at the issues of resistance and agency from both a Foucauldian and a psychoanalytic perspective, as well as one which is gendered. Deconstructing the epistemological foundations of psychoanalytic theory made clear that it drew upon modernist universalistic notions of the self as agentic. From a psychoanalytic perspective however, the self is not the unitary, rational modernist self, but one which is more akin to postmodernist notions of the subject, in that it is 'always becoming', albeit 'becoming' in a linear development. From a Freudian perspective, it is a thoroughly corporeal self, and within the context of the therapeutic material presented, it could be said that the subjectivity of these female patients *embodies* the conflict between modernist and gendered struggles between mind and body. However, the issue is perhaps less to do with rationality and more to do with control. In this vein, Foucault's theory of bio-power and the disciplines of the body are useful in thinking about ways in which the 'practices of femininity' (Bartky 1988) discursively produce gendered subjectivities—and, perhaps, eating disorders (Bordo 1988) through the installation of internal and external 'gendered panopticons'.

With respect to the idea that 'putting on a face' equates with 'donning' an identity, or 'performing' the self, I suggest that understanding the *tenacity* of an 'external face' requires adopting psychoanalytic notions of defence mechanisms such as splitting. Once the persona is in place for any length of time, it is no longer experienced as an agentic act, or positioning, but being 'acted on', or being positioned—or perhaps subjectified, in the Foucauldian sense of being *tied* to an identity. Further, when Laura made clear her need to 'be a self', to have some kind of way to categorise herself in order to develop a subjectivity in which she could relate either to herself, or to others, I suggest that adopting an eating disorder acts as an identity for her, in that it performed different functions which she was unable to either articulate or enact directly. However, it is more than an identity. It is also a defence mechanism which protects her from having 'no self'. Further, what might have been temporary defences—to eat or starve, to pretend—have become, through the accrual of secondary gains, entrenched identities.

Unlike post-structuralists, I would argue that there needs to be a self which is experienced as agentic, in order to perform *other* selves. Otherwise, there is a danger of misreading the celebration of performativity as a romanticisation of distress, or indeed as the equivalent of 'acting out' intrapsychic issues. This discrepancy is exemplified in the contrast between the ways in which, while reading and writing about psychotherapy are reflexive processes, the very fact that you and I as reader and writer, can take up multiple positions in relation to this chapter, shows that we do this by operating within a sense of agency. In contrast, while the women in the therapy group do, at times, experience their eating disorders as functional, it does not equate with a sense of agency in a *meaningful* way. Indeed, they seem to experience their subjectivities as occurring through being *positioned* through the eating disorders. As the therapist, I promote a psychodynamic discourse which also contains feminist elements which encourage the participants to reflect on themselves as agentic, albeit in quite complex and contradictory ways. Both contain pedagogic elements; that is, teaching the group members to think about themselves in particular kinds of ways, especially those that are *meaningful*.

Given that I want to offer a reading of text from the group which draws on both Foucauldian and feminist psychoanalytic theory, it is worth reiterating the differing ways in which the term 'resistance' is used, as it also clarifies the conflict between discursive constitution and unconscious structuring, thus explicating the tensions between the two perspectives. In psychoanalytic theory, 'resistance' refers to the manifestation of defence mechanisms, unconscious strategies which function in differing ways to protect aspects of 'the self' (Bateman and Holmes 1995). As such, eating disorders are understood as complex defences which are manifested in different behavioural strategies—starvation, bingeing and vomiting, compulsive eating—all of which enact *unconscious processes* (different constellations of good and bad Object Relations), concerned with struggles around separation and individuation. Given the ways in which classical Freudian psychoanalysis and ego psychology theorised eating disorders as failures to resolve femininity, feminists such as Orbach (1978, 1986) and Bloom et al. (1994) used the notion of resistance strategically, to make the political point that women with eating problems were not passive victims, but actively involved in managing tensions arising from gendered oppressions and sex inequalities. However, Bordo (1988) rejects Orbach's (1986) feminist theory of anorexia as 'hunger strike', arguing that anorexia is instead an 'overdetermined symptom', rather than a conscious political resistance to the 'disciplines of femininity'.

Moreover, Foucault's notion of power and resistance is not one in which power acts as an overt and structurally oppressive, transcendental force, but one in which power is an *effect* rather than a *cause*. Power is manifest in specific relational actions, and as such, power can only be manifested when there is *resistance* to it. Power is constraining, in that it constitutes subjectivities, while also appearing to be 'liberating', in that subjectification occurs through the construction of knowledge bases, including the constitution of the individual. Central to this is the notion of the 'disciplined individual' who takes up citizenship through taking part in the production, maintenance and reproduction of 'self' through discursive positioning. Crucial to a gendered understanding of power and resistance is Foucault's concept of discursive 'panopticons' (1978a), in that femininity becomes a disciplinary practice (Bartky 1988, Smith 1988). In this framework then, 'resistance' occurs through taking up differing discursive positions, albeit within whatever discourses are available. If we regard psychoanalytic theory as discourse, then resistance could be understood as a discursive tool used in the construction of the narrative of the psychoanalytic subject, a subject which is constructed retrospectively as intentional and instrumental. As such, the notion of the power of unconscious processes could only be made manifest through constructing a similar notion of defence mechanisms as indices of resistance, in order to present a coherent narrative of the psychoanalytic subject.

Where Foucault and Object Relations theory could be seen to inform each other in Bloom et al.'s (1994) gendered rendition of Fairbairn's persecutory object world (see Greenberg and Mitchell 1983). The authors draw on Bordo's (1988, 1990a, 1990b) feminist Foucauldian readings of women's disciplined bodies as constituted through gendered discourses, in order to theorise how women in consumer societies come to experience them'selves' as being 'in the wrong'. For Bloom et al., the 'disciplines of consumerism' construct women in particular ways that mean she is 'always becoming', but 'never is'. Moreover, she is 'always becoming' through her body, a factor which exacerbates a fluctuating 'sense of self', an understanding of which can be usefully informed through a feminist Object Relations analysis of the unconscious ways in which 'the self' experiences this (Orbach 1994).

From a combined therapeutic and discursive perspective, what is problematic—and crucial—is to enable patients to develop a 'sense of selves', through explicating the constitution of subjectivities—'*the point of contact* between identity and society' (Parker 1992: 117), and to promote the management of the myriad emotions which arise out of the inevitable tensions which result from being positioned through particular discourses about selves, gender, bodies. An understanding of the constructive function of language and the ways in which meaning is discursive would not liberate patients but enable them to know more. However, it would also mean that they knew more about the constructive nature of psychotherapy, which would involve challenging the discursive practice of the therapist being positioned as 'the expert'. For, despite the inter-subjective emphasis on combined knowledge, the therapist has a need to be the one who 'knows'.

My suggestion that psychoanalysis has a great deal to offer a discursive perspective is contentious from a postmodern or post-structuralist perspective, given the 'death of the subject', as well as the 'discursive formation' of psychoanalysis (Rose 1990, Flax 1990). However, I want to retain the possibility that there is agency (Butler 1992, Joy 1993), as well as 'pre-discursive', or 'unthought experience' (Cain 1993: 89), commonly known as 'unconscious processes' or. as Bollas (1987) describes it, 'unthought known'. At the same time, this narrative of the internal operates within an 'extra-discursive' or material reality (Gill 1995) which is gendered (Bartky 1988).

In this chapter I have offered both discursive and psychodynamic readings of text, using these strategically (discursively), to argue for the need to keep a foot in both camps. Foucault's notion of the gendered panopticon is an essential tool for understanding the practices of femininity, and the lack of boundaries between the public and the private. However, I have also suggested that it is necessary to make use of psychoanalytic notions of unconscious processes such as splitting, projection and the false self, in order to understand how embodied and gendered selves are simultaneously lacking in boundaries, as well as able to construct internal boundaries. What makes change difficult from a psychodynamic perspective is the inability to directly access the internal false boundaries from a discursive perspective, it is the inability to adopt a coherent psychoanalytic account of the self. At the same time, the struggle to construct an agentic self is a struggle to relate. Perhaps, as Mahoney and Yngvesson (1992) suggest, power and agency may be paradoxically located in the transitional space *between* the self and society.

Taking a discursive approach to clinical material provides a means to approach the text on different levels. While this may be similar to, it contrasts with a psychoanalytic approach. The psychoanalytic therapist must develop and incorporate reflexive ways of listening and relating to patients through adopting multiple positions in relation to the patient's conscious and unconscious communications, as well as her own. However, adopting a discursive perspective goes beyond understanding transference and countertransference responses, requiring taking a critical perspective on the theory and practice of psychotherapy. While Lacan (see Dor 1997) argued that the notion of 'knowing' oneself is impossible, since the self is constructed through language which inevitably separates 'I' from 'me', in contrast, I would suggest, within an Object Relations framework, that the internal world is populated by symbols *in relation*. I regard the project of psycho-analysis as facilitating an awareness of subjectivity, in order to develop a sense of self, and thus a sense of agency. While the self is constituted through language it could also be argued that language constitutes relationally (Mahoney and Yngvesson, 1992). As such, I would argue that, while the relationship is discursive, it is also dynamic and thus, 'always becoming'.

Notes

[1] While the terms are often subsumed within the one denominator 'post-structuralism', in this chapter I deliberately use both in order to distinguish between their different areas of concern.

[2] Names have been changed to preserve confidentiality.

[3] '(?)' indicates that the speaker or words are not identifiable

[4] Italics denote intonated speech.

BIBLIOGRAPHY

Acocella, J. (1998) 'The Politics of Hysteria' in *The New Yorker*, April 6th 1998: 64-79.

Arlow, J. (1984) 'The Clinical Base of Edith Jacobson's Contribution', in S. Tuttman, C. Kaye, and M. Zimmerman, (eds.) *Object and Self: A Developmental Approach. Essays in Honor of Edith Jacobson*, New York: International Universities Press.

Bartky, S. (1988) 'Foucault, Femininity, and the Modernization of Patriarchal Power', in I. Diamond and L. Quinby (eds.) *Feminism and Foucault: Reflections on Resistance*, Boston: Northeastern University Press.

Bateman, A. and Holmes, J. (1995) *Introduction to Psychoanalysis: Contemporary Theory and Practice*, London: Routledge.

Bateson, G., Jackson, D. D., Haley, J., and Weakland, J. (1956) 'Towards a Theory of Schizophrenia', *Behavioural Science*, I: 251.

Bateson, G. (1972) *Steps to an Ecology of Mind*, New York: Ballantine Books.

Baudry, F. (1994) 'Revisiting the Freud-Klein Controversies Fifty Years Later', *International Journal of Psychoanalysis*, 75: 367-374.

Beck, U. (1992) *Risk Society: Towards a New Modernity*, London and Newbury Park CA: Sage.

Bell, D. (1995) 'Emotion and Unconscious Phantasy', *British Journal of Psychotherapy*, 12, 2: 222-228.

Benjamin, J. (1966) 'Discussion of Hartmann's Ego Psychology and the Problem of Adaptation', in R. Loewenstein, L. Newman, M. Schur, and A. Solnit, (eds.) *Psychoanalysis, A General Psychology: Essays in Honor of Heinz Hartmann*, New York: International Universities Press.

Benjamin, J. (1995) *Like Subjects, Love Objects: Essays on Recognition and Sexual Difference*, New Haven CT and London: Yale University Press.

Benjamin, J. (1998) *Shadow of the Other: Intersubjectivity and Gender in Psychoanalysis*, New York: Routledge.

Bion, W. (1959) 'Attacks on Linking', in *Second Thoughts* (1967) London: Karnac.

Bion, W. (1961) *Experiences in Groups*, London: Karnac.

Bion, W. (1962) 'A Theory of Thinking', in *Second Thoughts* (1967) London: Karnac.

Bion, W. (1967) *Second Thoughts*, London: Karnac.

Bion, W. (1970) 'Attention and Interpretation'(1967) in *Second Thoughts* London: Karnac.

Bion, W. (1991) *A Memoir of the Future*, London: Karnac.

Blass, R. and Bennett, S. (1994) 'The Value of the Historical Perspective on Contemporary Psychoanalysis: Freud's Seduction Theory Hypothesis', *International Journal of Psychoanalysis* 75: 677-694.

Bloom, C., Gitter, A., Gutwill, S., Kogel, L. and Zaphiropoulos, L. (1994) *Eating Problems: A Feminist Psychoanalytic Treatment Model*, New York: Basic Books.

Blum, H. (1982) 'Theories of Self and Psychoanalytic Concepts', *Journal of the American Psychoanalytic Association*, 30: 959-978.

Bollas, C. (1987) *The Shadow of the Object: Psychoanalysis of the Unthought Known*, New York: Columbia University Press.

Borch-Jacobsen, M. (1997) 'Sybil—The Making of a Disease: An Interview with Dr. Herbert Spiegel', *The New York Review of Books*, April 24th, 1997: 60-64.

Bordo, S. (1988) 'Anorexia Nervosa: Psychopathology as the Crystallization of Culture', in I. Diamond and L. Quinby (eds.) *Feminism and Foucault: Reflections on Resistance*, Boston: Northeastern University Press.

Bordo, S. (1990a) 'Reading the Slender Body', in M. Jacobus, E. Fox Keller and S. Shuttleworth (eds.) *Body Politics: Women and the Discourses of Science*, New York: Routledge.

Bordo, S. (1990b) 'Material Girl: The Effacements of Postmodern Culture', in *Michigan Quarterly Review*, Special Issue, The Female Body, 24(4): 653-677.

Bott Spillius, E. (ed.) (1988) 'General Introduction' in *Melanie Klein Today: Developments in Theory and Practice*, Vol. 1: 1-11, London: Routledge.

Bowlby, J. (1969, 1973, 1980) *Attachment, Separation and Loss* (3 Volumes), London: Penguin.

Brandchaft, B. (1986) 'Self and Object Differentiation', in R. Lax, S. Bach, and J. Burland, (eds.), *Self and Object Constancy: Clinical and Theoretical Perspectives*153-176, New York: Guilford.

Breger, L. (1981) *Freud's Unfinished Journey: Conventional and Critical Perspectives in Psychoanalytic Theory*, London: Routledge and Kegan Paul.

Buhle, M. (1998) *Feminism and its Discontents: A Century of Struggle with Psychoanalysis*, Cambridge MA and London: Harvard University Press.

Burman I. and Parker I. (1993) (eds.) *Discourse Analytic Research: Repertoires and Readings of Texts in Action,* London: Routledge.

Burr, V. (1995) *An Introduction to Social Constructionism,* London: Routledge.

Butler, J. (1990) 'Gender Trouble, Feminist Theory, and Psychoanalytic Discourse', in L. Nicholson (ed.) *Feminism/Postmodernism,* New York: Routledge.

Butler, J. (1992) 'Contingent Foundations: Feminism and the Question of "Postmodernism"', in J. Butler and J. Scott (eds.) *Feminists Theorize the Political,* London: Routledge.

Butler, J. (1993) *Bodies That Matter—On the Discursive Limits of 'Sex',* London: Routledge.

Butler, J. and Scott, J. (1992) (eds.) *Feminists Theorize the Political,* London: Routledge.

Cain, M. (1993) 'Foucault, Feminism and Feeling: what Foucault can and cannot Contribute to Feminist Epistemology', in C. Ramazanoglu (ed.) *Up Against Foucault: Explorations of some tensions between Foucault and Feminism,* London: Routledge.

Cavell, M. (1993) *The Psychoanalytic Mind: From Freud to Philosophy,* Cambridge MA: Harvard University Press.

Chodorow, N. (1978a) *Feminism and Psychoanalytic Theory,* Cambridge: Polity Press.

Chodorow, N. (1978b) *The Reproduction of Mothering,* Berkeley and London: University of California Press.

Chodorow, N. (1994) *Femininities, Masculinities, Sexualities: Freud and Beyond,* London: Free Association Books.

Chodorow, N. (1999) *The Power of Feelings,* New Haven: Yale University Press.

Cottet, S. (1985) 'Présentation: Le plus novateur des analystes américains', in Heinz Kohut, *Les deux analyses de M.Z* (1979), tr. G. Laurent-Sivry and C. Léger-Paturneau, 7-28, Paris: Navarin.

Cottingham, J. (1995) in T. Honderich (ed.) *The Oxford Companion to Philosophy,* London and New York: Oxford University Press.

Dean, C. (1992) *The Self and its Pleasures: Bataille, Lacan, and the History of the Decentered Subject,* Ithaca NY and London: Cornell University Press.

Descartes, R. (1968) *Discourse on Method and The Meditations,* tr. F. Sutcliffe, London: Penguin.

Dinnerstein, D. (1976) *The Mermaid and the Minotaur,* New York: Harper and Row.

Dor, J. (1997) *Introduction to the Reading of Lacan: The Unconscious Structured Like a Language,* Northvale, New Jersey: Jason Aronson, Inc.

Ellenberger, H. F. (1994) *The Discovery of the Unconscious,* London: Fontana Press.

Elliott, A. (1992) *Social Theory and Psychoanalysis in Transition: Self and Society from Freud to Kristeva,* Oxford: Blackwell.

Elliott, A. (1994) *Psychoanalytic Theory, An Introduction,* Oxford: Blackwell.

Elliott, A. and Spezzano, C. (2000) *Psychoanalysis at its Limits: Navigating the Postmodern Turn,* London: Free Association Books.

Ellis, M. L. (1997) 'Who Speaks? Who Listens? Different Voices and Different Sexualities', *Br. J. Psychotherapy* 13, 3: 369-383.

Erlich, H. S. (1998) 'On loneliness, narcissism, and intimacy', *American J. Psychoanalysis,* 58: 135-162.

Erlich, H. S. and Blatt, S. J. (1985) 'Narcissism and object love', *Psychoanal. Study Child,* 40: 57-79.

Erlich, H. S. (1988) 'The terminability of adolescence and psychoanalysis', *Psychoanal. Study Child,* 43: 199-211.

Erlich, H. S. (1990) 'Boundaries, limitations, and the wish for fusion in the treatment of adolescents', *Psychoanal. Study Child,* 45: 195-213.

Erlich, H. S. (1991) 'Die Erlebnisdimensionen "Being" und "Doing" in Psychoanalyse und Psychotherapie', *Zeitschrift (J. Psychoanal. Theory and Practice),* 4: 317-334.

Erlich, H. S. (1993) 'Fantasy, reality and adolescence', *Psychoanal. Study Child,* 48: 209-223.

Evans, D. (1996) *An Introductory Dictionary of Lacanian Psychoanalysis,* London and New York NY: Routledge.

Fairbairn, W. R. D. (1941) 'A Revised Psychopathology of the Psychoses and Psychoneuroses', in W. R. D. Fairbairn, *Psychoanalytic Studies of the Personality,* London: Routledge and Kegan Paul (1952).

Fairbairn, W. R. D. (1943) *Psychoanalytic Studies of the Personality,* London: Routledge and Kegan Paul (1952).

Fairbairn, W. R. D. (1944) 'Endopsychic Structure Considered in Terms of Object-Relationships', in W. R. D. Fairbairn, *Psychoanalytic Studies of the Personality,* London: Routledge and Kegan Paul (1952).

Fairbairn, W. R. D. (1951) 'A Synopsis of the Development of the Author's Views Regarding the Structure of the Personality', in W. R. D. Fairbairn, *Psychoanalytic Studies of the Personality,* London: Routledge and Kegan Paul (1952).

Fairclough, N. (1992) *Discourse and Social Change,* Cambridge: Polity Press.

Fanon, F. (1986) *Black Skin, White Masks,* tr. Charles Lamm Markmann, London: Pluto.

Farrell, E. (1995) *Lost for Words: The Psychoanalysis of Anorexia and Bulimia,* London: Process Press.

Fast, I. (1998) *Selving: A Relational Theory of Self Organization,* Hillsdale, NJ: The Analytic Press.

Fenichel, O. (1941) *Problems of Psychoanalytic Technique,* tr. D. Brunswick, Albany NY: The Psychoanalytic Quarterly Inc.

Flax, J. (1990) *Thinking Fragments: Psychoanalysis, Feminism and Postmodernism in the Contemporary West,* Berkeley: University of California Press.

Flax, J. (1993) *Disputed Subjects: Essays on Psychoanalysis, Politics and Philosophy,* New York and London: Routledge.

Foucault, M. (1961) *Madness and Civilisation: A History of Insanity in the Age of Reason,* tr. R. Howard, London: Routledge.

Foucault, M. (1962) *Mental Illness and Psychology,* tr. A. Sheridan. London: University of California Press.

Foucault, M. (1972) *The Archaelogy of Knowledge,* tr. A. Sheridan, London: Routledge.

Foucault, M. (1978a) *Discipline and Punish: The Birth of the Prison,* tr. A. Sheridan, New York: Vintage Books.

Foucault, M. (1978b) *The History of Sexuality,* Vol. 1, tr. R. Hurley, London: Penguin.

Foucault M. (1984) 'Nieztsche, Genealogy, History' tr. D.F. Bouchard and S. Simon in D. Bouchard (ed.) *Language, Counter-Memory, Practice,* New York: Cornell University Press.

Foulkes, S. H. (1964) *Therapeutic Group Analysis,* New York: International Universities Press.

Foulkes, S. H. (1975) *Group Analytic Psychotherapy—Method and Principles,* London: Maresfield Library.

Freud, A. (1937) *The Ego and the Mechanisms of Defence,* London: Hogarth.

Freud, A. (1946) *The Psychoanalysis and Treatment of Children,* London: Imago.

Freud, A. (1966) 'Links Between Hartmann's Ego Psychology and the Child Analyst's Thinking', in R. Loewenstein, L. Newman, M. Schur, and A. Solnit, (eds.) *Psychoanalysis: A General Psychology.*

Essays in Honor of Heinz Hartmann, New York: International Universities Press.

Freud, S. (1900) *The Interpretation of Dreams*, S.E. IV and V, London: Hogarth.

Freud, S. (1905) *Three Essays on the Theory of Sexuality*, S.E. VII: 123-245, London: Hogarth.

Freud, S. (1911) 'Formulations on the Two Principles of Mental Functioning', S.E. XII: 218-226, London: Hogarth.

Freud, S. (1912) *Totem and Taboo*, S.E. XIII: 1-162, London: Hogarth.

Freud, S. (1914a) 'On Narcissism' S.E. XIV: 72-102, London: Hogarth.

Freud, S. (1914b) 'On the History of the Psychoanalytic Movement', S.E. XIV: 7-66, London: Hogarth.

Freud, S. (1915a) 'Instincts and their Vicissitudes', S.E. XIV: 117-140, London: Hogarth.

Freud, S. (1915b) 'The Unconscious', S.E. XIV: 159-215, London: Hogarth

Freud, S. (1916-17) 'Psycho-Analysis and Psychiatry', in *Introductory Lectures on Psychoanalysis*, S.E. XVI: 243-256, London: Hogarth.

Freud, S. (1917) 'Mourning and Melancholia', S.E. X1V: 237-260, London: Hogarth.

Freud, S. (1920a) *Beyond the Pleasure Principle* S.E. XVIII: 7-64, London: Hogarth.

Freud, S. (1920b) 'Psychogenesis of a Case of Female Homosexuality', S.E. XVIII: 145-172, London: Hogarth.

Freud, S. (1921) *Group Psychology and the Analysis of the Ego*, S.E. XVIII: 65-143, London: Hogarth.

Freud, S. (1923) *The Ego and the Id*, S.E. XIX, London: Hogarth.

Freud, S. (1926) *Inhibitions, Symptoms and Anxiety*, S.E. XX: 77:174, London: Hogarth.

Freud, S. (1933) 'The Anatomy of the Mental Personality', S.E. XXIII: 78-106, London: Hogarth.

Freud, S. (1940) *An Outline of Psychoanalysis*, S.E. XXIII: 141-207, London: Hogarth.

Freud, S. (1950) 'Project for a Scientific Psychology', S.E. I: 283-397, London: Hogarth

Fromm, E. (1978) *The Crisis of Psychoanalysis*, London: Penguin.

Frosh, S. (1987) *The Politics of Psychoanalysis: An Introduction to Freudian and Post-Freudian Theory*, London: Macmillan.

Frosh, S. (1989) *Psychoanalysis and Psychology: Minding the Gap*, London: Macmillan Education.

Frosh, S. (1991) *Identity Crisis: Modernity, Psychoanalysis and the Self*, London: Macmillan.

Frosh, S. (1997) *For and Against Psychoanalysis*, London: Routledge.

Frosh, S. (1999) *The Politics of Psychoanalysis*, London: MacMillan.

Gallop, J. (1982) *The Daughter's Seduction: Feminism and Psychoanalysis*, Ithaca NY and London: Cornell University Press.

Geertz, C. (1973) *The Interpretation of Cultures*, New York: Basic Books.

Giddens, A. (1991) *Modernity and Self-Identity: Self and Society in the Late Modern Age*, Cambridge: Polity.

Gill, R. (1995) 'Relativism, Reflexivity and Politics: Interrogating Discourse Analysis from a Feminist Perspective', in S. Wilkinson and C. Kitzinger (eds.) *Feminism and Discourse: Psychological Perspectives*, London: Sage.

Greenberg, J. and Mitchell, S. (1983) *Object Relations in Psychoanalytic Theory*, Cambridge, Massachusetts: Harvard University Press.

Grosz, E. (1994) 'Refiguring Lesbian Desire' in L. Doan (ed.) *The Lesbian Postmodern*, New York and Chichester: Columbia University Press.

Grotstein, J. and Rinsley, D. (1994) (eds.) *Fairbairn and the Origins of Object Relations*, London: Free Association Books.

Guntrip, H. (1961) *Personality Structure and Human Interaction*, London: Hogarth.

Guntrip, H. (1968) *Schizoid Phenomena, Object Relations and the Self*, London: Hogarth.

Guntrip, H. (1973) *Psychoanalytic Theory, Therapy and the Self*, New York: Basic Books.

Hacking, I. (1992) 'Multiple Personality Disorder and its Hosts' in *History of the Human Science*, 5: 3-31.

Hacking, I. (1995) *Rewriting the Soul: Multiple Personality and the Sciences of Memory*, Princeton NJ: Princeton University Press.

Hale, N. (1995) *The Rise and Crisis of Psychoanalysis in the United States: Freud and the Americans 1917-1985*, Oxford and New York NY: Oxford University Press.

Hamilton, V. (1996) *The Analyst's Preconscious*, Hillsdale, New Jersey: The Analytic Press.

Hammonds, E. (1994) 'Black (W)holes and the Geometry of Black Female Sexuality', *Differences* 6, 2 and 3: 25-144.

Hartmann, H. and Loewenstein, R. (1946) 'Comments on the Formation of the Psychic Structure' in *Psychoanalytic Study of the Child*, 2: 11-38.

Hartmann, H. (1939) *Ego Psychology and the Problem of Adaptation*, New York: International Universities Press.

Hartmann, H. (1950) 'Comments on the Psychoanalytic Theory of the Ego', *Psychoanalytic Study of the Child* 5: 74-97.

Hartmann, H. 1964 [(1950)] 'Comments on the Psychoanalytic Theory of the Ego', 1950: 113-141, *Essays on Ego Psychology: Selected Problems in Psychoanalytic Theory*, New York: I.U.P.

Hartmann, H. (1956) 'The Development of the Ego Concept in Freud's Work' in *The International Journal of Psychoanalysis*, 37, 6: 425-438.

Heenan, M. C. (1998) 'Discourse Analysis and Clinical Supervision', *Clinical Psychology Forum 114*, Division of Clinical Psychology, British Psychological Society, April, 1998.

Hegel, G. W. F. (1952 [1807]) *Phänomenologie des Geistes*, ed. Johannes Hoffmeister, Hamburg: Felix Meiner.

Hegel, G. W. F. (1977 [1807]) *Phenomenology of Spirit*, tr. A. Miller, Oxford: Clarendon Press.

Heidegger, M. (1990) *Being and Time*, tr. J. Macquarrie and E. Robinson, Oxford: Basil Blackwell.

Henriques, J., Hollway, W., Urwin, C., Venn, C. and Walkerdine, V. (1984) *Changing the Subject*, London: Methuen and Co.

Hollinger, R. (1994) *Postmodernism and the Social Sciences: A Thematic Approach*, London: Sage.

Hollway, W. and Featherstone, B. (eds.) (1997) *Mothering and Ambivalence*, London: Routledge.

Holstein, J. and J. Gubrium, (2000) *The Self We Live By: Narrative Identities in a Postmodern World*, Oxford: Oxford University Press.

Irigaray, L. (1985) *This Sex Which Is Not One*, tr. Catherine Porter, New York: Cornell University Press.

Jacobson, E. (1965) *The Self and the Object World*, London: Hogarth.

Jacobson, N. and Margolin, G. (1979) *Marital Therapy*, New York: Brunner/Mazel.

James, W. (1961 [1892]) *Psychology: The Briefer Course*, ed. G. Allport, NY: Harper and Row.

James, W. (1968) 'The Self', in C. Gordon and K. S. Gordon (eds.) *The Self in Interaction*, Vol. 1, New York: J. Wiley.

Joy, M. (1993) 'Feminism and the Self', in *Theory and Psychology*, 3(3): 275-302.

Kaufmann, P. (ed.) (1993) *L'apport freudien. Eléments pour une encyclopédie de la psychanalyse*, Paris: Bordas.

Kegan, R. (1982) *The Evolving Self*, Cambridge MA: Harvard University Press.

Kernberg, O. (1982) 'Self, Ego, Affects and Drives' *Journal of the American Psychoanalytic Association*, 30: 893-917.

Kernberg, O. (1984) 'An Overview of Edith Jacobson's Contribution', S. Tuttman, C. Kaye, M. and Zimmerman, (eds.) *Object and Self: A Developmental Approach. Essays in Honor of Edith Jacobson*, New York: International Universities Press.

Kernberg, O. (1997) 'Psychoanalysis in America' *Journal of European Psychoanalysis*, 5: Spring-Fall.

Kerr, J. (1992) 'History and the Clinician', 357-383 in T. Gelfand, and J. Kerr, (eds.) *Freud and the History of Psychoanalysis*, Hillsdale NJ: Analytic Press.

King, P. and Steiner, R. (eds.) (1991) *The Freud/Klein Controversies 1941-1945*, London: Routledge.

Kirk, S. and Kutchins, H. (1993) *The Selling of DSM: The Rhetoric of Science in Psychiatry*, New York: Hawthorn Press.

Kitzinger, C. and Perkins, R. (1993) *Changing Our Minds: Lesbian Feminism and Psychology*, London: Only Women Press.

Klein, H. and Erlich, H. S. (1976) 'Some psychoanalytic structural aspects of family function and growth', *Adolescent Psychiatry*, 6: 171-194.

Klein, M. (1926) 'The Psychological Foundations of Child Analysis', *The Psycho-Analysis of Children*, London: Hogarth.

Klein, M. (1935) 'A Contribution to the Psychogenesis of Manic-Depressive States', *Love, Guilt and Reparation and Other Works 1921-1945*, London: Hogarth.

Klein, M. (1940) 'Mourning and its Relation to Manic-Depressive States' in *Love, Guilt and Reparation and Other Works 1921-1945*, London: Hogarth.

Klein, M. (1946) 'Notes on Some Schizoid Mechanisms', in *Envy and Gratitude and Other Works 1946-1963*, London: Hogarth.

Klein, M. (1959) 'Our Adult World and its Roots in Infancy', in *Envy and Gratitude and Other Works 1946-1963*, London: Hogarth.

Klein, M. (1975 [1961]) *Narrative of a Child Analysis*, London: Hogarth.

Klein, M. (1997 [1955]) 'On Identification', *Envy and Gratitude and Other Works 1946-1963*, London: Vintage.

Kohon, G. (ed.) (1986) *The British School of Psychoanalysis: The Independent Tradition*, London: Free Association Books.

Kohut, H. (1971) *The Analysis of the Self: A Systematic Approach to the Psychoanalytic Treatment of Narcissistic Personality Disorders*, New York NY: International Universities Press.

Kohut, H. (1977) *The Restoration of the Self*, New York NY: International Universities Press.

Kohut, H. (1978 [1959]) 'Introspection, Empathy and Psychoanalysis: An Examination of the Relationship between Mode of Observation and Theory', in P. Ornstein (ed.) *The Search for the Self*, vol. 1, New York NY: International Universities Press.

Kohut, H. (1984) *How does Analysis Cure?*, ed. A. Goldberg, Chicago and London: The University of Chicago Press.

Kohut, H. (1990 [1979]) 'The Two Analyses of Mr. Z', in Paul Ornstein (ed.) *The Search for the Self*, vol. 4, New York NY: International Universities Press.

Kraemer, S. and Roberts, J. (eds.) (1997) *The Politics of Attachment*, London: Free Association Books.

Kurzweil, E. (1995) in P. Kutter, (ed.) *Psychoanalysis International: A Guide to Psychoanalysis throughout the World*, Vol. 2, Stuttgart: Friedrich Frommarin Verlag, 186-228.

Lacan, J. (1949) 'The Mirror Stage as Formative of the Function of the I as Revealed in Psychoanalytic Experience', in J. Lacan, *Ecrits: A Selection*, London: Tavistock, 1977.

Lacan, J.(1966a [1949]) 'Le stade du miroir comme formateur de la fonction du Je telle qu'elle nous est révélée dans l'expérience psychanalytique', 93-100, *Ecrits*, Paris: Editions du Seuil.

Lacan, J. (1966b [1953]) 'Fonction et champ de la parole et du langage en psychanalyse', 237-322, *Ecrits*, Paris: Editions du Seuil.

Lacan, J. (1967-68) *Le Séminaire XV: L'acte psychanalytique*, unpublished.

Lacan, J. (1968 [1949]) 'The Mirror-phase as Formative of the Function of the I', tr. J. Roussel, *New Left Review*, 51, September/October, 71-79. Reprinted in S. Zizek (ed.) (1994: 93-99) *Mapping Ideology*, London and New York NY: Verso.

Lacan, J. (1970 [1966]) 'Of Structure as an Inmixing of an Otherness Prerequisite to Any Subject Whatever', 186-200, R. Macksey and E. Donato (eds.) *The Languages of Criticism and the Sciences of Man: The Structuralist Controversy*, Baltimore MD and London: The Johns Hopkins University Press.

Lacan, J. (1975 [1973]) 'Introduction à l'édition allemande d'un premier volume des *Ecrits*', *Scilicet*, 5, 11-17.

Lacan, J. (1977a [1949]) 'The Mirror Stage as Formative of the Function of the I as Revealed in Psychoanalytic Experience', 1-7, *Ecrits: A Selection*, tr. A. Sheridan, London: Tavistock.

Lacan, J. (1977b [1953]) 'The Function and Field of Speech and Language in Psychoanalysis', *Ecrits: A Selection*, 30-113, tr. A. Sheridan, London: Tavistock.

Lacan, J. (1977c[1960]) 'The Subversion of the Subject and the Dialectic of Desire in the Freudian Unconscious', 292-325, *Ecrits: A Selection*, tr. A. Sheridan, London: Tavistock.

Lacan, J. (1981 [1953]) *Speech and Language in Psychoanalysis*, tr. with notes and commentary A. Wilden, Baltimore MD and London: The Johns Hopkins University Press.

Lacan, J. (1984 [1969]) 'L'acte psychanalytique 1967-1968', *Ornicar? Revue du Champ freudien*, 29: 18-25.

Lacan, J. (1988a [1953-54]) *The Seminar. Book I: Freud's Papers on Technique*, (ed.) J.-A. Miller, tr. with notes J. Forrester, Cambridge: Cambridge University Press.

Lacan, J. (1988b [1954-55]) *The Seminar. Book II: The Ego in Freud's Theory and in the Technique of Psychoanalysis*, ed. J.-A. Miller, tr. S. Tomaselli, notes J. Forrester, Cambridge: Cambridge University Press.

Lacan, J. (1990 [1963]) 'Introduction to the Names-of-the-Father Seminar', 81-95, (ed.) J.-A. Miller, tr. J. Mehlman, in J. Copjec (ed.) *Television/A Challenge to the Psychoanalytic Establishment*, New York NY: W.W. Norton and Company.

Lacan, J. (1992 [1959-60]) *The Seminar. Book VII: The Ethics of Psychoanalysis*, Edited by J.-A. Miller, tr. D. Porter, London and New York NY: W.W. Norton and Company.

Lacan, J. (1993 [1955-56]) *The Seminar. Book III: The Psychoses*, ed. J.-A. Miller, tr. R. Grigg, London and New York NY: W.W. Norton and Company.

Lacan, J. (1994 [1956-57]) *Le Séminaire. Livre IV: La relation d'objet*, texte établi par J.-A. Miller, Paris: Editions du Seuil.

Lacan, J. (1995 [1967]) 'Proposition of 9 October 1967 on the Psychoanalyst of the School', tr. R. Grigg, *Analysis*, 6: 1-13.

Lacan, J. (1998 [1957-58]) *Le Séminaire. Livre V: Les formations de l'inconscient*, texte établi par J.-A. Miller, Paris: Editions du Seuil.

Laing, R. (1969) *The Politics of the Family*, London: Tavistock.

Laplanche, J. and Pontalis, J. B. (1988) *The Language of Psychoanalysis*, London: Karnac.

Laurent, E. and Schneiderman, S. (1977) 'Parcours du self', *Ornicar? Revue du Champ freudien,* 11: 95-101.

Lear, J. (1998) *Open Minded,* Cambridge, MA and London: Harvard University Press.

Lévi-Strauss, C. (1950) 'Introduction à l'œuvre de Marcel Mauss', ix-lii, in M. Mauss, *Sociologie et anthropologie,* Paris: Presses Universitaires de France.

Levin, D. (1969) 'The Self', *International Journal of Psycho-Analysis,* 50, 41-51.

Litchenberg, J. D. (1983) *Psychoanalysis and Infant Research,* Hillsdale, NJ: The Analytic Press.

Mahler, M., Pine, F. and Bergman A. (1975) *The Psychological Birth of the Human Infant,* New York: Basic Books.

Mahoney, M. and Yngvesson, B. (1992) 'The Construction of Subjectivity and the Paradox of Resistance: Reintegrating Feminist Anthropology and Psychology', *Signs: Journal of Women in Culture and Society,* 18 (1): 44-73.

Malcolm, J. (1997) *In the Freud Archives,* London: PaperMac.

Malinowski, B. (1928) quoted in E. Jones, review of B. Malinowski, 'Sex and Repression in Savage Society', *Int. J. Psycho-Analysis* 9 : 365.

Mangabeira, W. C. (1999) 'On the Textuality of Objects in Disciplinary Practice: the couch in psychoanalysis' *Psychoanalytic Studies,* 1 (3): 327-354.

Marcuse, H. (1955) *Eros and Civilisation,* Boston: Beacon Press.

Masson, J. (1984) *The Assault on Truth: Freud's Suppression of the Seduction Theory,* London: Fontana.

McGuire, W. (ed.) (1991) *The Freud/Jung Letters,* London: Penguin.

McIntosh, D. (1986) 'The Ego and the Self in the Thought of Sigmund Freud', *Int. J. Psycho-Analysis,* 67: 429-448.

Merleau-Ponty, M. (1964) *Signs,* tr. R. McCleary, Illinois: Northwestern University Press.

Merleau-Ponty, M. (1986 [1945]) *The Phenomenology of Perception,* tr. Colin Smith, London: Routledge.

Merleau-Ponty, M. (1994) 'Phenomenology and Psychoanalysis: Preface to Hesnard's L'Oeuvre de Freud', tr. A. Fisher in K. Hoeller (ed.) *Merleau-Ponty and Psychology,* New Jersey: Humanities Press.

Miller, E. J. (1989) *The 'Leicester' Model: Experiential Study of Group and Organisational Processes,* Tavistock Institute of Human Relations: Occasional Paper No. 10.

Miller, J.-A. (1987) 'How Psychoanalysis Cures According to Lacan', *Newsletter of the Freudian Field*, 1(2): 4-30.

Mitchell, S. A. (1993) *Hope and Dread in Psychoanalysis*, New York: Basic Books.

Mitterauer, B. and Pritz, W. (1978) 'The Concept of the Self', *International Review of Psycho-Analysis*, 5: 179-188.

Moore, B. and Fine, B. (eds.) (1990) *Psychoanalytic Terms and Concepts*, New Haven: The American Psychoanalytic Association and Yale University Press, 154-172.

Morrow, R. and Brown, D. (1994) *Critical Theory and Methodology*, London: Sage.

Muller, J. (1996) *Beyond the Psychoanalytic Dyad: Developmental Semiotics in Freud, Peirce and Lacan*, New York NY and London: Routledge.

Muller, J. and Richardson, W. (1982) *Lacan and Language: A Reader's Guide to Ecrits*, New York: International Universities Press.

NN (1996) 'Le self contre le moi', in Association Mondiale de Psychanalyse (ed.), *Les pouvoirs de la parole*, Paris: Editions du Seuil, 301-307.

Nobus, D. (2000) *Jacques Lacan and the Freudian Practice of Psychoanalysis*, London and Philadelphia: Routledge.

O'Connor N. and Ryan, J. (1993) *Wild Desires and Mistaken Identities: Lesbianism and Psychoanalysis*, London: Virago.

Ogden, T. (1994) *Subjects of Analysis*, London: Karnac.

Orbach, S. (1978) *Fat is a Feminist Issue*, London: Paddington Press.

Orbach, S. (1986) *Hungerstrike*, London: Faber and Faber.

Orbach, S. (1994) 'Working with the False Body', in A. Erskine and D. Judd (eds.) *The Imaginative Body: Psychodynamic Therapy in Health Care*, London: Whurr.

Padel, J. (1986) 'Ego in current thinking', G. Kohon, (ed.), *The British School of Psychoanalysis: The Independent Tradition*, London: Free Association Books.

Parker, I. (1992) *Discourse Dynamics: Critical Analysis for Social and Individual Psychology*, London: Routledge.

Parker, I. (1997) *Psychoanalytic Culture: Psychoanalytic Discourse in Western Society*, London: Routledge.

Phillips, A. (1988) *Winnicott*, London: Fontana.

Porter, R. (1997) *The Greatest Benefit to Mankind: A Medical History of Humanity from Antiquity to the Present*, London: HarperCollins.

Potter, J. and Wetherell, M. (1987) *Discourse and Social Psychology: Beyond Attitudes and Behaviour*, London: Sage.

Ragland, E. (1995) *Essays on the Pleasures of Death: From Freud to Lacan*, New York and London: Routledge.

Ragland-Sullivan, E. (1986) *Jacques Lacan and the Philosophy of Psychoanalysis*, Urbana/Chicago: University of Illinois Press.

Rangell, L. (1982) 'The Self in Psychoanalytic Theory', *Journal of the American Psychoanalytic Association*, 30, 863-892.

Richards, A. (1985) 'Editor's Introduction' *Sigmund Freud: On Metapsychology Theory*. London: Penguin.

Riley, D. (1983) *War in the Nursery*, London: Virago.

Rioch, M. J. (1975) 'The Work of Wilfred Bion on Groups', A. Colman and W. Bexton (eds.), *Group Relations Reader*. San Rafael: GREX: 21-33.

Roazen, P. (1974) *Freud and His Followers*, London: Allen Lane.

Rose, N. (1990) *Governing the Soul*, London: Routledge.

Rose, N. (1996) *Inventing Our Selves: Psychology, Power, and Personhood*, Cambridge: Cambridge University Press.

Rosenfeld, H. (1964) 'On the psychopathology of narcissism: a clinical approach', *Int.J. Psycho-Analysis*, 45.

Roudinesco, E. (1990 [1986]) *Lacan and Company: A History of Psychoanalysis in France 1925-1985*, London: Free Association Books.

Roudinesco, E. and Plon, M. (eds.) (1997) *Dictionnaire de la psychanalyse*, Paris: Fayard.

Rustin, M. J. (1995) 'Lacan, Klein and Politics: the Positive and Negative in Psychoanalytic Thought', A. Elliott and S. Frosh (eds.) *Psychoanalysis in Contexts*, London: Routledge.

Sandler, J. (1983) 'Reflections on Some Relations Between Psychoanalytic Concepts and Psychoanalytic Practice', *Int. J. Psycho-Analysis*, 64, 35: 36-43.

Sandler, J. (1986) 'Comments on the Self and Its Objects', in R. Lax, S. Bach, and J. Burland, (eds.) *Self and Object Constancy: Clinical and Theoretical Perspectives*. New York: Guilford Press, 97-106.

Sandler, J. (1987) *Projection, Identification, Projective Identification*, New York: International Universities Press.

Sandler, J. and Rosenblatt, B. (1962) 'The Concept of the Representational World' *Psychoanalytic Study of the Child*, 17: 128-148.

Sandler, J., Holder, A. and Meers, D. (1963) 'The Ego Ideal and the Ideal Self' *Psychoanalytic Study of the Child*, 18: 139-148.

Sandler, J., Holder, A., Dare, C. and Dreher, A. (1997) *Freud's Models of the Mind: Psychoanalytic Monograph No. 1.*, London: Karnac.

Saravay, S. M. (1975) 'Group psychology and the structural theory: a revised psychoanalytic model of group psychology', *J. Am. Psychoanal. Assn.*, 23: 69-89.

Schafer, R. (1976) *A New Language for Psychoanalysis*, New Haven: Yale University Press.

Schwartz, J. (1999) *Cassandra's Daughter: A History of Psychoanalysis in Europe and America*, London: Allen Lane/The Penguin Press.

Searles, H. (1959) 'The Effort to Drive the Other Person Crazy—An Element in the Aetiology and Psychotherapy of Schizophrenia' *Collected Papers on Schizophrenia and Related Subjects*, (1986) London: Maresfield.

Segal, H. (1973) *Introduction to the Work of Melanie Klein*, London: Hogarth Press.

Seu, B. (1998) 'Change and Theoretical Frameworks', in B. Seu, and C. Heenan, (eds.) *Feminism and Psychotherapy: Reflections on Contemporary Theories and Practice*, London: Sage Publications.

Shane, M. and Shane, E. (1980) 'Psychoanalytic Developmental Theories of the Self: An Integration, in A. Goldberg (ed.) *Advances in Self Psychology*, New York: International Universities Press.

Sharff, D. and Fairbairn Birtles, E. (eds.) (1994) *From Instinct to Self: Selected Papers of W. R. D. Fairbairn, Vol. 1.*, Northvale, New Jersey: Jason Aronson Inc.

Siegel, A. (1996) *Heinz Kohut and the Psychology of the Self*, London-New York NY: Routledge.

Smith, D. E. (1988) 'Femininity as Discourse' in L. G. Roman and L. K. Christian-Smith (eds.), *Becoming Feminine: The Politics of Popular Culture*, London: Falmer Press.

Socor, B. J. (1997) *Conceiving the Self: Presence and Absence in Psychoanalytic Theory*, Madison CT: International Universities Press.

Spence, D. (1982) 'Turning Happenings into Meanings: The Central Role of the Self' in P. Young-Eisendrath and J. Hall (eds.), New York: New York University Press.

Spillers, H. (1997) 'All the Things You could be by now if Sigmund Freud's Wife was your Mother' in E. Abel, B. Christian, H. Moslen (eds.) *Female Subjects in Black and White*, California: University of California Press.

Spruiell, V. (1981) 'The Self and the Ego', *Psychoanalytic Quarterly*, 50: 319-344.

Spruiell, V. (1995) 'Self' in B. E. Moore and B. D. Fine (eds.), *Psychoanalysis: The Major Concepts*, New Haven CT and London: Yale University Press, 421-432.

Steiner, J. (1988) 'The Interplay between Pathological Organisations and the Paranoid-Schizoid and Depressive positions', in E. Bott Spillius, (ed.) *Melanie Klein Today: Developments in Theory and Practice, Vol. 1*, London: Routledge.

Stern, D. N. (1985) *The Interpersonal World of the Infant*, New York: Basic Books.

Stolorow, R. D., Brandchaft, B. and Atwood, G. E. (1993) 'Intersubjectivity in Psychoanalytic Treatment', in N. Gregory Hamilton (ed.), *From Inner Sources: New Directions in Object Relations Psychotherapy*, Northvale, New Jersey: Jason Aronson, Inc.

Sullivan, H. S. (1964 [1950]) 'The Data of Psychiatry' in *Fusion of Psychiatry and the Social Sciences*, New York: Norton.

Taylor, C. (1989) *Sources of the Self: The Making of the Modern Identity*, Cambridge: Cambridge University Press.

Tong, R. (1989) *Feminist Thought: A Comprehensive Introduction*, London: Routledge.

Treurniet, N. (1980) 'Kohut's Psychology of the Self', *International Journal of Psycho-Analysis*. 61.

Turquet, P. M. (1975) 'Threats to identity in the large group', in *The Large Group: Dynamics and Therapy*, L. Kreeger (ed.) London: Constable.

Tuttman, S. (1984b) 'The Significance of Edith Jacobson's Self and Object World in Contemporary Object Relations Theory', in S., Tuttman, C. Kaye, and M. Zimmerman, (eds.) *Object and Self: A Developmental Approach. Essays in Honor of Edith Jacobson*, New York: International Universities Press.

Tuttman, S. (l984a) 'A Historical Survey of the Development of Object Relations Concepts in Psychoanalytic Theory', in S. Tuttman, C. Kaye, and M. Zimmerman, (eds.) *Object and Self: A Developmental Approach. Essays in Honor of Edith Jacobson*, New York: International Universities Press.

Walton, J. (1997) 'Re-Placing Race in (White) Psychoanalytic Discourse', in E. Abel, B. Christian, and H. Moslen (eds.), *Female Subjects in Black and White*, California: University of California Press.

Weedon, C. (1987) *Feminist Practice and Poststructuralist Theory*, Oxford: Basil Blackwell.

Wells, L. (1985) 'The-group-as-a-whole perspective and its theoretical roots', in A. D. Colman and M. H. Geller (eds.), *Group Relations Reader 2*, A. K. Rice Institute: 109-126.

Wilden, A. (1968a) *Jacques Lacan and the Language of the Self: The Function of Language in Psychoanalysis*, PhD Thesis, Baltimore MD: The Johns Hopkins University.

Wilden, A. (1968b) *The Language of the Self: The Function of Language in Psychoanalysis*, Baltimore MD and London: The Johns Hopkins University Press.

Winnicott, D. W. (1950) 'Aggression in Relation to Emotional Development', in D. W. Winnicott, *Through Paediatrics to Psychoanalysis*, London: Hogarth.

Winnicott, D. W. (1956) 'Primary Maternal Preoccupation', D. W. Winnicott, *Through Paediatrics to Psychoanalysis*, London: Hogarth .

Winnicott, D. W. (1958) *Through Paediatrics to Psycho-analysis*, London: Hogarth.

Winnicott, D. W. (1963) 'Communicating and Not Communicating Leading to a Study of Certain Opposites', D. W. Winnicott, *The Maturational Process and the Facilitating Environment*, London: Hogarth.

Winnicott, D. W. (1965) *The Maturational Process and the Facilitating Environment*, London: Hogarth.

Winnicott, D. W. (1971) *Playing and Reality*, New York: Basic Books.

Winnicott, D. W. (1986) *Home is Where We Start From: Essays by a Psychoanalyst*, London: Penguin.

Yalom, I. D. (1970) *The Theory and Practice of Group Psychotherapy*, New York: Basic Books.

Index